The Guide to Online Due Diligence Investigations

The Professional Approach on How to Use Traditional and Social Media Investigations

By Cynthia Hetherington

Facts on Demand Press
PO Box 27869
Tempe, AZ 85285
800-929-3811
www.brbpublications.com

Facts
ON DEMAND
PRESS

The Guide to Due Diligence Investigations
The Professional Approach on How to Use Traditional and Social Media Investigations

©2015 Cynthia Hetherington and BRB Publications, Inc.
ISBN: 978-1-889150-61-1

Written by: Cynthia Hetherington
Contributing Editors: Joann M. Wleklinski and Michael L. Sankey
Cover Design by: Robin Fox & Associates

Cataloging-in-Publication Data
(Provided by Quality Books, Inc.)

Hetherington, Cynthia, author.
    The guide to online due diligence investigations :
the professional approach on how to use traditional and
social media resources / by Cynthia Hetherington ;
contributing editors: Joann M. Wleklinski and Michael L.
Sankey. -- First edition.
    pages cm
    ISBN 978-1-889150-61-1

    1. Business enterprises--Evaluation--Handbooks,
manuals, etc. 2. Business enterprises--Information
resources--Handbooks, manuals, etc. 3. Business--
Research--Methodology--Handbooks, manuals, etc.
4. Reasonable care (Law)--Handbooks, manuals, etc.
5. Private investigators--Handbooks, manuals, etc.
I. Wleklinski, Joann M., editor. II. Sankey, Michael L.,
1949- editor. III. Title.

HD30.4.H484 2015   338.7
                       QBI14-2200

Table of Contents

In my career as a fraud-fighter and co-founder of the Association of Certified Fraud Examiners, I have seen thousands of cases of fraud that could have been prevented if the victim had only done some basic due diligence on the employee, partner, or customer who ultimately defrauded them. People are very trusting by nature, and that is what the fraudster is counting on. An enormous amount of information is available on individuals and businesses. Organizations are foolish not to use this information to their advantage.

Cynthia is a recognized expert on gathering intelligence online. Her guidance on how to obtain the information you need to protect yourself is invaluable and can help prevent you from being the victim of fraud.

James D. Ratley, CFE
President and CEO
Association of Certified Fraud Examiners

Acknowledgements

My dear family is my solid foundation – and my sounding board – which I rely on daily. We often give deep thoughts to a matter, but in the end, just go for it! Someone always has your back. In an industry where a moral compass can sometimes spin 360 degrees, I find my bearing and best common sense in my own first responder and loving boyfriend, Mickey.

My extended family is my office team – the mission command that keeps me grounded. Though I travel 200+ days a year, they make sure the clients are happy, the work flows, and deadlines are met. Our Administrator, Paul Atkinson, has shown incredible clarity in our operations management while daily keeping me in Tootsie Rolls and mint tea as I hacked my way through this book, chapter by chapter. Kim Miller, Investigations Manager and Ph.D. candidate, proofed for investigative corrections, page by page. Kim is as vigilant an investigator as I have ever met; her critical thinking skills and impressive resilience are matched only by her loyalty to our company.

It is one thing to talk about writing a book, and entirely another thing to do it. When I can accomplish that on my own, I will let you know. Till then my chatty Jersey style is tamed by the ever-present and brilliant editing team of Michael Sankey, CEO of BRB Publications, Inc., and Joann Wleklinski, owner of Wleklinski Information Services. I am absolutely grateful for their red pens, easy style, and knowledge of proper grammar.

Finally, the first responders, the corporate security professionals, and fellow investigators and analysts are what drive me to write and lecture; knowing that what we learn together helps stop terrorism and fraud, prevent crime, and protect our citizens. Time and budgets may constrain us, integrity and vigilance will always reflect in our work.

You have all made this book possible. Thank you.

—Cynthia Hetherington

Introduction

In God we trust; all others we monitor.
—Naval Intelligence

Due diligence investigations examine the backgrounds of corporate entities and the principals who manage them. Due diligence investigations are applicable to all professionals involved in investigations: insurance and risk managers, attorneys, security practitioners, and every-day consumers. Regardless of your investigative ability, learning the critical thinking tactics to research and conduct due diligence analysis will empower you with the information to make proactive decisions in life and business.

Information is power. The most accurate, up-to-date, strategic information on a competitor or an industry can give you a solid, strategic advantage to help your business succeed and not merely exist.

In my twenty years of conducting online due diligence, I have seen the proof time and again: Those who conduct methodical investigations, ignore distractions, and stay informed, do in fact maintain their competitive advantage and avoid business failure. An hour spent on substantive due diligence prior to engaging a potential client will save appreciably on both budget and reputation should said client, in the future, turn out to be nefarious.

Unfortunately, not everyone conducts thorough due diligence before engaging in business contracts. The news is littered with reports of tragic business decisions made by executives who didn't take the time to research their clients – the Bernard Madoff scandal being but one example of how even the most business-savvy of executives were drawn into a perilous investment. Conducting some due diligence beforehand might well have alerted these investors to the risky situation Madoff represented.

Due diligence can be applied to not only financial investments but many areas of life. Conducting research on any professional you may have to hire – contractors, lawyers, healthcare workers – can save you time, money, aggravation, and give you peace of mind.

Information is power. Use this book as an instruction manual for how to find the information that can often give you the power of competitive advantage.

Ch 1:

A Successful Approach to Due Diligence

Success is a journey, not a destination.
—Ben Sweetland

If you run a Google search on the words "Due Diligence" you will find many interesting and drawn- out definitions. According to Wikipedia:

> "Due diligence is an investigation of a business or person prior to signing a contract, or an act with a certain standard of care."

(en.wikipedia.org/wiki/Due_diligence)

I conjecture that if you use only Wikipedia to get the definition of due diligence you are not doing due diligence. Wikipedia, though interesting, is far from being an authoritative and comprehensive encyclopedia.

A more authoritative and respected resource would be Black's Law Dictionary. Its reference tool, used extensively by attorneys and legal practitioners, includes legal references as part of its definition. For example, Black's defines Due Diligence as:

> "Such a measure of prudence, activity, or assiduity, as is properly to be expected from, and ordinarily exercised by, a reasonable and prudent man under the particular circumstances; not measured by any absolute standard, but depending on the relative facts of the special case." *Perry v. Cedar Falls*, 87 Iowa, 315, 54 N. W. 225; *Dillman v. Nadelhoffer*, 1G0111. 121, 43 N. E. 378; Hendricks v. W. U. Tel. Co., 120 N. C. 304, 35 S. E. 543, 78Am. St. Rep. 058; *Highland Ditch Co. v. Mumford*. 5 Colo. 330.

(thelawdictionary.org/due-diligence)

The difference between these two definitions leaves a great expanse for interpretation. Although Black's quotes case law and makes it an authoritative definition, it takes a few reads to fully understand.

Simply put, my definition of due diligence is:

> "The thorough research of a topic utilizing the tools available and the resources that are accessible."

Part of finding and knowing the best tools and resources is also an expectation that the chances for better results and more thorough answers will increase with new developments. Working in due diligence is an exercise in due diligence in and of itself. How often and regularly it occurs is also a consideration. The field is constantly evolving and expanding as new sources become available, or disappear, using progressive computing, science, and analytical methods. What we could not even imagine twenty years ago as being possible has become routine in today's investigations.

Conducting due diligence on the human genome was a study in futility until April 2003, when the Human Genome Project (HGP) completed the mapping of the full DNA of a person. (genome.gov/10001772) This was not to say scientists were wasting time; in fact, they were conducting due diligence with the best resources they had up until the later discoveries that opened up the possibility to map the human. The ability to map DNA and draw markers from it, allows us to identify with specificity individuals. Hence the improvements of the HGP work carried over into the law enforcement world leading to a breakthrough in investigations. For ages, the law enforcement community has been arresting and prosecuting people based on the limited information they could collect; it was the best due diligence of the time. Once DNA matching was admitted into criminal court, thousands of cases overturned. According to Sara L. Crowston, "DNA forensics identifies potential suspects using evidence left at crime scenes, exonerates those wrongly accused, enables the identification of crime and catastrophe victims, and establishes paternity."[1]

A few years ago if I researched criminal offenders in Kansas, I had to call the Kansas Bureau of Investigations and wait days for their search results. Today I can visit kbi.ks.gov/registeredoffender and search for sex, violent or drug offenders by their name, phone number, Facebook account, email or by geography. The access to this database of offenders emphasized to me that conducting due diligence means not only do I have to consider finding the answers to my questions, but involves a constant pursuit of new resources and tools to conduct due diligence at the highest level.

This book will help with that. A major portion of this book is focused on working with online and open sources found through the Internet. Hence my definition of **online due diligence** is:

> "The analytical use of public records and information found in databases, open sources, fee-based resources, and Web 2.0 sites."

---

[1] ndsu.edu/pubweb/~mcclean/plsc431/students99/crowston.htm

The What, Where, and How of Conducting Due Diligence Investigations

What triggers the topics needed for your due diligence investigation? What merits the spending limits on resources to conduct a due diligence investigation? For how long should the investigation be conducted? And how do you know if you have enough facts? There really is no definitive answer to these questions since much of the answer depends on the circumstances, budget, and time.

Here is a simple yet practical example of due diligence used in everyday life. I was prepared to hire a deck contractor to update my deck. His advertisement in the local paper was all I had to refer to, but it appeared professional. A visit to his Web site showed work that was well done and professional. He appeared to be a suitable contractor. He was registered and licensed in the State of New Jersey, which requires him to carry certain insurances. Then I visited his personal Facebook account and read several racist rants he posted, which struck me as callous and unprofessional. The man is entitled to his own opinion, but my meager due diligence of him changed my opinion on his suitability to be my contractor.

In the world of professional investigations, I believe the *what* and *how long* come down to two factors: comfort and budget. The real reasons any investigator is hired are to bring resolution and a sense of comfort to the client. Simply stated; they are unsure. Clients do not fully know or understand the circumstances around a person, an event, or a company. We are hired to conduct these investigations to make sure our clients are comfortable with decisions to be made. The client's desire to learn more drives them to our office and opens up their wallets – and they also must decide how much money they are willing to invest to obtain that comfort level.

The discussion of how much money to spend should be considered. I've heard investigators talk about conducting due diligence investigations on a single person for fees ranging from $100 to $10,000. Certainly there are very brief investigations, where the client spends little but is given a small but potent level of comfort in return.

As a budget consideration when hiring non-management employees (line workers, customer service reps, hospitality workers), most large companies choose to do minimal background checks, which I refer to as compliance checks. In order for a large manufacturer to obtain the best insurance for the lowest price, it does inexpensive background checks on its workforce. Yet, the same company who is hiring a new CEO or CFO will spend thousands of dollars in order to insure this high level staffer has the credentials to run and represent the company.

The amount of money the client is willing to spend depends on who is being investigated, the position they are being hired for, and where they live. Yahoo could have spent a few more dollars verifying the education of their potential new CEO Scott Thompson before a news story surfaced that he lied about his education. He claimed to have a Bachelor of Science Degree in Computer Science, which he doesn't. That headline embarrassed Yahoo, caused internal fights with their investors, and had business ethics professionals spinning on their heels.[2]

Thompson is not the only executive to lie about his past and not get caught. Headlines surface often about individuals sneaking past sleeping companies who don't thoroughly vet their potential hires. There are doctors, lawyers, industry leaders who walk among us without ever having obtained the required qualifications to hold their jobs. A New Jersey doctor, who was convicted of manslaughter in England, had been performing spinal surgery (badly it appears) on numerous individuals, crippling them. He wasn't even qualified in spinal surgery; his area of study was as an anesthesiologist. Surprisingly the State of New Jersey does not conduct background checks on physicians, until after something happens. Kansas, where the doctor first tried to get his license to practice, does conduct background checks and the state did deny him a license.[3]

Dr. Nutjob

Many years ago I received a call from a distraught woman who was recommended to me by a well-respected fellow investigator. She asked me for a very simple assignment: "Will you obtain a copy of my PhD in psychiatry?" I thought this an odd request, and even asked her if she had a copy hanging on the wall over her desk or in her waiting room. To which she replied, "I did until the fire." Apparently it was the second fire that took the license. Which was my first indication that the woman was a little odd. It is rare indeed to have one fire, but to have two fires in the home, makes me really suspicious about her behavior. Does she smoke in bed? Does she run a heater near the drapes? So I was curious to work with her and cautious to move ahead.

I explained that she could simply call her school and ask for a certified copy to be sent to her for a fee. I even offered to give her the phone number for her school's registrar office. But she was "too busy to do these mundane tasks."

Being young and hungry, I took the assignment, but with a retainer up front because she was definitely an odd bird and I wanted to make sure I got paid.

I spent a week looking for her PhD. I called the registrar, the associated school's registrars, current administration, and past employees of the

[2] dailymail.co.uk/news/article-2141099/Yahoo-CEO-apologises-lying-past-education-apparently-doesnt-bother-resign.html

[3] northjersey.com/news/pompton-lakes-pain-doctor-a-shocking-story-of-damaged-patients-and-weak-oversight-1.584714

school. No one could vouch knowing her. The only fact I uncovered was an employment record for one Spring semester at the school library. Finally I had to confront her.

"Ma'am (I'd stopped calling her Doctor), do you remember walking in procession to receive your diploma?"

"Do you remember paying for classes?"

"Do you remember writing and defending your dissertation?"

She couldn't answer honestly to any of these questions, because she wasn't a doctor. Her response was that she hung out at the school so much during the time she might as well be a doctor. This woman had actually testified in court for 15 years before a judge ordered to see her credentials. She'd been treating children for just as long.

A year later, a Chief Medical Examiner in another state hired me to investigate her. She was doing the same thing somewhere else.

People Are the Key

Conducting due diligence on companies and events really comes down to investigating the people who run them. The company doesn't fail – the people who are employed there do. Our investigation into due diligence will turn to and use the resources, databases, Web sites, and social media that allow us a view of these people. This mind set can apply to your professional work as well as your personal life. Remember the deck contractor story? There really is nothing off limits to my investigative eye. If you call me and I don't recognize your number, I will research it before answering. I will look into the background of doctors, lawyers, and professionals before hiring them. Even if I choose to donate money to a charity, I will review its tax returns to see if they give as much as they receive. Digging into this level of detail gives me insight into the person I'm investigating. If my family member needs to find a doctor, lawyer or a deck repair company, after my due diligence I am going to know that business owner better than he knows himself.

Phases of Due Diligence

As mentioned there are varying levels of intensity in due diligence investigations. On one hand, you can check out someone's Facebook page or LinkedIn profile and get a sense of who he is. On the other hand, you can spend thousands of dollars on a battalion of investigators to ferret out every last bit of information available on the person. Being involved in both styles of investigations for years, I now use a systematic approach when explaining the possibilities to clients so they can quickly understand how our work can meet their needs. This approach is called the *Phased*

Approach. Phases of due diligence occur naturally when investigations are done correctly. Breaking down the job into investigative phases is a good way to not only help the client better understand the job, but also to give the client a sense of control and a cutoff point when he is satisfied with our work.

Phase One – Preliminary Due Diligence (aka Online Due Diligence)

Phase One involves the steps in a typical preliminary due diligence including Internet research, searches of social networks, individual U.S. government databases, local media searches, and online litigation research for the relevant jurisdictions. The results should be compiled in a written memorandum summarizing the issues identified. Phase One will also focus on any new activity mentioned in social networks using non-traditional Internet resources.

The following are some, but not all, specific identifiers that should be researched on the subject.

Personal Identifiers and Assets

- Name (including any aliases or former names)
- Date of Birth
- Social Security number
- Home address (including past addresses)
- Contact numbers
- Family members
- Corporate ownership or partnership, or any business involvement
- Identify any donors and their beneficiaries of gifts valued at more than $1,000
- Professional association affiliations, position held and time served
- Educational certification and membership verification
- Automobiles, vessels, and planes
- Property ownership

Financial History

- Personal debt of the subject and its principals
- Real property interests including mortgages held
- Outside business interests of subject and its principals
- Local, state, and federal tax liens
- Other recorded judgments and liens
- Bankruptcy or financial insolvency records

Civil and Criminal Filings

- Any criminal convictions
- Any pending or post-civil, criminal, or administrative actions
- Proceedings involving any violations, racketeering, or unfair trade practices.
- Any Federal or state regulatory actions
- Any association to known organized crime affiliates or politically exposed persons

Sources

Phase One can access over 3,000 databases including but not limited to the following topics:

- Academic records
- Board appointments
- Business and personal affiliations
- Civil filings
- Corporate records
- Criminal filings
- Financial records
- Government litigation history
- Intellectual property
- Liens, Judgments, and UCCs
- Media history
- Non-profit participation
- Online and social networks
- Physical assets
- Political and charitable causes
- Property records
- Regulatory history
- SEC, FINRA, and State Securities filings
- State specific regulatory agencies
- Subsidiaries and franchises
- Vendor and supplier relationships
- WorldCompliance ®

Phase One can be quite comprehensive and should be done before any other work; it is the basic intelligence-gathering portion which all other investigations should follow. After Phase One, a report is issued to the client, then a review of the work conducted and information found is considered. The assignment might end here or the client may wish to continue to Phase Two.

Phase Two — Comprehensive Due Diligence (aka Boots-on-the-Ground)

In Phase Two, a continuation of the work done in Phase One, the investigator will start contacting references of the person or company. The investigator will also hire and send court retrievers into every jurisdiction in which the person lived or worked to ensure the investigator has captured every redundant detail and record. Redundancy is necessary when working on cases needing thorough research because many counties (or cities or boroughs) do not produce an online means to their complete public record database. In fact, per the Public Record Research System[4], 32 percent of courts are not online.

AUTHOR TIP **What is a *Public Record Retriever*?**

According to the Public Record Retriever Network (one of the largest U.S. trade organizations representing professionals in the public record industry):

"Simply put, PRRN Members are professionals who visit government agencies on-site—such as local, federal, and state courts or recorder's offices—to do name searches and/or obtain copies of file documents. Retrievers are often hired in conjunction with the pre-employment screening, investigations, lending, litigation, or for legal compliance (e.g., incorporations)."

prrn.us/Home.aspx

Outside the U.S.

When searching within the United States, you can locate a great deal of information and feel reasonably assured all resources were covered with a Phase One due diligence investigation. In fact, most of an investigator's daily work is strictly in Phase One.

However, when there is a need to look for information outside of the United States, going to Phase Two is absolutely necessary because Phase One public record databases in foreign countries are sparse and privacy laws are severe.

Regardless of whether due diligence is conducted inside or outside of the U.S., once Phase Two is completed, a report or a verbal update of the investigation's findings could occur, depending on the nature of the engagement.

---

[4] https://www.brbpublications.com/products/Prrs.aspx

Phase Three — Recommended Next Steps

After the information is gathered and analysis has brought the details from Phases One and Two together, there can be more questions that develop, depending on the type of case and the person or company who is the subject of the due diligence. At the end of each Phase, the report usually includes a Recommended Next Steps section.

For example: Let's say you are performing due diligence on the background of a manufacturer of diet supplements. Your investigation would require reviewing financial strength, manufacturing ability, current management and other business, scientific, and manufacturing sources. During the course of reviewing your gathered information, you might come across a newspaper article, social media post, or other open source (rumor) information. Perhaps the information suggests the CEO spends all his time gambling and jet-setting. Then a Recommended Next Step in the investigation would be to take a closer look at the CEO's background to see how it may directly relate to his ability to lead in the future. The company could find itself in dire straits if its potential CEO were to begin draining capital from the company to support his gambling habits.

In summary, the Recommended Next Steps section often includes recommendations to continue monitoring the subject to see if any future information develops that will add to knowledge regarding the investigation. Also Recommended Next Steps can also include comments on leads that seemed tangent to the investigation. For example, perhaps the individual worked for a company three years earlier, but currently does not have a relationship with that company. Then Phase Three would recommend contacting and interviewing the former employer and co-workers. A Recommended Next Step might also include an interview with the subject to find additional data not found online or on the ground.

Phased Approach Summary

Using the three Phases outlined above—the Phased Approach—gives the investigator a linear, stepping-stone method to develop more information on the subject at hand, gathering information that is often scattered, spread out, and not easy to understand. The Phased Approach also helps clients manage what is happening in their hired investigation and where they can expect to see results. The client can order a Phase One Due Diligence Investigation, and hold off on ordering Phases Two and Three—or not order the last two at all. The Phased Approach will allow the client to see a report following each phase, and the results of Phase One, the Online Due Diligence, may very well suffice. Or, Phase One may also jump straight to Phase Three, first conducting online due diligence in Phase One, and then next monitoring or following up on online items in Phase Three, with no Phase Two required.

The Necessary Skill Set for Online Due Diligence

My goal is to give you the insight and education to perform quality due diligence investigations. With this book, you will learn a certain necessary skill set, including analysis techniques and how to solve research challenges. You will also be introduced to hundreds of Web sites, social media and online resources. However, beyond reading, writing, and looking up a Web page, there are other skills necessary to have when conducting due diligence investigations.

A good investigator must understand various businesses, their principals, industries, economics, finances, and risks. Expert knowledge is not required in each area, but a strong basic knowledge in these corporate worlds is necessary so that when investigating, valuable information is not missed. When researching specific businesses, the challenge comes as you work to understand the specific type of industry in which your target company is involved. For example, one day you might be investigating a clothing manufacturer with locations in China, Mexico, and California. You will then need to learn about and become familiar with the clothing industry, the players in the business, and the language of retail and manufacturing for those particular countries. Legal issues and the implications of having businesses located in those countries may also come into play during the investigation.

Necessary Ingredients

There are four key areas that are indispensable to a due diligence investigator:

1. **Critical/analytical thinking, some imagination, and raw determination** are needed. Needing these traits is especially true when investigating cases involving crimes, fraud, or deception. An investigator's dogged determination is the catalyst to keep pushing through the mounds of information that need to be uncovered. An investigation is not for the lazy, but is for the individual who is easily consumed in picking apart minutiae—one fact at a time—and reviewing it.

   Tracking lead after lead can be mentally exhausting, especially when cases drag from days to weeks to months and beyond. But when a fact makes itself apparent, and you then realize that the marathon research you have been doing to get there was the sole reason for finding that key piece, you feel like you have won the lottery. That is the moment when you will hear a hearty "Yahoo" coming out of my office.

2. **Proficiency with a computer** is another necessary skill, and can sometimes be a struggle. Knowing word processing, spreadsheets, Web browsers, email, and social media are basic tools for an online investigator. Everyone eventually learns these skills, but a good investigator must take a step beyond. Your work will greatly benefit from having a deeper knowledge level of how the Web works, how email is transmitted, and how information

is stored. Think about it: most of today's crimes involve a computer in some way.

3. **Good investigators speak the language**. Understanding the business community and the industries you may be associating with will help you win over clients, as well as give you a firm knowledge base from which to perform solid due diligence investigations. You also need to understand the difference between a docket and a disposition. It takes time to learn the language of the courts and the other government bodies that warehouse public records. When speaking about the public records, filings, and other administrative memos retrieved and used in an investigation, a seasoned investigator will often sound like an attorney.

4. **Access to the best databases and services** is a necessity to accomplish your due diligence investigation. Investigators often find it necessary to spend a considerable amount of money on professional databases with thorough and extensive access to public records, business reports, and other pertinent information needed as a case develops. In some matters, the service may be free, such as accessing LinkedIn to view the online resume of a person. In other matters, not so free; you may use LexisNexis's aggregated database of public records to see if what was documented in LinkedIn does indeed match the public record to then validate the fact. For example, a LinkedIn profile may say the candidate worked for a company for three years. You can look at the People at Work feature found at Accurint (accurint.com/hr.html) or IRBsearch (irbsearch.com/searches.html) to help verify that employment detail.

Have a Toolkit Worth Carrying and Know How to Use it

You do not need to subscribe to thousands of databases to be a smart and successful due diligence investigator. The databases that I believe are necessary to conduct investigations intelligently are highlighted throughout this book. However, you will need to intimately know the services you are using to answer the on-the-spot questions from your clients about your reports. Knowledge of where information comes from and how to obtain the most current sources possible are also necessary.

AUTHOR TIP **Staying Abreast With What is New**
Every time I lecture, the question arises: "How do you keep up with the newest Web sites and sources?" My answer is always the same: "Keep your nose in the news, read the journals, buy books on research, venture into industries you are not immediately tied to, join associations, and communicate." When I teach and share my sources, I always get two sources in return.

Due diligence investigators must maintain an information edge as they run their own businesses. For example, an arson investigator is a professional who is hired to assess how a fire occurred and moved throughout a building. He is paid for his analysis of what occurred, for presenting the evidence, testifying in court, and writing reports or depositions. But an arson investigator should also be an expert in this unique field so that he can examine a building and offer suggestions to prevent fires from happening.

The edge in knowledge is to know. Know more about the tools you use, know more about the products coming out on the market, know your client's needs and know your limitations.

I once spent three months examining a company and its leadership. I had every last public record but one to establish that this company was fraudulent. The project went from Phase One - Preliminary Due Diligence to Phase Two - Boots-on-the-Ground with a record retriever obtaining a key public record from a Georgia court which I believe was going to confirm the senior leader of the company was also a convicted felon, Ponzi-scheming mastermind. The cost of obtaining documents from the retriever was $150 including the materials. The client said, "No, we don't want to pay anymore, and we're going to stop this case." After months of effort, with moderate success in our work, the frustration of having the plug pulled before the song ended was awful. But the client hit his limit. Without the one final document in hand, I could not say that this was the same man as our subject, or someone with a similar name. I will forever wonder if the court record we wanted to pull held the key information that would have proven the fraud scheme was occurring again. An investigation never has an endless budget or an unlimited amount of time.

The lesson to be learned from my example is to thoroughly plan your due diligence investigation from the start. A good plan will give you a giant step forward to help you accomplish as much as you possibly can within the allotted timeframe and budget. Chapter 2 talks specifically about how to intake a due diligence investigation and set up a plan of attack to execute the best work possible.

The Role of Social Media and Online Due Diligence

Social media is not merely the playground of 15 year-olds and bored housewives. With hundreds of millions of customers, online services such as Facebook, Twitter, Instagram, and LinkedIn are treasure troves full of useful information, right alongside the pointless posts. Companies are now using social media platforms to announce new products and shifts within its industries, even before the more traditional press releases are used. On one hand, the company itself is embracing and encouraging its employees to move into this medium, and that gives the due diligence investigator an entirely new area to find excellent leads on corporate shifts. On the other hand, employees who are dissatisfied with their work, or their management, or are simply too chatty online with social media, readily give investigators an inside view to the company structure and workplace culture that, in the past, would have been kept behind closed doors—because there wasn't a public forum available.

As this book progresses, I will continue to draw upon the current and sometimes future social media applications that can be used during the course of an online investigation to demonstrate how to investigate within the service, and also how to apply and verify the information.

A Few Final Comments

Know and clearly understand what **due diligence** is all about before you decide to start offering it as a service. The next chapter defines the difference between due diligence and other business online investigations. Once you comprehend the big picture, approaching the investigation in Phases will prove helpful to both you and your client. This systematic approach to discovering and reporting your findings will help with controlling costs and expectations.

Finally, regardless of your own personal interest in social media, keep in mind due diligence has been expanded by the application of the many social media resources and their offerings. Do not dismiss what they have to offer and what benefit it might give your case. Also, pay close attention on how to utilize these resources to the benefit of your due diligence investigation.

Ch 2:

What Makes Due Diligence Different from Other Investigations?

The business of America is business.
—Calvin Coolidge

Do you know the difference between a due diligence investigation and a competitive intelligence search? Knowing the key elements associated with different types of investigations is an important first step in establishing or setting up your investigation methods for a client.

Types of Business Investigations

Investigators are as diverse as doctors. You have foot doctors, head doctors, and witch doctors. Each doctor specializes and produces a different result; so too with investigators. As you will learn throughout this book, there are several approaches to take when performing business investigations, and all depend on the type of investigation requested.

The many names investigations fall under are unique and sometimes perplexing. For example, there are background investigations, due diligence investigations, competitive intelligence, market intelligence, and background checks, to name a few. I have always believed the type of investigation depends on what the customer wants. The customer has a question and we find the answer. That is what we do.

How much information I find and how the report gets written define what we can do for a client. As in the case of our Phased Approach to investigations, the more in-depth you go, the more effort and expense is required. Some work inherently requires a deeper dive and more thorough effort to get to the bottom, and I would say due diligence is just that.

A typical phone call from a potential client goes something like this: "I would like to know more about ABC Company." The investigator's follow-up questions should be "Why do you want to know about ABC Company? Is it a competitor, a potential acquisition, or a defaulted company? Are the principals of that company individuals you want to examine closer?" The client's answer should trigger a response from the investigator that clearly identifies how the investigator should handle the investigation and what information edge is needed. Particularly if the client's focus is on the CEO, or a specific individual, of the company, the client might not be looking at the entire enterprise, but only one part (the person) and those reasons can vary.

AUTHOR TIP Over time, I have learned that clients often will ask for what they think I can find, and not for what they really want. There is a difference. When taking on an assignment, be sure to ask the client what is expected in the investigative report. Each possible answer will guide the investigator in a different direction; the approach will not be the same for every case. There is crossover and many times a margining of the different types of investigations that follow. Each one of these approaches though, will include online due diligence.

Below are descriptions of different types of investigations with examples of how I would begin each of investigation based on the clients' needs.

Competitor Investigations

The need for Competitor Investigations usually occurs when a new company enters your client's particular market, or a preexisting company starts to out-perform your client's company. A suspicion of fraud or regulatory cheating will also prompt a competitor to scrutinize the other players in his market.

If I am asked to investigate a competitor, I begin by drawing an outline of the competitor company, with an emphasis on supply chain vendors, clients, and revenue streams. In addition, I look for new trends, or establish existing trends in the market, to formulate where it is heading in the next six months to a year. I also review the past six months to a year, laying the stepping stones to the current investigation. Finally, I analyze this information and write a SWOT (Strengths, Weaknesses, Opportunities, and Threats) analysis[5], emphasizing the company's position in the market compared to similar companies. My report will offer recommendations for continued monitoring of the company to avert any surprises for the client.

---

[5] See Chapter 3 for an explanation of SWOT analysis.

Competitive Intelligence

Competitive Intelligence is similar to Competitor Investigation, except the investigation covers more than one company; it will also cover the industry as a whole for a comparison. In an Competitor Investigation for example, I may be looking at one peanut processing plant in Central Mexico. In Competitive Intelligence, I would be evaluating a few peanut processing plants in central Mexico, as well as the industry in all of Mexico, and perhaps even globally. Thus, Competitive Intelligence will require a good deal of knowledge about the industry you are researching, as well as a deep understanding of statistical and analytical models.

An excellent organization representing the competitive intelligence industry is the Strategic and Competitive Intelligence Professionals association (SCIP). At SCIP's Web site (scip.org), you will find all sorts of industry information, including an excellent array of books and techniques specific to conducting competitive intelligence work.

Potential Acquisition

Sometimes the goal of an investigation is to research a company acquisition – by the client or another party. Potential Acquisitions has its own investigative pattern. Since a company's reputation can be as important as its financial status in business, I first search various media, including the Internet. I look for information to insure that the company has not come under fire for any malpractices or misdeeds, and that its principals have not been accused of criminal misconduct such as fraud or collusion. I then examine the company's financial health to determine if it is suitable for an acquisition. Perhaps it is on its last dollars of venture capital investment, and is desperate for a new company to purchase it. Finally, looking at the company's marketing strategy, Web site, and industry reviews, I learn about its products and services, and assess, through analysis, how it compares to its competition in the market. Perhaps it is a technology company with some cutting-edge software. But, the management is incompetent and cannot market its product effectively. If I see positive reviews of the software, but notice that the product is not selling as much as its competition, this indicates management does not understand the product it is selling. Perhaps the company has incredibly brilliant software developers, but its marketing is targeting the wrong industry, which could be a sign the company is struggling, just waiting for a more competent competitor to acquire it. The company might also be a shell or a front for another enterprise. Potential Acquisition investigations will consider all of the above issues.

Fraudulent or Defaulted Company

Sometimes the goal of a client investigation is to research a company that owes the client money; a company defaults on payments, and so the client intends to sue for compensation or collect on a judgment. Fraudulent or Defaulted Company investigations will involve tracking company assets – assets that could have been moved into the personal funds of the shareholders. My investigation will involve tracking the assets. I will identify all the responsible parties, and then examine these principals, including their wealth, vehicles, including watercraft and aircraft, homes, other expensive business interests, families, associates, tangible and intangible assets such as property, trademarks, and patents.

All items that hold value can potentially be assets my client can seize with the proper judgment. My task is to locate all fiscal, tangible, and physical property associated to the defaulted parties – and done within the limits of the law. I can locate physical property through public records without any hesitancy, yet the Fair Credit Reporting Act (FCRA) does not allow me to look for bank accounts or other fiscal trusts, and similar, without a judgment.

Judgments, FCRA, and permissible access all can trigger a compliance issue – an important aspect in investigations. Compliance rules alone will steer you towards one type of investigation or another. There are many items to consider as you talk to your client about what can and can't be accomplished in your investigation.

Compliance

An acquisition or defaulted company investigation will sometimes involve compliance issues. Companies are required by various compliance rules, such as the Sarbanes Oxley Act of 2002 (SOX)[6] and the Foreign Corrupt Practices Act (FCPA)[7], to hire outside vendors to remain unbiased when information reporting needs arise. The conflict-of-interest issue is avoided because, for example, compliance laws such as SOX do not permit an accounting firm to conduct compliance due diligence on the same client it audits. Consequently, corporate clients will often look for independent investigators to conduct impartial, business investigations. The compliance investigations market is open to those investigators with the right resources and the necessary skill set.

Once the parameters of an investigation are established, you will know what type of investigation you will be pursuing, be it due diligence on a person or a company, or a competitive intelligence analysis on several emerging companies, or finding out who is funding the latest project for a competitor company. Each type of investigation will have a different starting and ending point.

Many investigative resources will be repeatedly used in your search, no matter the type of investigation being conducted. However, as you get into the minutiae of an investigation, what type of investigation – acquisition, asset, or business background – will certainly dictate other resources specific to that type of investigation that you must use.

---

[6] gpo.gov/fdsys/pkg/PLAW-107publ204/html/PLAW-107publ204.htm
[7] gpo.gov/fdsys/pkg/STATUTE-91/pdf/STATUTE-91-Pg1494.pdf

Information Retrieval Language

There are many terms used throughout this book. Some terms refer to investigative resources; other terms refer to reporting detailed results to clients. The following selected terms and definitions will help you better understand some of the unique information gathering processes used in due diligence investigations. These terms represent important components within the unique information world where investigators reside.

Information Aggregators

Information aggregators gather, warehouse, and resell data. The information is collected from multiple sources of public records. Dun & Bradstreet (D&B), Experian, TransUnion TLO, Westlaw, and LexisNexis are large enterprises that aggregate disparate public records from across the country and format the information into readable and usable reports. With their easy-to-use search interfaces, these aggregators are considered the go-to sources for business investigators – regardless of the type of investigation.

However, since aggregators cannot collect data from every U.S. county and city, they cannot provide a complete turnkey service offering – which is actually a benefit to investigators; if there were one completely comprehensive tool available to everyone, there would be no need to hire an investigator.

The types of reports created by aggregators from comprehensive searches can be classified into two categories: Business Reports and Comprehensive Reports. For the sake of clarity in this book they are defined as follows, but with the understanding vendors of all types often use both titles to describe their services.

1. **Business Reports**, generated by services such as D&B and Experian, focus on company information. These aggregators obtain their data from public records, vendor-supplied information, self-reporting, government filings, and limited research.

2. **Comprehensive Reports**, generated by companies such as TransUnion TLO and IRBsearch, focus on individual persons information. This type of report is created from aggregated data collected from public records.

Visit the online services of these aggregators for an explanation of their record-collection techniques as well as the coverage, scope, and limitations of their databases.

AUTHOR TIP There are many Web sites touting their proprietary databases as being the largest or most complete, holding everything from national criminal records data (this doesn't exist) to public information going back to the 1800s (also doesn't exist). How do you know if these databases are truly primary resources? If they fail to disclose where their information comes from, then be careful before paying for their services.

In truth, all information comes from public records and open sources. The vendor should not be afraid to share its information sources with you. We do not subscribe to these services because they have special access; we subscribe to them because they aggregate many of the needed records into one easy-to-retrieve report. It is a matter of function, not secret magic resources.

Data Mining

Data mining (also known as data warehousing) is the researching of specific data and analyzing it for trends, using data from high-end databases and analytical tools to cull through their big data and apply predictive analytic methods. Suppliers constantly gather sales data at each store in real time to determine which products are hot and which ones are not. Data mining occurs when a company, such as Wal-Mart, conducts market basket analysis to find out which product sells the best in conjunction with another, during certain periods of time. Often told and readily understood is the story about the combination of beer and diapers sold as a set on Friday nights at Wal-Mart. The store knows from its data mining and analytics, that as men are sent out to buy diapers on a Friday night, they are easily enticed to buy beer which is strategically placed in the store close to the diapers.[8]

The actual data mining is performed with specialized software such as Cognos or MicroStrategy in the business world, and i2 or Palantir in the intelligence and investigative worlds. Databases such as SAS and Oracle also create their own data mining interfaces.

Whether the asset is diamonds, coal, or information, mining is never random.

Information Anxiety

Information anxiety is what most pedestrian searchers attempting due diligence on their own experience as they click through Web page after Web page, trying – and often failing – to gain insight into their query. As a business investigator, you are the antidote to the information anxiety the executive client experiences. Your task is to gather the data from the ether called the Web, verify this data until you know that it is factual information, and then analyze and translate the factual information into knowledge as you write your report for your client

Below is an image of the ecology of turning data into knowledge.

---

[8] information-management.com/news/1006133-1.html

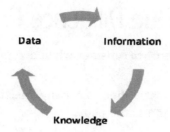

Data   Information

Knowledge

Direct Evidence

Direct evidence relates to the smoking gun in the hand of the criminal, the full statement with signature and confession, and the public records retrieved from government offices. All these items can be brought into court and used as evidence in a court trial. They can still be questionable, but there is a high level of confidence based on their validity.

Intelligence

Intelligence is information that is valuable to building the case, but the confidence level is not as high as that for evidence because intelligence information needs stronger validation. Confidential Informants (CIs) often provide intelligence information on a case, and are usually good reporting sources, but CIs may have suspect backgrounds.

Hearsay

Hearsay is rumor – perhaps an overheard conversation – and unless you can substantiate the data gathered, either by primary or secondary research, you should always cite it as hearsay and unverified information in your report.

Primary Research

Primary research is first-hand experience: interviewing, collecting data onsite, or pulling records from a courthouse. Primary research is the traditional method of most investigators and interviewers – it is what occurs in Phase Two mentioned earlier in this book.

Secondary Research

Secondary research is the use of databases, online services, Web sites to gather information, plus the gathering of information from books, magazines, and other second-hand sources. When using secondary research sources for your investigative reports, verify the information you are relaying or quote the source used. Secondary research is what occurs in Phase One mentioned earlier in this book.

How to Receive a Due Diligence Project

There are several key steps to consider when accepting a project that requires a due diligence investigation.

1. First and foremost, when receiving incoming work the client's objective should be clear and to the point.

2. The amount of the retainers and the manner in which documented statements of work are to be presented should be established BEFORE you start your investigation in order to avoid wrong expectations and non-payment.

Working With an Experienced Client

If you are working with another seasoned investigator, attorney, or security professional, the call and request for due diligence is usually clearly stated. The question they always ask is, "What's your cost and turnaround?" For example, "Cynthia, we have a company in Pittsburgh, Pennsylvania that is being considered as a supplier for our client. We want to know the background of the company and its three top executives. What's your cost and turnaround?" These are the best types of client; their expectations are likely as predictable as mine.

Although I know there are four items to investigate in the above sample request, I will double-check and ask if all four items are located in the United States.

AUTHOR TIP Always verify that your target (person or company) is in the United States before quoting a price. Once a case leaves the United States the price starts increasing because of your need to engage a foreign investigator. The price can go as high as five times your normal rate.

Working With a Newbie

If your client has never hired a private investigator before, the client may act like a priest in the confessional or an attorney checking for thoroughness. The client no doubt will have a long-winded and rather detailed story to share with you. Patience is absolutely necessary; buried in the long-winded tale could be key points that will help form your investigation.

Be aware of the emotional client. Sometimes emotional clients will hire you just to tell you their problems and when you cannot find the answers for them, they might not pay you.

The Bakery

Buried in the life story of the new client I am now listening to, I hear that he wants to invest a good deal of money into a suggested business venture. Mixed in are the details I really don't care about. The business venture is actually the client's oldest friend's daughter who is opening up a bakery in an up-and-coming neighborhood. I get to hear about the friendship, the daughter, the history of everything. In this case, my investigative ear hears that the client wants to help the friend's daughter and wouldn't mind making a return on the investment. My job is to look at the viability of a bakery in the community chosen. I will examine the area for crime, new business development, new residential encouragement, major construction permits being issued, and any major road changes, such as moving an exit ramp from a nearby highway.

I will also ask the client if he wants me to look into the background of the young baker, but chances are he knows this person well enough to feel comfortable with the investment risk.

Planning the Investigation

At this point, your client has now relayed the case requirements. Your task is to explain the Phased Approach, which will help you manage an efficient and cost effective investigation.

As you can see from the many lists of sources and topics reported in Chapter 1 of this book, deciding where to start and which path to follow for an investigation can be daunting. Though I'm not a fan of check-box investigations because I feel it creates a lethargy that squelches creative thinking (a necessary tool in investigations), an investigative plan will definitely help keep you on target and prevent errors.

Below is a simple plan of attack on a due diligence investigation of a company and its principals. Subsequent chapters in this book will cover the due diligence investigation in much more detail with extensive specifics, such as the databases and the investigative methods to be used.

Begin your investigative work by identifying the target company and its location. Often you can simply look online at the company's Web site and read its Contact Us page. A simple way to verify that the company is actually located where it says it is, or that you are not looking at the franchisee, subsidiary, or any other attached firm, is to visit the Secretary of State's Web page for that state and retrieve the company's business filings. The addresses should match or be in reasonable proximity to each other. For example, my business address is 12 Main Street, Anytown, NJ. On the Secretary of State filing with New Jersey, my business address is registered at P.O. Box 123, Anytown, NJ. I don't immediately think of the address discrepancy as being awry, but I will look to see if any other businesses are registered to the same post office box number.

AUTHOR TIP

Checking the Address

Always check the business addresses of the companies you are investigating. Fraudulent entities will often have multiple companies registered at the same address. Also, check to see if the physical address really is for a building, or perhaps it is a Mailboxes, Etc. or UPS store location. Nothing fraudulent in that, but know there isn't a real presence for your company at that location. Even if it is a real building, it could also be a short term rental lease. Co-op office spaces are rented out by the hour, the day, or longer. Fraudulent companies that prey on want-to-be models and musicians will set themselves up on high-end addresses in New York and Los Angeles for a day or a week. They'll put pictures on the walls, hang gold records up. They'll get these want-to-be kids to come in and, to the kids, it all seems legitimate. Then they tell the want-to-be, "I can make you a star, but you have to pay me $10,000 to get your production started." After the money changes hands, the fake promoter leaves the office as if he were never there.

When reviewing the business filings for a company you may see the firm listed as a Foreign Company. That means it is foreign to the state, not to the country. An example is a company operating in New Jersey as a foreign firm, but is legally incorporated in Delaware. The firm will have tax and/or legal obligations in both states. The process is common with companies having a physical presence (such as an office) in more than one state. Of course, large companies often use Delaware as a tax shelter.

For many investigators planning the investigation can be the most daunting task. You want to tell a client that the work will take seven days and cost $1,000, however, at the onset, you won't really know about the work at-hand, and therefore won't know the real plan until you start the investigation. The case may become not one principal but six people to investigate. Or, if the company has an overseas branch, now non-U.S. entities need to be examined.

Once you have outlined your plan, but before you start your investigative work, create a Statement of Work (SOW) for the client. In it, outline specifically what you as the investigator are responsible for, what your investigative approach will be, and how often and in what format you will be making reports to the client. The SOW is not a contract; it is the outline of the investigation. The SOW will help you manage your client's expectations of the investigation.

How to Manage Client Expectations

There are three primary reasons for hiring an investigator, or any consultant for that matter:

1. The client is low on manpower and is hiring your services to fulfill his contract.

2. The client does not have a unique skill set or resource, so he is farming out a piece of the project to get the job done.

3. Plausible deniability; the project is risky, the client is edgy, or compliance laws require the client does not conduct his own audit, so the client hires you to do the heavy lifting, and if you drop the ball, the client can then blame you.

With every new project you should determine your role in it using the above three reasons; doing so will help immediately establish your relationship, and the client expectations will then fall into place.

To illustrate the first point listed above, my firm has been hired many times by a law firm, whose budget is tight, to conduct clerical work simply because we charge a less-expensive hourly rate than an attorney. As my firm conducts our work, I may suggest other opportunities where we can assist that lawyer, but will not hard sell him because I know I am there to shuffle papers.

Another scenario for hiring an investigator will illustrate the second point listed above: Perhaps another investigative house calls my office with a request to check specific databases for needed information. I'm not going to volunteer to run the whole case for the client house; they can do their own analysis. I will, however, share with them facts from other databases they might not have access to – or even know exist. For example, we get calls to locate import/export data from the PIERS (Port Import/Export Reporting Service) database. I would then offer to also search the Panjiva, Zepol, and ImportGenius databases for the client.

The third point listed above, plausible deniability, occurs when a company hires you to manage the case or the research for them. The compliance law (FCRA or SOX, for example) requires the audit and/or investigation be farmed out to prevent a conflict of interest in having the company investigate itself. However, sometimes our work could be in an area that makes the client very uncomfortable. If we find material that makes them or their organization look bad, they may prefer to have an outside firm do this report.

Working within the client's expectations and your own comfort level are important considerations. You may be deep into an investigation and still do not know what the outcome will be. Sometimes surprising information surfaces, such as finding out the CEO lied about his background, or that the CFO is diverting funds to his own private venture. Maybe a department head is posting nasty rants on a Facebook profile page. All sorts of strange facts about the past and present may come to light once you start your investigation. Perhaps the investigation is to locate and prove where the company's own staff is inept. Then the report will reflect the employer is not thriving because the staff doesn't know how to do their jobs properly.

I am careful to never guarantee the results the client expects. If I uncover what they hope I find, then life is grand. But if my investigation finds contrary information, then I will only report the facts perhaps using ambiguous language such as "based on the research, the results appear to be...."

I will however guarantee that we will do our best work and the client will get nothing less than 100 percent of effort. But I never assure the client the answer is just waiting for us once we start digging. Sometimes the answer never happens, and there you are handing the client an empty report and an invoice—however, since all research is documented, there is no question as to whether the work was done. A simple analogy is seeing a doctor: if you go to the doctor because you are sick and he cannot find anything wrong with you, you still have to pay him for his time and expertise.

Ch 3:

The Correct Approach to Research and Due Diligence Analysis

We must ask where we are and whither we are tending.

—Abraham Lincoln

Research and analysis are necessary steps in any type of investigation. Research requires knowledge of available sources and services to accurately answer the questions asked. Analysis is the ability to critically discern the gathered information and decide which possible conclusions to offer.

Whether you are a researcher, a special agent, or private investigator, implementation of consistent methodology is a must. A systematic approach to your research must include recording your findings and reporting your analysis in an accurate and easy-to-understand manner. Your reporting must be aligned correctly. For example, don't comingle the paragraph for Mr. John Doe with the paragraph for ABC Company; keep them in separate and distinct sections.

Initial Research Strategy

Strategically-directed research is a key component to successful investigations. Conducting investigative research today requires identifying the best resources associated with specific topics. Some resources are geared toward the legal market while others focus on fraud or motor-vehicle reconstruction, or Internet investigations; the subject focus is many and varied.

When I teach a research class, one of the first areas I cover involves directing investigators on:

- where to obtain information,
- how to know its limitations, reliability, and biases,

- how to compile all the information that is available.

Research tools and in-depth training aids are helpful to investigators in taking an organized approach to research. Among them are:

1. Case management software

2. Books on managing investigations

3. Training offered by professional associations

4. Downloadable checklists.

The various state and national associations will advise, endorse, or recommend on any of the four points above. *PI Magazine* presents an excellent list of investigative organizations and resources at pimagazine.com/links.htm.

Using Online Sources

The Internet tends to make us lazy. Log onto CLEAR or Experian and we can easily download a report on a subject. Gone are the days when we had to write letters requesting alpha searches to be conducted county-by-county, and then wait weeks for the results. I do not wish to return to that inefficient way for the bulk of my information gathering, but accessing offline sources is an important methodology that should be taught to all new investigators.

Reports From Online Database Sources

Most of the database services I utilize for my investigations do not create information – they aggregate or retrieve content from public sources. Reports from CLEAR, LexisNexis, Westlaw, and others are produced from public records (i.e., county courthouse and state motor vehicles). A team of investigators at LexisNexis does not provide me with dossiers on subjects I am evaluating. Supercomputers gather information from thousands of sources to create a single document or report.

The most sizable report I can purchase from a database vendor, such as CLEAR or IRBsearch, is called a *comprehensive report* as mentioned in Chapter 2. Comprehensive reports are used to enlighten the investigator about the subject (person or company) under investigation. A typical report contains addresses, relatives' names, business associates, phone numbers, etc., and is a catalog of information aggregated from various federal, state, county, and other vendor databases. For example, a comprehensive report on myself includes data from the New Jersey Division of Motor Vehicles, credit report companies (i.e., Experian, TransUnion, Equifax), the local Recorder of Deeds, the U.S. Postal Service, my phone provider, coupon-card distributors, and data from other agencies that sell personal information to commercial entities.

Investigators often stake a high level of reliance on these comprehensive reports. However, there can be instances when they improperly interpret what can be misleading statements. Granted, they find most of what you find independently going from site to site. For example, a report indicating a series of *None Found* statements, like the one below, may be interpreted several ways or may even indicate a misreporting of findings.

```
Driver's License:
    None Found
Motor Vehicles Registered:
    None Found
Florida Accidents:
    2 Found
Concealed Weapons Permit:
    None Found
```

There is a distinct difference between when a record is not found (the subject is clean) versus when a record is not available. Let's say the above example concerns a subject living in Utah. However, Utah has no concealed weapons permit searchable database. Also the vehicle ownership data from Utah is not sold to the aggregator who produced the above fact. So, should the investigator assume there are no records reportable in a search, or assume the aggregator simply couldn't find a source? The answers to these questions should be determined before the report results are passed to a client.

Big Brother Aggregators

In June, 2012 the *New York Times* published an article titled "Mapping, and Sharing, the Consumer Genome on marketing aggregator Acxiom ."[9]

The sum of the article was an in-depth report citing how Acxiom manages the world's largest database of consumer data. They know your height, weight, gender, shopping preferences, past and can predict your future. Not only is your shopping behavior analyzed through those value cards you use to save dollars on groceries, but also through the *Likes* and *Friends* you have in Facebook.

The thought of Acxiom playing Big Brother (and indeed they have capability) upset so many of the *Times* article readers, that the company had to respond. Although Acxiom sees themselves as a mom-and-pop operation out of Arkansas, they truly are the world's largest data warehouse of personal data.

[9] nytimes.com/2012/06/17/technology/acxiom-the-quiet-giant-of-consumer-database-marketing.html

In the true sense of transparency, Acxiom reacted to the general concern with a Web site aboutthedata.com in which Axiom openly discloses the company's marketing data to those asking to see their personal information and permits data edits. At this site, you can type in your particulars (don't worry, they already have your information!), and review the types of information they have on file for you. You can update it, edit it, and delete it. What I value on the site is the deep explanation of how they actually gather the various public records and private activity information and, form it, form a profile.

A conversation with their Chief Privacy Officer, Jennifer Barrett Glasgow (an amazing professional who has been with the company since 1974) relieved much of my consternation about their use of Facebook Likes within their data on us. Acxiom does not directly connect a social media profile when creating their Big Brother reports. Through predictive analytics, they surmise your buying habits based on a number of categories such as demographics, age, sex, and income.

You can view own profile after registering at <u>aboutthedata.com</u>.

Do Not Discount the Use of Social Media

As mentioned in Chapter 2, social media searches open a laundry list of due diligence leads. Sometimes these leads can be confirmed by a public record search and will help change the direction of your investigation. Consider this Facebook post by a subject of an investigation: "Here we are painting our new house!" The next steps of retrieving and verifying this new deed might lead to the information you need to make your case.

Recently my office conducted a discreet due diligence case on an executive. Nothing found in the paperwork and public records was very revealing. But one primary concern was why he had a leadership role in six companies within eight years. So we sifted through social media sources and found dozens of former company workers who complained about his management style and distinct lack of leadership. This led us to begin looking at his ability to run the next company.

AUTHOR TIP **Let's Define Predictive Analytics**

Predictive analytics is concerned with the prediction of future possibilities and treands. The following defininition is taken from reference.com

"Predictive analytics encompasses a variety of techniques from statistics and data mining that analyze current and historical data to make predictions about future events. Such predictions rarely take the form of absolute statements, and are more likely to be expressed as values that correspond to the odds of a particular event or behavior taking place in the future.

In business, predictive models exploit patterns found in historical and transactional data to identify risks and opportunities. Models capture relationships among many factors to allow assessment of risk or potential associated with a particular set of conditions, guiding decision making for candidate transactions."

The Importance of Using Offline Sources

The World Wide Web is not taking over the role of the library, archives, or a county court docket index. So do not consider this useful but often frustrating tool the only source to use.

There are a bevy of available sources that never make it to the Web. For example, this book mentions several time that 32 percent[10] of the courts in the U.S. do not provide online access to case files or to the record index. One must visit the court in person and search public records still in file cabinets and microfiche. At the corporate level, annual reports and market research analysis are deliberately kept in a printed format to curtail copyright infringement.

Knowing how to search offline sources is both a skill and a necessity. If your investigation leads you to research at the local level, a town library is a good place to usually find localized data cataloged, indexed, and archived. Some towns maintain history rooms or designate a few shelves in their town halls for books written by local authors, and small-town newspapers often report stories from the local residents' perspective. If General Motors decided to close plants in Springfield, Illinois, the *New York Times* might report on GM's financial burden to maintain such large facilities as the purpose for the closings. However, a newspaper in suburban Springfield is more likely to report on the families losing jobs and incomes due to the closings. It is common for investigators to visit local libraries, or hire a local researcher to comb through microfilm or microfiche articles of the local regional newspaper, to find that one vital article not databased anywhere.

AUTHOR TIP Locate a town's public library using an Internet phone book source or call the information operator. Then call or email the reference librarian to inquire about the local collection. It might take a visit to view the actual documents, because your answers may be sitting in an old file cabinet rarely used or noticed.

---

[10] Per The Public Record Research System https://www.brbpublications.com/products/Prrs.aspx

Collecting and Tracking Information

When starting your investigation, create an initial keyword list of terms and expressions. This technique will help you later expand your list with additional, helpful words.

For example, I had a case involving maintenance men who had been involved in escalator accidents. The client did not want information about accidents involving patrons, of which there are hundreds, but, specifically, he wanted to know about the workers who repair and maintain movable floors and stairs.

Using a Taxonomy

A taxonomy is a classification system. Using the above example, search Google or another search engine for these key terms: construction, accident, and maintenance. You soon will realize there are other terms that can work for this search as well. You are now developing word taxonomy – meaning a list of all possible terms and expressions that can get you closer to the answers you need.

Organized into three columns, your taxonomy list for the escalator example would look like this:

Construction	Accident	Maintenance
building	injure	worker
	hurt	laborer
	harm	employee
	dead	mechanic
	killed	repairman
		union
		contractor
		foreman
		apprentice

Keep this list on your computer or in a notepad. Within this same document, insert descriptive notes for yourself. You may be searching in one direction and find a new lead to pursue. However as enticing as the new lead appears to be, you will be better served if you first finish the original inquiry, and then pursue the new lead. Remember to document every step and you won't have to explain from memory what you did three days, three weeks, or three years ago. A disciplined to-the-end approach will keep you from wasting time with scatterbrained and wandering searches on the Internet.

AUTHOR TIP When searching the Internet or using an electronic database, it is easy to wander off on a lead and forget your original location. Use a notebook or notepad program to record where you were visiting. Copy and paste the results, and leave yourself a note. You also can capture a Web page as an Adobe Acrobat document and save it for later printing.

Whichever method works for you, be consistent so you will always know where you left off. This technique is very helpful if another investigator has to finish the work.

Using one document to track your words and leads will always pay dividends when you have to follow up later in the investigation and need to refer to your notes. You can search one document versus digging through a pile of notes, post-it stickers and saved documents. If you electronically manage a word and subject directory, you can easily incorporate within your final report those items you searched and where you looked.

Recording Your Findings

An important component of research is to establish a **methodology** that keeps you attuned with your research results. I recommend a combination approach of finding and recording information in the initial stages of the gathering mode in this manner:

- Record the findings in a consistent way so that you can return to the search and repeat the steps. Recording your findings in a consistent manner will help you create a more professional looking report that will benefit the client.

- Choose an actual style manual, such as in Chicago Manual of Style or APA Style Guide, or create a style guide that is clear and consistent.

- Place a date and time stamp on your reports/notes and add the location of where you searched: 7/14/2014, Wayne, NJ. This will establish a location in case there is a challenge to your report. Google and Bing have servers all over the country, and your results will vary based on your location.

- It might be redundant, but date the document itself and title it properly using terms such as *preliminary report*, *final report*, and *draft report*.

If you are uncertain whether or not your reports display an acceptable level of quality, show your report style to a colleague and ask for feedback on flow, content, and readability. The reason I mention "report style" and not the actual report is because the information you are reporting should be subject to non-disclosure.

Know the Market or Industry

There is an old saying: "I may not have a lot of knowledge, but I know where to find mountains of information." This statement rings true with due diligence investigations.

Good due diligence investigators locate information by knowing where to focus their research efforts. Looking for data about an insurance company or an auto manufacturer will still require a Dun & Bradstreet report. Knowing that A.M. Best Company and ACORD represent industry standard sources for rating insurance companies will enhance the report compared to off-the-shelf generalist information.

Hoover's (hoovers.com) is a great resource tool for performing industry and corporate research and searching for general-business information. Hoover's free and fee-based services offer quick and concise information. Hoover's provides key points such as geography, industry, people, company description and competitor identification; however, it will not report how a company compares to its competitors.

While you may find hundreds of news articles written about Ford Motor Company, you will not see any detail of union concerns or gain insight as to why its plants are closing. You must search further to find and read the trade magazines that focus on auto manufacturers.

A Case Study With Peanuts

Over the years, you will be exposed to many new, unique markets that you knew little about before you started a case. When you finish your final report, you will feel like an expert. In one particular case, I was tasked with locating peanut processing plants in South America. My client wanted to sell his peanut factory and requested I find the top three likely purchasers. I started by searching for peanut processors, but my approach was too limited. So using the taxonomy principle, I built a word list that included the term nut. However, searching for nut processors broadened the search too much resulting in a list that included all legitimate and inappropriate contenders. Once I realized that I was searching too broadly, I stepped back and decided to educate myself on the peanut industry. I went to Hoover's and searched by industry keyword nuts. The results come back as follows:

- Crop Production (found within Agriculture)

- Fresh Fruit & Vegetable Production (found within Agriculture - Crop Production)

- Hardware & Fastener Manufacturing (found within Industrial Manufacturing)

- Industrial Manufacturing

- Snack Foods (found within Food)

- Steel Production (found within Metals & Mining)

Choosing Crop Production offered an insight into the peanut industry, since it defined companies that grow, harvest, process, and package agricultural crops for both food and non-food products. Further research also steered me to the following:

- Most-Viewed Crop Producers

- Other Industries Related to Crop Production

Using a combination of taxonomy, tracking, and common sense research, I was able to get a sense of the market including who the major the players were and other industries associated with peanuts.

Using Industry Journals

Specialized trade journals, reference sources, and industry-specific publications offer in-depth analysis of the minutiae within their targeted industry. Industry journal writers are generally experts in their respective fields. If article writers are also business developers, company presidents, or chief executive officers, they tend to write at a higher level of specificity. Generalization is exchanged for details. Interviews with key people turn into personal exchanges between interviewer and interviewee. Mutual trust and respect between journalist and interviewee increases because each speaks the same language, resulting in a knowledge exchange that can be very insightful. This level of peer respect creates a potential bond which might lead to useful information. Other industry journal elements to review are sections where movers and shakers in the industry are profiled and who is moving to which company, or firms bought or sold, or what new products are being released. These specialized journals are published by trade associations, industry-targeted publishers, or companies. Of course, keep in mind advertisers need to be appeased, so there will be some bias.

See the Lists of Additional Resources section in the back of this book for a listing of resources connected to construction and the building trades.

AUTHOR TIP I use *Fulltext Sources Online* by Infotoday.com and the *Gale Directory of Publications* (gale.cengage.com/DirectoryLibrary) to locate industry publications. These sources and possible alternatives should be available at your local library.

Using Government Agency Resources

Data from government agencies are an important component and standard source used in business investigations. Most investigators immediately think of public records, such as court cases, business registrations, or Securities and Exchange Commission (SEC) filings, when they hear the words government documents. Often these types of government documents, or at least an index of the documents, are available on various government agency Web sites for free or for a nominal cost. A one-stop site for an enormous and updated collection of free searchable U.S. sources is found at brbpublications.com.

Other publicly available government publications are industry reports, government studies and surveys, military reports, historical documents, and white papers. Every single industry, country, scientific, or medical endeavor has some government documents written about it. Locating these documents can be cumbersome. Much of this data can be found at various Web sites, and the perfect place to start your search is through the U.S. Government search engine.

If you are diligent, you will want to visit the U.S. government depository library Web site gpoaccess.gov/libraries.html. Government depositories are excruciatingly complex information arsenals. Since the government produces more paper, media and source material than standard publishers, it has created its own classification system called the Superintendent of Documents (SuDoc). SuDoc numbers change with every new administration. Before the creation of the Department of Homeland Security, most agencies fell under the Department of Treasury, Department of Justice or other law enforcement organizations. Classification for Department of Justice documents all began with the letter J until the Department of Homeland Security was formed. Now, that same type of document is classified as HS.

Visiting a government depository can be a vital part of your research assignments. But avail yourself to the specialized government-documents librarian who can help you navigate through the vast amount of source material and help find what you need. Go to a library depository location near you (see gpoaccess.gov/libraries.html). The first visit should be in person in order to establish a relationship with this valuable research asset.

Vendors With Government Documents

LexisNexis, Westlaw, and Dialog are three strong enterprises providing government information that would not be easily accessible without their aggregation cataloging and indexing services. Time is an important budget item for the professional researcher; with a subscription to these services information can be accessed rather quickly. You can visit your local depository for a report on a Congressional hearing, but it is faster to search Dialog's Web site and download the same available document for a fee. Depending on your needs and usage, aggregators can be expensive. Between the government, Internet, media, and other available sources, there are more than enough places to find research information.

Definitive information about finding and using certain government information sources is found throughout this book, by topic chapter.

The Basics on Analysis

Business investigations that focus on mergers and acquisitions, competitive intelligence, vendor and supplier evaluations, or data mining research all require analysis. Simply collecting information and making claims is not an investigation; it is just finding and reporting "stuff."

The Returning Client

A longtime client called me after he had taken a few months' hiatus. When I asked him if work had been slow, or if he had chosen another company, he admitted that he had tried a cheaper investigative firm. My reply to him was, "Did the new firm disappoint you? Did you get what you paid for?"

He agreed that he had been disappointed. The other firm reported to him through a series of haphazard emails and phone calls that related the facts as they occurred, which made it impossible for him to track and manage the case. He brought his business back to my firm.

Unfortunately, stories such as these are all too common. Some investigators can find details, but they lack the ability and critical thinking skills to analyze and report their findings properly. If a case has time limits, contacting the client when key information in the investigation is uncovered is welcome. The client is then part of the process and can make decisions based on the findings. The professional method for closing the investigation is to follow up with a prepared report that includes all findings plus your analysis.

Often the true analysis occurs during the report writing procedure. Detailing the daily events keeps an investigator stay focused on the purpose of the content. First and foremost, your report must answer the initial question(s) your client hired you to find.

Using high-level analysis methods will make investigations easier to write. Getting acquainted with the different methods for the different types of case request needs allows you to offer a higher level of sophistication and confidence.

Three Recommended Analysis Methods

There are many books dedicated to analysis methods; consult the online store of the Society of Competitive Intelligence Professionals (scip.org) for titles. In the meantime, we'll review three methods below.

1. SWOT Analysis

SWOT is an acronym for—

- **S**trengths
- **W**eaknesses
- **O**pportunities
- **T**hreats

SWOT is a popular method of analysis especially handy for due diligence investigations. It allows for evaluating an item, person, or business, as compared to others. As the investigator gathers details and facts about his target, he considers which part of the analysis his investigative detail falls into. For example, the company may have strict 9 to 5 hours, but excellent customer service during those hours. I may write that up as, "Customer service during normal business hours is a strength with this company; however, with service not available in evening hours to those customers who cannot reach them during the day, limited daytime hours becomes a threat."

SWOT is flexible, easy to learn, and included within investigative reports. The analysis can itself be a report or included within a larger investigative report.

SWOT Advantages and Disadvantages

SWOT is the simplest of analyst methods and offers more benefits than merely the analysis itself. As an investigator, don't get caught up in the details of the information; consider comparing information to similar circumstances.

The SWOT analysis allows an investigator to analyze details in a manner that can lead to other investigative tracks. For example, if a company is showing $750,000 in annual revenue, but similarly-sized companies of the same type in the same market are bringing in $1.5 to $2.0 million, this could indicate a weakness or a threat. Perhaps the sales force is ineffective, the company is young to the market, or a bad reputation is involved. With a SWOT analysis, the client is properly prepared for your work and will anticipate a formula in the report you prepare.

There is one caveat to the SWOT analysis method: When your investigation requires creative and critical thinking – say, in cases concerning deception (fraud) – a check-box-style analysis, of which SWOT is one, is not useful. SWOT can negate the creative and critical thinking that some investigations require.

The Orange Grove Example

An orange juice producer is considering a Florida orange grove as an attractive acquisition. Using the SWOT method, the investigator will analyze the issues related to that grove, but only after gathering all the necessary researched data and facts.

- Strengths would include location, size of grove, and a present and established workforce.

- Weaknesses could include old on-site machinery, which might need repairing or replacing, or the trees themselves may be older and declining in productivity.

- Opportunity comes in the future potential to purchase adjacent property and expand the grove into a larger producing farm.

- Threats could possibly be present if the FDA were to test produce for bacteria-related illnesses due to bad well-water.

All of these points come into play in the decision to purchase. The client will use the information the investigator has gathered and verified.

Several more examples of SWOT analysis appear at the end of this section.

Writing Benefits

Filling in the blanks for the SWOT analysis helps the investigator write his report. In addition, the details of the SWOT identify issues that might otherwise not have been noticed. For example, let's return to the earlier-stated orange grove case, which was a real case of mine. By filling in the Opportunities section of the SWOT for the case, I was forced to consider possible opportunities – of which I was finding very little. By filling in that section, I came across the adjacent properties available for sale. Had I been writing a standard, detailed report about the orange grove case, I wouldn't have been focusing on opportunities, not known of the properties for sale, and thus, not mentioned it to the client who would then have missed out on the opportunity.

Presentation Benefits

The SWOT analysis helps create a final report that reads smoothly, is easy to navigate, and looks attractive. The client will appreciate being able to easily locate key information in the report, whether that be the Weaknesses or the Threats section of the report to read about a competitor, or the Opportunities section to read about a potential acquisition.

Marketing Benefits of SWOT

Using a SWOT analysis to create your report lets you speak to your client in business language (rather than in investigator's lingo), letting the client have an easier time understanding your proposal – and a happy client is often a repeat client.

Sample SWOT Analysis on a Company

Big Cola Company realizes the beverage market is moving towards healthier drinks and away from sugary sodas. Big Cola recently purchased a bottling company with an existing water product, Clifton Springs Water, which is sold in the U.S. in three states. In the below example, we can see how Big Cola Company would conduct a SWOT analysis to gauge the viability of keeping or changing the name of the water product. Among the factors considered in the analysis are the product's name, and the product itself.

Big Cola Company SWOT Analysis

Strengths

- Clifton Springs Water has a regional market which can be expanded.
- Clifton Springs Water has production and branding in place.

Weaknesses

- Clifton Springs Water is a single point of distribution, which can be interrupted.
- The name Clifton may not convey to consumers the concepts of fresh and healthy, especially when compared to the names of other water products.

Opportunities

- Clifton Springs can be drawn into a larger product offering, under a larger brand name.
- With production already in place, the product can be rolled out quickly.

Threats

- The market for water and energy drinks is very competitive. Clifton Springs Water will need to be quickly turned into a viable product and heavily promoted in order to gain market share.

The market for water and energy drinks is very competitive. Clifton Springs Water will need to be quickly turned into a viable product and heavily promoted in order to gain market share.

The market for water and energy drinks is very competitive. Clifton Springs Water will need to be quickly turned into a viable product and heavily promoted in order to gain market share.

Sample SWOT Analysis on a Person

SWOT analysis works well for employee reviews; it highlights both the positive areas as well as those areas that need improvement. For example, Sally Smith, a four-year company employee, asks for a raise in pay. She is in charge of project management and is currently the Project Manager of several key ongoing developments. The SWOT analysis would involve the following:

Sally Smith SWOT Analysis

Strengths

- Sally is a loyal and dependable employee.

- Sally is very literate in her work and understands the nuances of her projects.

- She has four years of client experience and is very good at her project deadlines.

Weaknesses

- Sally's self-confidence is low, and she is easily threatened by new co-workers.

- Sally doesn't like to promote the business outside of her comfort zone, which is by phone and email only.

Opportunities

- Stepping up and promoting the company to produce more sales will quickly give Sally an opportunity to gain additional income from bonuses.

- Training junior workers to take over the more mundane of her tasks will free up Sally's work load and allow her to move into a more senior position.

Threats

- Several other Project Managers, some with less experience, are looking to be promoted into better positions and are willing to make the sacrifices necessary to gain a new position.

From our SWOT analysis, we see that Sally is somewhat of a loner who is excellent at her job and will most likely stay with the company for a long time. But Sally cannot break out of her shell in order to gain promotion. Given the knowledge and value that Sally offers, yet understanding her introverted ways, the employer may choose to offer Sally mentoring to help her gain insight about the role she wants to grow into.

2. Supply Chain and Value Chain Analysis

Supply Chain Analysis

A **supply chain** is a system of organizations, people, activities, information, and resources involved in moving a product or service from supplier to customer.

Supply chain analysis looks at logistics, both inbound and outbound, operations, support teams, human resources, infrastructure, and technology. Using a combination of locating the information for each of these areas, and defining the respective roles within the company, this analysis method will indicate a company's strengths and weaknesses within its supply chain. Used properly, supply chain analysis will also indicate where there are opportunities to enhance production or services.

Adapting supply chain analysis to a due diligence business investigation will help assess who is providing assets to the company, whether financially or as a vendor. It also can be instrumental in security assessments and business-continuity planning. The following is a list of the key components of supply chain analysis, along with major considerations to be given for each component.

1. Logistics Inbound – Warehousing and Internal Handling of Products

What are the warehouse conditions? Be ready to define how the product is handled and stored. If refrigeration is necessary, is that addressed? Which vendors are used to service and repair the air conditioners? If the company produces a controlled substance, food, or a potentially hazardous product, then consider which oversight agency (EPA, FDA, local labor commission, union heads, etc.) would be on-site and writing reports about the internal logistics.

2. Logistics Outbound – Distribution

How are the products shipped? Are the products packaged and shipped by the company? Does the company use an outside contractor as part of the fulfillment procedure, such as transporting the products to distribution centers, stores, or some other final location? Is there a shipping department? How are shipped products tracked?

3. Operations – Product Development and Manufacturing

Who is making the product? Is there special machinery involved in the creation of the manufactured good? Keep in mind that many products, such as cola and beer, are not actually manufactured by the parent company, but are made and shipped from a participating vendor or supply partner. For example, a company like Georgia-based Coca-Cola contracts with companies all around the world to manufacturer its product (keeping the production in accordance with its recipe and standards), and to bottle and distribute locally.

4. Support Teams – Research and Development, Manufacturing-Related Groups, and Unions

Recognize that the workforce for the product could be made up of research and development in one country, and union workers in another country. Software companies also may be spread out in this fashion. Perhaps the research and development labs are located in New York or Tel Aviv, the customer support in India, and the products actually packaged and shipped from China. Discovering where all the employees are will help locate and determine if any regional laws or rules apply.

5. Human Resources – Support for Support Teams and Management

This is also known as management analysis. The sole purpose of management is to make sure that the staff is provided with the proper environment to work in, the tools and resources needed to conduct the work, and adequate leadership to guide the company. Analysis of the management will help discern if the management is able to create a productive environment and produce a consistent product.

6. Infrastructure – Location, Security, and Risk Management

Consider what would happen if a catastrophe were to strike the building where the products were manufactured or stored. What contingency plans are in place to get the business back to manufacturing? Are compliance and security policies in place and are the employees aware of the standard operating procedures for emergencies?

Most manufacturing companies abide by the technical standards that were established by the International Organization of Standardization (ISO). They meet and are qualified for an international standard that is accepted as a benchmark for companies in their respective industries. Qualification is an expensive and painstaking process. For investigators, finding a company ISO-qualified indicates that the plans of operation are on file with the standards board.

Also, any large plant operating in a community will have emergency plans on file with local law enforcement, the zoning commission, or another oversight agency.

7. Technology – Tracking Products, Customer Intelligence, and Market Basket Analysis.

Customer Relationship Management (CRM) tools are standard for companies selling products. The CRM allows a purchaser access to his account to purchase more supplies, manage the shipments, and analyze the usage.

Wal-Mart is famous for its Retail Link®, (retailersolutions.com), which allows suppliers to globally access sales data and manage their product inventory.

Tying all seven pieces of supply chain analysis on a company investigation can demonstrate weaknesses that otherwise would not be apparent in the traditional "who, what, and where" investigative report.

Value Chain Analysis

Created from the seminal 1985 book, *Competitive Advantage*, by Michael Porter, Value Chain Analysis (VCA) is a stable methodology used in many industries to analyze a company's logistics and operations in order to measure the value they offer and try to increase profit margins.

The value chain components are the additions (value) a product receives in its handling as it goes from production to market. For example, a farmer grows oranges and sells them to a juicer who extracts the juice and sells that to the bulk receiver who then bottles the juice and sends it out to market. Value chain analysis is the examination of the farmer, the juicer, and the bottler, and the value that each brings to the product before it goes to the consumer.

For the purposes of investigations, VCA is very similar to Supply Chain Analysis. It differs from SWOT because VCA performs specific functions within certain tasks. For example, VCA can be used to examine the core competencies of internal to external resource allocation – i.e. how a client manages, builds, maintains, ships, sells, and protects products.

Investigators need only a portion of this analysis to help identify key players in a business, or potentially fraudulent vendors and suppliers. If the investigator is looking at the value of the shipping process of widgets, he is not examining the entire manufacturing of the widget. At this point the investigator may notice that shipping is overpriced, inefficient, or being redirected as in product diversion to grey markets.

I prefer to call supply chain analysis a simplified version because it identifies the suppliers and the vendors involved within the specific business process.

Investigators must keep in mind Value Chain Analysis is looking at only one part of the process. In the orange juice example above, the farmer and the juicer may pass inspection, but the bottler needs to be scrutinized for inefficiency or fraud.

Woes

The ABC Needle Company is responsible for manufacturing pediatric hypodermic needles. It has created a special process to make custom, tiny injectors and is the sole supplier of the product to Farley Pharmaceutical Co. These needles are so precise that Farley uses them exclusively for its infant insulin-injector guns. Part of Farley's process involves the plungers, stoppers, and other mechanics used in making insulin guns for babies.

One day in Little Town, Kansas, where ABC is located, a tornado severely damages the roof of ABC's building and well as causing devastating to the community. The damage affects not only the immediate products, but also the manufacturing equipment and machines. ABC cannot produce any new needles until the equipment is fixed. But, even if the equipment worked, the employees are too overwhelmed by their own grief and troubles to go to work, since they are dealing with the damage to their own homes.

The company president realizes the only viable products he has left are the tractor-trailers that were away from the factory at the time of the storm. Because he cannot immediately get his machines repaired and operating, he will be unable to continue producing the hypodermics in the short term. Therefore, he will have to contact a competitor, if there is one, or expect to lose the contract with Farley, and potentially file for bankruptcy.

As a protection, Farley now must look for another needle manufacturer. Without a supplier that can provide needles to its specifications, Farley will be unable to produce the infant insulin-injector guns.

Finally, without infant insulin-injector guns available, doctors will be forced to find alternatives for families who rely on the insulin guns to treat their children.

If that story sounds a tad preposterous, then consider the challenges associated with the U.S. supply of influenza vaccines. Per the Centers for Disease Control and Prevention (cdc.gov/flu/about/qa/vaxdistribution.htm):

"Influenza viruses change from year to year, so influenza vaccines must be updated annually to include the viruses that will most likely circulate in the upcoming season. Once the viruses are selected for the new formulation, manufacturers operate under a very tight timeline for producing, testing, releasing and distributing the vaccine. Due to these time constraints, any problems encountered during production may cause shortages or delays, and in fact, such problems have impacted the supply in prior influenza seasons."

Supply chain analysis looks to find the weakest link in a supply chain. The analysis first establishes whether all links are substantial, or offer redundancy, or have solid contingency plans. It then identifies the weakest link and further posits a worst-case scenario based on the link's failure. In the supply chain analysis of your client report, be specific that the scenario is only a supposition of events that may never occur, however, the client must be aware of all possibilities that could affect his supply chain.

3. CARA Analysis

The third analysis model is known as CARA, and is used for analyzing individuals. CARA is the acronym for:

- **C**haracteristics
- **A**ssociations

- **R**eputations
- **A**ffiliations.

Characteristics

Characteristics give a sense of the subject's personality. Look at his professional rank or position, or even the type of car he drives. Is he litigious? Has he been convicted of any crimes or rewarded for any heroic acts?

Associations

Associations, either professional or personal, with other people help in understanding the socio-economic position of the subject. For example, associations can indicate if the subject is wealthy, or an average worker, or a criminal.

Reputation

Reputation searches present the best opportunities to hear what people say about the person and his affiliates.

Affiliations

The affiliations a person has with certain companies, organizations, associations, and educational facilities can be quite telling and offer insight into the person's character.

Whether you are investigating a person or a company, reputation and associations are important. We are judged by association – you are the company you keep. Establishing with whom your target individual associates, consorts, does business, or maintains relations are important details your client will want to know.

Presenting CARA Analysis

With all of the information gathered in your CARA analysis, examine any unusual relationships between the associates, addresses, or businesses. Fraudulent people will go to great lengths to hide common threads linking them with other parties.

For leads that seem to go nowhere, be prepared to explain to your client your search strategy and your pursuit of a false lead that ultimately resulted in a dead end or an unexpected outcome.

Be careful and use common sense when presenting your analysis. Do not make bold statements based solely on research findings. You cannot say for certain that Mr. So-and-So is a mob lawyer. Instead, convey the information as you interpret it based on your CARA analysis. For example, you can state:

> "Based on today's research and the ever changing Internet, it appears that Mr. So-and-So is an attorney with a high net worth, and he is considered to be a savvy businessman. He has attended, according to the media, six recent social engagements, all organized by reputed mob bosses and their families."

An example of a CARA analysis report is shown at the end of this section.

A Word of Caution When Combining Social Media and CARA

Social media research can help strengthen a CARA analysis. LinkedIn and Facebook offer clear connections to friends and associates, as do Instagram and similar personal social networks. However, do not make assumptions based solely on social media friends and connections; verify any connections you find in social media. Some individuals will Friend anyone and pay no attention to whom they are connected. Also Profile Page fraud in Facebook and LinkedIn is rampant; the person you think you are connected to is not in reality who he claims he is. I connected to the retired CEO of a pharmaceutical company, who listed himself as an Angel Investor and excited by the prospect of conducting due diligence for his potential future investments. However, his posts seemed odd, and his other connections were widespread and unfocused. Then I realized the name of the pharmaceutical company was misspelled; he was a fraud.

A 2014 article from the American Bar Association (ABA) made an impact on the use of social media. Released as *Formal Opinion 466 April 24, 2014 Lawyer Reviewing Jurors' Internet Presence*[11] the Opinion gave attorneys permission to look at some importance factors: Who are their jurors talking to, who are they Friends with on Facebook, and what are they saying online about the case?

Since the release of the Formal Opinion, one may expect to see a greater use of social media in character evaluations pertaining to juror selection. Please note the one important section of this Formal Opinion: the attorney or his agent cannot friend or communicate with the juror – they can only look at the juror's online content.   However, an open social media account will allow a due diligence investigator to find a subject's friends, points of contact, associations and associates. Social media was built for CARA analysis.

A Sample of CARA Analysis

An excellent tool for providing a quick, simple method of profiling a subject on his associations, CARA analysis does come with a caveat: *Not all things are what they seem to be.*

With social media profiles so readily accessible today, CARA methodology has made some business and legal decisions easier. For example, potential jurists now have their profiles scanned via CARA before selection by attorneys of jury trials.

Imagine a defense attorney examining Bob Smith, potential jury member on a murder case. The case involves a 36-year-old, foreign-born husband who is accused of murdering his 34-year-old wife. The couple is poor and the husband has been arrested in the past for domestic violence and public drunkenness.

---

[11]

Americanbar.org/content/dam/aba/administrative/professional_responsibility/formal_opinion_466_final_04_23_14.authcheckdam.pdf

As the attorney examines Bob Smith's background, he will look at Bob's social media status, and any available open source information via Google searches.

Bob Smith CARA Analysis

Characteristics

- Potential jury member Bob Smith drives a Lexus, lives in the good part of town, and wears expensive suits into court.

Associations

- Bob's friends on LinkedIn all point to business executives, attorneys, and corporate leaders.

Reputation

- Bob's posts on his Facebook show a self-made successful man who does not believe in charity or handouts. He has liked several close the border groups who stopped helping undocumented citizens in the U.S.

Affiliations

- Affiliations for Bob are conservative parties, gun rights groups, and racist organizations.

From our CARA analysis, Bob doesn't appear to be the best candidate for our defense attorney. His profile paints a picture of a man who may be deeply anti-sympathetic to the man on trial.

CARA analysis can also be used to evaluate the corporate culture of a company. Faith-based companies will show strong characteristics. Affiliations and associations can be automatically assumed for some liberal or conservative companies.

AUTHOR TIP Try a simple SWOT or CARA analysis on a company or person with whom you are well acquainted. As you build the analysis, observe how the information fleshes out in the report.

These analytical methods are meant to enhance – not replace – the research and reporting you are doing. By themselves, the analytic tools do not carry the full intensity of your in-depth research and analysis, which are the real foundation of your reports. Analytic tools, however, can help quickly paint a picture when you need to prove a point or demonstrate an idea.

Due Diligence Analysis

Due diligence analysis is a combination of all above analytical methods plus a little more. With the suppositions gathered from social media, the news outlets, and other open sources, we start to draw a story about the company or person we are analyzing. That information coupled with public records, business and credit reports, potentially litigation history, SEC (or other regulatory agency) filings, and other published findings will give the analyst a proper foundation to start an investigation.

In a due diligence investigation, you spend 80 percent of your time gathering information from every resource available to you. However, it is the analysis, interpretation, and reporting of the data that is the core of any good investigation. The client ultimately wants to know something, if not everything, about the venture he hired you to investigate. Many times our reports come back rather blasé, but that is not because we didn't find anything, but rather it's reflective that the company or person is respectable, or at least average. The reality might also be that the company does not have an Internet presence. If it is not out there, we cannot find it

The Analysis Process

Let me outline below a typical scenario and how the analysis process works for me.

 After the assignment is given I identify the target of the investigation and start to retrieve the profile reports, also known as *comprehensive reports* (see Chapter 2), from our public record vendors (i.e., TLO, LexisNexis, and CLEAR).

If the target of the investigation is a company, I also look up the corporate database reporting systems and pull those reports, such as Hoover's, D&B, LexisNexis, and Kompass, to name a few.

Using the leads generated form those reports, I visit key online database within the state and county(s) where the company is located and where the key players live. Using BRBPublications.com I look up each county to see what extra public record information can be retrieved.

All reports and public records are saved into a folder and sorted through piece by piece to add and later compare with one another. I am specifically looking for consistency of information from vendor to vendor. It might not be exciting to see the same home address reported in each document, but it probably means the person lives at that address.   The details are recorded in the report thusly:

> *Based on proprietary databases, Bob Smith lives at 12 Main Street, Anytown, CA 90123.*

If there are more consistent details to add, such as Social Security number, wife's name, and other pieces of data, this information should also be reflected in the report.

> *Based on proprietary databases, Bob Smith, born January 12, 1964 (Social Security # 123-45-XXXX), currently resides with Sally Smith at 12 Main Street, Anytown, CA 90123. They own the residence, purchased on January 9, 2013 and valued at $200,000.*

The above information came from public records and was reported in all of the vendor databases, as well as a search of the property deed found using BRBPublications.com.

In the next phase I identify as many potential relatives, work associates, friends, and other personal connections as possible. The connections are developed using social media and the profile reports I have pulled.

I then attempt to locate and verify a number of items, including:

- Assets
- Criminal history
- Regulatory history
- Litigation history
- Media history
- Social Media findings

Each item is researched and reported. In addition to the information being stated, I also need to be very clear in describing any limitations of our sources.

For example, the N.Y. State Unified Court System has a very attractive series of databases known as eCourts (https://iapps.courts.state.ny.us/webcivil/ecourtsMain). The site seems quite comprehensive with separate database searches for civil, criminal, housing, and family court matters. However, unless you read the details about each of these databases, you may not realize several of the databases only have current docket data, and not historical case data. If you assume their WebCrims option has historical records, and using this as your primary source you report no records, you could have a problem. If your subject had a criminal matter several years ago, the WebCrims will not provide that information. The alternative is the subscription service for historical data which currently costs $65.00 per search.

When stating a finding, be sure the language is clear in describing what is and isn't available. For example:

> *According to the New York State Online Court eCourts database, it appears Bob Smith does not currently have any ongoing legal matters. We recommend an onsite visit to the court system to verify if any past litigation or criminal matters exist.*

If the name is common, this sentence will be added into the report:

> *Due to the ambiguity and commonality of the name, it is not possible to confirm or deny if the results pertain to the subject.*

Such an admission is simply stating the truth, and it protects the investigator from a possible Errors or Omissions claim being made by the client. The report stated what was available online and recommended the client research further to insure Bob Smith has no serious offenses in his past.

The actual report of my due diligence will then have a cover sheet, followed by a confidentiality statement, then followed by the first page of the actual report – where the key findings are disclosed. If the investigative analyst finds that Bob Smith has been convicted of a weapons charge, plus charged with securities and regulatory violations, and he was a state lottery winner 10 years ago, I will write these key findings at the very beginning of the report to immediately draw the client's eye to what may be important or notable items in Bob Smith's history. The most negative information is placed first in the Key Findings section; for example a criminal weapons charge trumps a traffic ticket.

It's Not Me

My firm received the signed authorization, with all the key primary identifying indicators (DOB, SSN, and name) included from a particular fellow applying for a job with our client. In the margin of the form, the applicant wrote in, "I'm not the Robert Smith from Anytown, ST who was convicted of child molestation. I have the same name and it comes up often."

We did our due diligence and background investigation and discovered there were two Robert Smiths from the same town and our guy wasn't the child molester. It was wise of the applicant to give us a heads up. We would have eventually reached the same conclusion, but an initial report to the client would have caused a lot of noise or concern.

Since then, I have a blank-lined section on my forms, without instructions, just in case someone wants to add to his or her history.

In Summary

Analysis methods, resources, and databases are all helpful and necessary for performing essential online due diligence. However, nothing replaces critical thinking and common sense.

New investigators rely on the methods and training they receive to do the best job possible. However, in talking to a seasoned due diligence investigator, you will notice that the breakout of CARA and Supply Chains, the language, and the reporting to the client all presented in this book, are all intuitive in the seasoned pro's work.

If you are a new investigator, start by conducting trial due diligence investigations on non-essential companies and people. In other words, don't practice on real clients. If you are already attuned to conducting due diligence investigations, but are interested in diversifying your portfolio of report writing then start adding in CARA or Supply Chain Analysis.

Ultimately accuracy and consistency are the most important items to reflect in your work.

Ch 4:

Investigating People Connected to Businesses

Too bad that all the people who know how to run the country are busy driving taxicabs and cutting hair.
—George Burns

Investigators find facts and analyze information about legal, financial, and personal matters. An important function of due diligence investigations is examining the backgrounds of corporate entities and the principals who manage them. People are always at the heart of a due diligence investigation. Although a business investigation includes a company's corporate filings, lawsuits, subsidiaries, etc., the real subject of the investigation is people. Buildings do not commit fraud or make dubious business decisions, humans do. Any investigation into a corporation will have the investigator researching the individuals behind the scenes.

While this book covers tools and resources that pertain to all investigative targets – business entities as well as individuals – this particular chapter takes a close, detailed look at certain highly-specialized resources that are concerned with the investigation of individuals – whether a CEO and board president of a multi-national corporation, or a local electrician.

First, Know the People Types

Early in their careers, investigators learn there are four types of individuals who are researched as part of any investigation. Know these classifications; they will help steer your investigation to the right possible sources to find the data you need for good leads.

The four classification types are:

1. Unremarkable
2. Lime-Lighters
3. Fraudulent
4. Incompetent

Unremarkable

There is very little published about this individual. He is rarely a corporate giant, but if so chances are he is new to the role. This individual has not enough significance for reporters to interview and write about, or for him to appear in the news in any way. He does not sign many official documents, and his legal background is minimal, if at all. He steers clear of most activity that can be recorded.

Unremarkable is the ideal position for an individual trying to avoid a paper trail. With all the data services you use, you likely will find little if anything on him. An open-source researcher will come up flat.

The exception is the corporate leader who has been well groomed to insure his statement is consistent. For example, usually the only comments this officer makes are when he is discussing company business. No personal comments are addressed to reporters. His wife and kids are not a topic for conversation. He is meticulous about the events he attends, and cooperative with his own corporate security and legal counsel on all travel, personal safety, and public-profile issues. An example of this type of individual is an American foreign diplomat. There are mountains of information written about this individual; however, you will gather very little from the public statements and personas you obtain through the embassy's Web site.

This individual can also be the local mechanic or tradesman who is not really attracting any attention, nor wanting it. Rarely will this person have any sort of online social media persona, or a minimal one at that, as he appreciates his privacy. Investigating this type of personality will have you focusing on public records for his assets (homes, vehicles, etc.) and family social media profiles, which may give you insight into the family life, if not on the unremarkable person.

Lime-Lighters

Many morning news programs show the crowds gathering outside the networks' studios. NBC's Today Show, for example, makes use of this crowd and often shoots part of its program among the masses. As the cameraman pans the crowd, everyone gets a bit giddy and starts screaming and waving because they can see themselves on TV. Being on national television and holding up a Love You Mom banner is not an everyday occurrence for most people; so it is no surprise that everyone jockeys for position to get in front of that camera.

A similar pattern emerges for those subjects, such as celebrities who cannot avoid the camera. They realize their images are tied to the public perception. They strive for as much camera time, press releases, and "look at me" action as they can possibly receive.

Researching the Lime-Lighter type of person can be tricky. These people often know how to work the media and they will massage their imagines to be perfect for what they are seeking. The TV reality shows are ripe with Lime-Lighters. Where a handful of the hundreds of reality stars are actually more than lackluster, the majority are merely everyday people doing ridiculous actions in order to get on TV.

The key Lime-Lighters in the business world are Chief Executive Officers (CEOs) of companies. You might recognize Donald Trump, Martha Stewart, and Emeril Lagasse right away. However, can you name the CEOs of McDonald's, Coca-Cola, or Starbucks? Their notoriety is often a matter of how they use the media to showcase their companies, products, or even themselves.

AUTHOR TIP When investigating the CEO or any upper-management executive Lime-Lighter, a few focus points are necessary to keep in mind.

First, if the stories you are reading are press releases distributed by PR Newswire or similar wire services, then consider the stories have been paid for by the company and are protentially biased.

Second, discount any talking points coming directly from the executives, or quotes located on the company Web sites. They are masters of ceremony and will always take an opportunity to self-puff about the business, its brands, or themselves.

The best way to truly find info about a Lime-Lighter is to check what is being written about him by others. For every celebrity, there is a critic. In business, the critics come from multiple places such as competing companies, industries or trade sources, conference proceedings, and even magazines and product reviews. Look for older articles that mention the individual; early articles often offer a bit of insight into what the person was like before he was C-level (CEO, CIO, CFO, etc.). Early stories might give you a sense of the character of the professional you are investigating.

Fraudulent

Hiring an experienced investigator is prudent before money is invested or promises are made. However, all too often the investigator is hired as part of the asset recovery process.

Who Are You?

An executive client called me recently, fresh from an investment seminar in his community. My client was so impressed by the presenter's intelligence and charisma that he spoke with the presenter after the seminar and was then offered a follow-up meeting to discuss some investment opportunities.

> My client asked me to check out the presenter. A quick search showed that this Wall Street-wise presenter was also known by a federal prison number. The year prior, the presenter was convicted of various corporate crimes.

Does it get more obvious than this? While it seems straightforward, you also have to take into account you could initially be misreading your subject as a Lime-Lighter, and then it turns out he is Fraudulent. In fact, most Fraudulent characters are Lime-Lighters. One of the greatest talents of a fraud is his charisma and need for attention. As he is touting what a great person he is, or how great his company is, or the superior product he has to offer, what you are really buying into is the charisma of the Fraudulent person.

Incompetent

There are a few reasons to be considered Incompetent. Perhaps the executive is too busy to manage all his tasks and mistakenly thinks someone else is taking care of the details. Or perhaps the executive is entering an unfamiliar realm and is unaware of the various compliance laws that apply to his new project (i.e., SOX, HIPAA). Or maybe he is a go-getter who hopes the ends justify the means, and in order to achieve his goal he ignores all legal and ethical concerns.

The more investigations you do the more you might shake your head and wonder how some executives have made their way into their current positions. Many times an investigation starts with the premise that something nefarious or fraudulent has occurred. But what you eventually find is the person driving the project is more likely unprepared to handle the task. As the saying goes, "Ignorance of the law is not a defense." However, it certainly explains why some executives do stupid things.

For the Incompetent type of individual – and for that matter for all four – take a hard look at the different roles the person may take, the information that surrounds him, and the circumstances that have affected his business and personal decisions.

The next portion of this chapter examines certain resources used for diligence investigations involving corporate- or business-related people.

Researching Board Positions

Who are the Board of Directors? According to investorwords.com, Board Members are:

> "Individuals elected by a corporation's shareholders to oversee the management of the corporation. The members of a Board of Directors are paid in cash and/or stock, meet several times each year, and assume legal responsibility for corporate activities."

There is no schooling or training involved to become a board member. They help run the company establish and maintain the organization's mission. The general sense is that board members get their seats based on their influence. And while they do use their influence to help run the organization and establish merit for the company, sometimes you will find they merely fill seats and keep out of the way.

But corporate board members do have a fiduciary responsibility to care for the finances and legal requirements of the corporation. Their focus is to remain true to the goals set forth by the shareholders. Many board members are often major investors in the company. For example, a start-up technology company most likely will have one or two of its biggest investors sitting on its board, because the want to oversee their investment.

Board members are often picked because they are well-respected captains of industry, such as scientists, writers, sports figures, or celebrities. Having their name on your board will bring instant name recognition and credibility to your company.

The keeping-out-the-way seat holders are those family members who do not need a job because they are wealthy, but it looks good if you have them occupied in a useful function. These board members tend to sit on philanthropic boards. Political figures often have their spouses involved with non-profit organizations, such as a board member of an ABC fund-raiser.

When investigating a company, it is important to determine who the board members are, and what their roles are on the board. Investigators especially will want to look for collusion among board members or corporate officers. Your investigation should focus on such questions as:

- Do they sit individually or together on other boards?
- Have they been investigated in the past or accused of any type of corruption?
- Are any of them also a vendor for the company?
- Have they or their companies/families or organizations received any special treatment or pricing?
- Who appointed each board member and when?
- Are relatives on the board?

Finding out who sits on which boards, as well as getting the lists of corporate officers, is not so difficult, depending on the sources you have at hand. The next portion of this chapter takes a look at the resources available to find this information.

Key Resources for Investigating Board Positions

The Company's Web Site

The Company's Web site should always be your first source to check. There is really no reason to hide the board from the general public, especially since having a board gives a sense of credibility to the company. You will find board members under one of three common links: About Us, Investor Relations, or Management.

Securities and Exchange Commission (SEC) Filings for Public Companies

If a company is publicly traded, then there is an overseeing national authority for the stock exchanges, such as the SEC in the United States or SEDAR in Canada. The SEC is a resource for factual data about not only board members but about the company itself. If the company is not publicly traded, then state filings or the company Web site and literature are key resources of research material.

More information about using the SEC for investigations is found in Chapter 6.

Annual Reports

Publicly traded companies issue annual reports. Past and present reports will be of value. The annual report will list board members, their backgrounds, and if they sit on other boards. The annual report also will disclose ongoing investigations.

Visit sec.gov, search by company name, and then obtain the company's proxy statement, also known as the DEF-14 filing. The proxy will show the compensation for each board member and corporate officer.

Researching Other Management People

The following are key organizational lists or resources to be used when finding and investigating corporate officers.

Phone Lists of Private Companies

Services found at infousa.com and hoovers.com (a Dun & Bradstreet company) offer mailing-list services. Through various public records, news accounts, and telephone interviews, D&B has amassed a large amount of very specific contact information that can be purchased by the batch or in small doses. Although the lists are targeted for marketing purposes, investigators can use purchased lists to locate a target or subject by occupation, geography, or hobby.

Former Employees and Officers

If it is an option, do not hesitate to try to interview former employees to find out who may be still working at the company. Do not discount the importance of researching at least several good names of individuals who are either on the employee roster, are former board members, or are now, or were in the past affiliated with the company.

Finding these former employees may create additional leads to former workers who are disgruntled, or to others who love to talk about the past and all the problems their companies suffered, or all the great people they worked with. Until you actually speak to them, it will not be clear what information they can provide.

You can locate former employees by searching through Zoominfo and LinkedIn. Both sites publish employee and employer information. Indeed (indeed.com) has a section for employee reviews of a company. Although names are not given, the location might help.   The Wayback Machine, located at archive.org, might have older versions of the Web sites with the employee names listed.

Political Affiliations and Donations

According to Socialist Oscar Ameringer:

> *Politics is the gentle art of getting votes from the poor and campaign funds from the rich, by promising to protect each from the other.*

The higher in power your executive subject rises, the more politically involved he or she will become by choice or as a result of a position in the senior-management group. Companies spend billions of dollars every year on lobbyists to help their company succeed. Certainly petroleum companies most likely want to dig into the Alaskan wilderness to tap into the rich supply of oil underneath the earth's crust, even though these wild preserves are on government protected land. Conversely, animal-rights groups, such as People for the Ethical Treatment of Animals (PETA), are supported by name-brand products that you see on the store shelves every day. Why do I mention this? Because researching a corporate employee's sponsorship of certain political parties and non-profit organizations may very well be of concern to the investigation.

A fast way to locate information about the political donations and activities of an executive is to use the Federal Election Commission's Web site at fec.gov. Under the Campaign Finance Reports and Data tab, you will see the Disclosure Database. This database can be searched by party, by contributor, or committee. If you want to find all the contributors for a particular company, use the advanced search feature and search by company. Investigators also can download an entire list of people and view it in comma-delimited format through File Transfer Protocol (FTP), a common way to move large files via the Internet. The list can be sorted and viewed easily in applications such as Microsoft Excel.

The Federal Election Commission administers and enforces federal campaign-finance laws, insuring that companies, parties, and persons do not abuse campaign-finance laws. If a company offers an automatic withdrawal from an employee's paycheck and donates that money to a campaign, then it must report this transaction to the FEC in its annual reporting.

The form below is an example of an actual report filed. Although we have redacted all the form's names and addresses, it does give you an idea of what is available.

Image# 14942369760

SCHEDULE A (FEC Form 3) **ITEMIZED RECEIPTS**	Use separate schedule(s) for each category of the Detailed Summary Page

FOR LINE NUMBER: (check only one) PAGE 27 OF 94

[X] 11a [ ] 11b [ ] 11c [ ] 11d
[ ] 12 [ ] 13a [ ] 13b [ ] 14 [ ] 15

Any information copied from such Reports and Statements may not be sold or used by any person for the purpose of soliciting contributions or for commercial purposes, other than using the name and address of any political committee to solicit contributions from such committee.

NAME OF COMMITTEE (In Full)

A. Full Name (Last, First, Middle Initial)

Mailing Address

City   State   Zip Code

FEC ID number of contributing federal political committee.   C

Name of Employer   Occupation
None

Receipt For: 2014
[X] Primary   [ ] General
[ ] Other (specify)

Election Cycle-to-Date   250

Date of Receipt
11 / 01 / 2013

Transaction ID :

Amount of Each Receipt this Period   250

B. Full Name (Last, First, Middle Initial)

Mailing Address 83 Old McLeod Bridge Road

City   State   Zip Code

FEC ID number of contributing federal political committee.   C

Name of Employer   Occupation

Receipt For: 2014
[X] Primary   [ ] General
[ ] Other (specify)

Election Cycle-to-Date   500

Date of Receipt
11 / 18 / 2013

Transaction ID :

Amount of Each Receipt this Period   500

C. Full Name (Last, First, Middle Initial)

Mailing Address 14 Highgate St W

City   State   Zip Code

FEC ID number of contributing federal political committee.   C

Name of Employer   Occupation
None

Receipt For: 2014
[X] Primary   [ ] General
[ ] Other (specify)

Election Cycle-to-Date   1000

Date of Receipt
12 / 31 / 2013

Transaction ID :

Amount of Each Receipt this Period   1000

SUBTOTAL of Receipts This Page (optional)...   1750.00

TOTAL This Period (last page this line number only)..............................

FEC **Schedule A (Form 3)** (Revised 02/2009)

(Source: Federal Election Commission at fec.gov)

Two excellent private Web sites to find political donations are FollowTheMoney (followthemoney.org) and OpenSecrets.org (opensecrets.org). More Web sites are available, but these two are very comprehensive and good places to start when tracking contributions at the state level.

After searching the federal, state, and local contributions, as well as the vendor sites where possible, then start a media search. Is the executive talking openly about a political issue or attending fund-raisers sponsored by the Democrats or Republicans? These executives are not shy about whom they support. In fact, knowing their attendance at rallies and fund-raisers most likely will be reported in the media, they use their positions to lend support to their party. How to perform a media search is covered in Chapter 10.

Be aware it is not unusual to see a company, or its executives, supporting multiple parties. Contributors know they have a greater chance of winning influence if they play both sides of the coin. As Will Rogers once said, "A fool and his money are soon elected!"

Charitable Works

Look for any charitable works involving your subject executive. Of course these charitable interests may be sincere, but they could also be a front for laundering money.

A Profitable Non-Profit

An East Coast building developer was the recipient of every major, new building project within the city limits. Just about every school, hospital, or government building was built by this developer or by his father, since the developer was a second-generation company owner. His major competitor believed something underhanded or unfair was occurring that was leading every new project to this man's company. So he hired me to investigate.

After days of researching his business reports and filings, I learned that the developer's buildings were structurally sound, he had few negative stories written about him in the press, and his legal troubles were minimal. Since his history seemed to be free of trouble, I investigated potential involvement in non-profit organizations. He had a non-profit organization named after him and the organization was receiving more than $1 million a year in donations. The leading donator was his own company. He recently had won building contracts with the schools and hospitals that were also the recipients of these donations. The Form 990 revealed a highly suggestive kick-back scheme connected to the projects he won contracts to build.

Investigating Business Assets

There are three types of assets:

1. Physical
2. Financial
3. Intellectual.

Physical Assets

Physical assets include automobiles, vessels, airplanes, real estate, property, personal possessions, and collectibles. The "stuff" that people associate with status and wealth, whether driving a nice car, living in a beautiful home or owning an incredible baseball-card collection, are considered to be assets and can be insured or repossessed.

Each of these physical possessions is usually associated with some type of public record, thus a paper trail is created. For example, cars, boats, and planes all must be registered within an operating jurisdiction. State motor-vehicle agencies register for cars and pleasure boats, the U.S. Coast Guard registers commercial boats, and the Federal Aviation Administration registers planes. Real estate property records are kept at the county, parish, or city level, depending on the state.

Other personal property includes collections or business equipment. These assets will not show on a public record unless the owner has borrowed against them and the lender has recorded a lien known as a Uniform Commercial Code (UCC) filing.

Financial Assets

Personal financial assets are trust accounts, UCCs, stocks and securities, retirement plans, insurance clauses, funds, and other financial entities that you invest in or own. The assets are evidenced by the paperwork mélange that people accumulate in their lives while try to increase net worth as they near retirement.

Only so much data about financial assets are available in open source for the investigator. Bank accounts and financial statements are protected by the Fair Credit Reporting Act (consumer.ftc.gov/sites/default/files/articles/pdf/pdf-0111-fair-credit-reporting-act.pdf).

However, other financial documents are accessible from the government agency where the liens are recorded. A good place to perform a name search of a lien index is at the local recorder's office or at a state agency such as the Secretary of State. Other legal filings to investigate that will lead to assets include bankruptcies at federal courts, divorce proceedings and other civil lawsuits at the local level. Additionally, you will see financial information in the Federal SEC filings, if the person is a corporate officer as mentioned earlier.

Other important open source avenues for checking for leads are Google and newspaper stories or press releases. Using these sources, one can search for stories about donations to charities, or hosting events such as fundraisers, or purchasing a new home, property, or a yacht. Sometimes individuals reveal more than should be mentioned in the press, or take pictures in front of their fancy new boat or car. The open source searches can generate useful leads to finding actual assets. One case I recently worked involved a homeowner who renovated his pool area, and the company that did the work took pictures for their Web site and included the homeowner's name and town.

Intellectual Assets

In some cases, intellectual property is more valuable than homes, planes, and stocks. Imagine investigating an individual whose physical assets amount to a home in the suburbs, a three year-old car, and a 401K plan.

Searching intellectual property might seem to be a limited venue. But if you determine your subject holds a patent or the trademark of a valuable item, you may have uncovered hidden or undisclosed wealth. If you were investigating Thomas Edison, genius that he was, you would find he was very smart (or perhaps rude) about registering other people's ideas in his name with the United States Patent and Trademark office. When comparing Facebook to Twitter as an asset, Facebook exceeds Twitter twentyfold, because Facebook holds hundreds of "patents" compared to Twitter's smaller collection.

Information on how to investigate assets is covered in-depth in Chapter 7.

Connecting Criminal and Civil Records to Your Subject

Although the topic of how to search for court records is covered in detail in the next chapter, it certainly bears mention in a discussion of corporate officers and key personnel. Legal research of criminal and civil records is fruitful and necessary for any investigation, and especially to corporate investigations. It is important to know where companies have fallen down, lost sight of their ethics, or got caught with their hands in the cookie jar. Not to give too much weight to the defense side, the company you are researching could be litigious, frequently suing other companies or persons for debts unpaid, trademark infringement, contract disputes or any number of pertinent issues.

Both criminal and civil research should be done carefully, as the availability to information changes from jurisdiction to jurisdiction. The rule of thumb is to start online, but always finish the research in person.

When researching overseas companies, try to locate an investigator in that particular country who can assist you in understanding the legal system there, and help you conduct the research on-site.

To discuss the differences between criminal and civil research, I have borrowed text from *The Criminal Records Manual* by Derek Hinton and Larry Henry. Their work, from which I've learned a great amount, includes the chart below which they has graciously allowed us to reprint, and will help demonstrate the differences between the two types of cases.

Subject	Criminal Case	Civil Case
Who brings the case	A government prosecutor.	A private party, normally through an attorney.
Name of case	People vs. Smith (if state court) or the United States of America vs. Smith (if federal court).	Adams vs. Smith (names of the parties)
Outcome if Plaintiff successful	Criminal sanctions, including imprisonment, fine and probationary terms.	Monetary damages. In some lawsuits, the plaintiff may be seeking injunctive relief.
Jurors who must agree with the plaintiff	All twelve jurors - unanimous verdict.	Nine jurors out of twelve.
Standard of proof	Government must overcome the presumption of innocence by proving guilt beyond a reasonable doubt.	Plaintiff only needs to show that his side is more convincing, and that it's more probable he's right.

Again, see Chapter 6 for additional details on how to conduct criminal and civil record investigations.

Sanctions

Sanctions are administrative actions, usually involving punishment or restrictions, taken against an individual or entity by a government agency or trade-related association.

Sanctions come from many places and are imposed for many reasons. Law enforcement, compliance, professional disciplinary actions, as well as regulatory enforcements, are all forms of sanctions. Depending on the type of professional you are researching, the sources you check will vary.

Chapter 6 covers in depth the investigation of various sanctions, but it is worth mentioning here certain examples of what is available to research online:

- The Excluded Parties List System (EPLS) managed now by System for Award Management available at sam.gov is a great U.S. government site. Exclusions are categorized into four Classification Types: Firm, Individual, Vessel, and Special Entity Designation. The last category is a miscellaneous category for any organization that cannot be considered a Firm, Individual, or Vessel, but still needs to be excluded. For example, the organization Terrorists Against the USA does not fit into any of the previous categories and would be considered a Special Entity Designation.

- Many Professional License Sanctions can be found online via state agency Web sites. In fact, over 5,000 of the nearly 8,800 state boards offer an online verification of individuals' licensing, some report on disciplinary actions including lawsuits filed for malpractice. View these links at https://www.brbpublications.com/freeresources/pubrecsitesOccStates.aspx. While most professions are regulated by state licensing boards, there are certain, specific occupations that involve the federal regulation, such as the air-traffic controllers regulated by the FAA.

- For many years the U.S. Congress has worked diligently to protect the health and welfare of the nation's elderly and poor by implementing legislation to prevent certain individuals and businesses from participating in federally funded health care programs. The Office of Inspector General (OIG) established a program to exclude individuals and entities affected by these various legal authorities as per contained in sections 1128 and 1156 of the Social Security Act, and maintains a list of all currently excluded parties called the List of Excluded Individuals/Entities.

- The key oversight committees for securities and financial markets are the SEC and the Financial Industry Regulatory Authority (FINRA). Oversight groups, such as FINRA, monitor brokerage houses and brokers. The SEC Web site has a litigation section to peruse, but at the moment it redirects you to the FINRA Web site. Each state also monitors securities dealers in its jurisdiction; that is the next step to researching your subject. Visit sec.gov/litigation.shtml.

Several Recommended Database Sources

Professional, albeit expensive, service sites such as Capital IQ (capitaliq.com) from Standard & Poor's and BoardEx (corp.boardex.com) from Management Diagnostics Limited are phenomenal in their coverage of people and companies. Their analysts offer summarized data and biographies in their reports.

Random data Web sites such as They Rule (theyrule.net) make a great attempt to pull information and report, but be aware there can be limitations.

Access to public records at the IRBsearch Web site at irbsearch.com is a great resource for private investigators. Yes, the site offers many of the same public records searches offered by all the major information companies servicing the investigative profession. However, one unique service that puts this vendor above the rest is its People-at-Work search. The database is aggregated from secretary of state filings, Web site registrations, credit headers, and other public records.

Another great source for free searching is ZoomInfo (zoominfo.com). Information is collated from the Web sites ZoomInfo software bots (also known as intelligent agents) have captured and matched to a particular person or company. You can search by company, person, or industry and truly, it is the most useful specialist search engine on the Internet. You can locate an abundance of "who's who" straight from ZoomInfo. Keep in mind, though, that this information is being generated from other Web sites and needs to be verified before being incorporated in the final report.

Using Social Media Sources

As a resource for performing background investigations on individuals, social media sites – where people broadcast all sorts of information about themselves – can be quite the useful resources. Don't dismiss it too quickly; social media is not just for teenagers.

LinkedIn

LinkedIn is a social media site that focuses more on the professional work of a person. After joining LinkedIn via subscription (free or fee), members upload their professional profiles – including a photo – and highlight their skills. In addition to listing where and when they worked, LinkedIn users/members also share, often in a short narrative, the sorts of things they were responsible for while at each company. Users also profile their education and academic accomplishments. Essentially, it is one's resume on the Internet.

A LinkedIn premium subscription (currently $25 per month) allows a user to see who is viewing his profile while keeping himself anonymous when viewing others' profiles. Otherwise, subscribers have to choose one or the other view status.

To search for an individual on LinkedIn, start with a simple name search on the site. You can also search for employees of a company, by searching on the company name. LinkedIn can be a tremendous treasure trove of valuable leads and unanticipated information for the investigator. For example, I was reviewing a candidate's resume and verifying the data that he entered. When I compared his resume to his LinkedIn profile, he had listed on LinkedIn that he was also the owner of a delicatessen. A public records search confirmed that the individual was indeed a business owner of a food business. Whether this was an investment, a side business, or a family venture, it wasn't disclosed in his original application – and gave us something to talk about in the interview.

Another useful function of the LinkedIn profile is the user's professional endorsements. Your colleagues can endorse you for all sorts of professional skills – and you can endorse them right back. There are no limitations or vetting processes for these endorsements (but it sure looks nice to have a string of colleagues endorsing you on your profile). If you are investigating someone, look at his LinkedIn profile and record all of the individuals who have endorsed him for a skill. These most likely won't be the person's closest friends or family, but they most likely will be associated one way or another with the person through work or professional life.

Below is a sample of a LinkedIn profile's endorsements list.

Skills

Top Skills

99+	Private Investigations
99+	Fraud
99+	Executive Protection
99+	Investigation
99+	Evidence
99+	Security
99+	Forensic Analysis
69	Police
66	Skip Tracing
64	Risk Management

Some Investigative Notes for LinkedIn

- You must have an account with LinkedIn in order to conduct a search, and to get the most out of your search.
- LinkedIn's Terms of Service states they do not want you to technically or socially circumvent their security by creating a false profile.
- Most LinkedIn profiles are not privacy secured, leaving them opne for scrutiny.
- People tend to use their full and proper names on LinkedIn, as they would on their resume.
- In the LinkedIn URL, LinkedIn lists the full name after the /in/... Example: Linkedin.com/in/cynthiahetherington
- Read everything; the devil is in the details.
- Look for inconsistencies on the LinkedIn profile; compare it with what you already know.
- If you have the individual's resume, compare and contrast it to what he is posting on LinkedIn.
- Find out whom the individual recommends and who recommends him.
- Review the LinkedIn Skills section to see who endorsed the individual, and is thereby a potential friend, client, or associate.
- Look for leads to other professionals also searched on, listed in the right-hand column of the LinkedIn screen.
- LinkedIn's Premium subscribers, at $25 per month, can see who is viewing their profile while keeping themselves anonymous to those they view. Otherwise, subscribers have to choose one or the other view status.
- I recommend you stay anonymous all the time.

Facebook

Facebook is a social media site that focuses more on the, well... social side of a person's life. While you do need to sign up with an account on Facebook, that process is free and open to anyone. You can leave your account open, available to anyone who wants to view it, or connect with you (Friend you, in Facebook parlance). You can also select options that will place some security on your account; you can control who sees what.

When using Facebook for investigation, many companies, and countries (Germany for one), will not permit the employer to view a potential employee's Facebook profile. It's wise to check with the employer first. If it isn't forbidden, looking at a person's Facebook account can be very telling for the investigator. Some subjects can be quite forthcoming. On their Facebook page (Facebook parlance for account), they may give you all sorts of data (date of birth, sexual orientation, physical capabilities, etc.) that, were you conducting a pre-employment background check, you would not be able to use due to equal opportunity laws. However, investigating someone through Facebook you might find asset allocation such as buying expensive cars and going on extravagant trips. From a person's Facebook account, you could build a list of associates via their Friends list, to help establish connections they have. Behavior can be established as well, especially if the person seems to demonstrate himself in compromising situations on a regular basis. I wouldn't judge someone for posting their college keg party photo of 10 years ago. However, if the person has a new drunk picture every weekend, complete with a groggy Monday morning hello post, such behavior might indicate he might not be the best candidate for whatever work position he is being considered via my background check.

Searching in Facebook is different than other sites because it uses graph searching. The plus side: I can look for the Cynthia Hetheringtons who live in New Jersey. The negative side: I can't simply put in Cynthia Hetherington and expect a keyword search to produce all Cynthia Hetheringtons.

AUTHOR TIP **Some Investigative Notes for Facebook:**

- To search for a name, you must type PEOPLE NAMED followed by the name in the search box, and then click on the magnifying glass at the end. For example, type in PEOPLE NAMED Cynthia Hetherington.
- Often, placing a person's name in the URL will produce a viable result. For example: type in www.facebook.com/johnsmith.
- If a person's name is common or has been taken, there will be a number that follows. For example: www.facebook.com/bradsmith2.
- When you don't locate your target, try searching on the names of family members, friends, and colleagues.
- Use the lists of Friends, which are available in most cases, to research for additional contacts.
- Look at the networks your subject is a member of as a possible place for more information.
- If you don't easily find a person in Facebook, or through a Google search, try using Bing.com to locate the person and/or his account.
- If your subject is updating his Facebook account from his cellphone and from his computer, he might not have the security settings set on both devices; one or the other might offer up unsecured information.
- If you don't see Friends listed, look at any Likes and Comments associated with posted photos of the subject.
- Beware of trying to Friend a subject whose account is set to private. Facebook has strict terms of service that discourage you from creating a false profile to circumvent security applications in order to Friend a subject whose account is set to private.

- According to Facebook terms of service, Facebook will not share with the users who is looking at their profile.
- BE AWARE: If you look at someone's profile often enough, Facebook will assume you are acquainted with that person and will then start to recommend you to your target as someone to connect with on Facebook.
- HOWEVER... if you look at someone's profile enough times, Facebook assumes you are friends and starts to recommend you as someone to connect with on Facebook to your target.

Instagram, Pinterest, and Twitter

A trio of popular social media sites, Twitter, Pinterest, and Instagram rely mostly on smartphone activity. Gaining access into someone's account can be as easy as looking them up in the respective services with these three sites. A simple way to find a person's profile is to search for him in Google; for example, search on "Cynthia Hetherington." Using the quotation marks around the name indicates the two words must be searched together, so that we can focus our search on only Cynthia Hetheringtons (and not Cynthia Lennons or Joey Hetheringtons). Google usually displays the most popular sites first in its search returns, and so anything social media related will most likely come out at the top of the list. In the returned search results, you will see Pinterest and Twitter results mixed in with LinkedIn and Facebook results, as well as results from other social media sites you may not be familiar with.

Twitter can be the easiest of the search sites. You do not need a Twitter account, nor do you need to Follow (Twitter parlance for being connected to the person) the Twitter user, in order to see what the person has posted – if the person's account security settings are set to open. You can look back as far as 3,200 posts in the person's Twitter stream (parlance for what the person has posted to his Twitter account). Searching directly on Twitter is possible, but using third-party applications can be more productive. My preferred Twitter search tools are Tweettunnel (tweettunnel.com), Topsy (topsy.com), and Twazzup (twazzup.com). Tweettunnel manages to draw down the most recent 3,200 Twitter posts (with dates next to them) in a manner that is easy to capture and save. Topsy can search other social media sites, but its Twitter-only search allows you to look at Twitter posts by specific dates. Twazzup has a smooth interface for topical searching and search results appear quickly.

Pinterest does not offer myriad search sources. However, Pinterest's users quite often create their Pinterest account via their Facebook or Twitter accounts, which then connect the multiple social media platforms for that user. For the investigator, the real benefit of Pinterest is in seeing what the user pins (Pinterest parlance for user posts) to his account, the theory being what he pins is what he likes. So, if you notice a good deal of kitchen improvement photos, new car photos, or exotic vacation destination photos being pinned to your target's Pinterest account, this could possibly be where your target plans to spend money in the near future.

Instagram originally seemed to be a photo-taking application for young adults, however, over time it has developed into an application appealing to all age markets. Individuals use Instagram on their smartphones to take a photo, apply a filter (sepia, black-and-white, grey scale, or a frame) to those photos, and then upload the photos to their Instagram accounts. Similar to Pinterest, Instagram accounts are quite often connected to Facebook and Twitter accounts, so that when a photo is uploaded to Instagram, it would also be uploaded to Facebook and Twitter. For an investigator, multiple posting sites can prove quite useful as a work-around when the target has locked his Facebook account from prying eyes (the investigator's) but has left his Instagram account wide open. I will be able to view photos – and potentially identify the location where those photos were taken, thanks to metadata. Also any Friends who Comment, Like, or Share (more Facebook parlance) those photos will also be identified (exposed). There are several services available for viewing Instagram photos, starting with Iconosquare (iconosquare.com), Websta (websta.me), and FinderGram (findergram.com).

Try social media resources for investigations; you will often find them quite useful. For a closer look at social media investigations of people and topics, see Chapter 10 of this book.

Ch 5:

Businesses, Corporations, and Other Due Diligence Focuses

I went looking for trouble, and I found it.
—Charles Ponzi

Due diligence investigations are rooted in corporate background research; understanding all that you can know about a company's founding, financial status, scalability, security, and reputation. Beyond that, it is learning about what makes the company successful and how that can effect you as a competitor, a merger, or otherwise. This section on business investigations and other due diligence focuses on the best of what is available online to help answer the corporate questions that might linger.

Companies come in all sizes, with multiple jurisdictions, different ownership, and different sectors. The quest for information about companies will vary depending on how long the companies have been in business, how large they are (measured by the number of employees, profits, and other factors), how many customers they serve, where they are located, and the principals behind them. Narrowing the structure and logistics of the company you are investigating will set the stage for the budget and timeline for your investigation. Having in-depth knowledge on all aspects of a company is nearly imperative for an investigator.

Chapter 5 will examine, in detail, the following topics:

- Types and structures of business entities
- Publicly- and privately-owned companies
- Large companies vs. small companies
- Location issues

- Locating company headquarters
- Subsidiaries, divisions, satellite offices, affiliates, and plants
- Non-profits and foundations
- Recommended online investigative resources.

Identify the Type of Business Entity

Determining the entity's structure will give you an invaluable sense and understanding of what is available from an information perspective and how to launch your investigation. A few norms can be supposed:

- Generally, a publicly traded company has more information readily available, and the data is apparent and easy to obtain. However, these types of companies also tend to be large, multi-layered organizations that can be cumbersome to examine as you attempt to peel away the layers of management, subsidiaries, and partnerships.

- Investigating private companies is challenging since there are fewer regulations that demand these firms file or report publicly available data, especially financial records. Private company financial information gathered from off- the-shelf business services is always questionable because of the self-reported value.

- A company based in the U.S. will be easier to investigate than a foreign entity.

- Small and/or young companies are difficult to research because of the lack of available company information. You will have to search deeper into the history of the principals' prior companies.

To lay a proper foundation, let us examine the types of U.S. business entities that you will encounter as an investigator.

Corporations

A corporation is a legal entity or structure created under the authority of state law. A corporation is owned by shareholders or stockholders. A corporation can enter into contracts, sue or be sued, and is liable for its own debts and obligations, including income taxes. When ownership changes in a corporation, the corporation does not dissolve.

There are two common forms of a corporation – a C corporation and a subchapter S corporation with several important differences. A C corporation pays income tax as a legal separate entity, but with limited personal liability for business debts. An S corporation is not a taxable entity; the corporate earnings and profits are passed directly to the personal tax return of the shareholder on a prorated basis equal to the share of ownership.

About the Term "Foreign Corporations"

Also referred to as an out-of-state corporation, a foreign corporation is an existing corporation registered to do business in another state. A foreign corporation is able to operate in multiple states or jurisdictions as one organization. (Do not confuse this with a corporation formed and operating in a foreign country; these are two entirely different types of entities.) The alternative – to register a separate corporation in each jurisdiction where operations are taking place – would be extremely cumbersome.

Non-Profit Corporations

A non-profit corporation is formed to carry out a specific purpose that is charitable, educational, religious, literary, or scientific in nature. A non-profit corporation does not pay federal or state income taxes on its profits because the IRS perceives that the public derives benefits from this organization. Non-profits are often referred to as a 501C3 which comes from Section 501(c)(3) of the Internal Revenue Code.

Partnerships

A partnership is a business with two or more owners who have not filed papers with the state to become a corporation or a limited liability company (see below). A partnership is not a separate tax entity like a C corporation, but instead is a *pass thru* entity, like an S corporation or a sole proprietorship.

There are two basic types of partnerships – **general partnerships** and **limited partnerships**. A general partnership is the simplest and least expensive co-owned business structure to create and maintain. One of the major drawbacks of limited partnerships, however, is that they require a general partner that has unlimited liability for the debts of the partnership. Now most states allow the creation of a specialty partnership known as a **limited liability partnership** (LLP). In an LLP, one partner is not responsible or liable for another partner's misconduct or negligence.

A **limited liability limited partnership** (LLLP) is a relatively new modification of the limited partnership, a form of business entity recognized under U.S. commercial law. Like a limited partnership, an LLLP is a limited partnership and, as such, consists of one or more general partners and one or more limited partners. Many LLLPs are associated with real estate ownership and management.

Limited Liability Company

A limited liability company (LLC) combines the advantages of a corporation with the tax advantages and management flexibility of a partnership. Similar to a corporation, an LLC is created by a state filing, protects personal assets from business liabilities, has few ownership restrictions, and is not taxed as a separate tax entity. Perhaps the biggest difference between LLCs and corporations is that

LLCs do not issue stock. Like partnerships, LLCs are simply owned by the members and/or the managers of the company.

Because of the simplicity and flexibility, an LLC is very popular for both start-up businesses and more mature businesses. In many states, the number of new LLCs being formed is outpacing new corporation filings.

AUTHOR TIP

Watch for Trade Names, Fictitious Names, and Assumed Names

Trade name is a relative term. Trade names may be referred to as fictitious names, or assumed names, or DBAs (doing business as). States (or counties) allow business owners to operate a company using a name other than its real name. Registering the trade name insures two entities will not use the same or close to the same name.

Typically, the state agency that oversees corporation records usually maintains the files for trade names. Most states will allow verbal or Web status checks of names. Some states will administer fictitious names at the state level while county agencies administer trade names, or vice versa.

Researching Publicly Owned Companies

A publicly owned company is a corporation whose securities, i.e., stocks, are available for sale to the open market. These shares are exchanged on stock markets, such as the American Stock Exchange (AMEX), the New York Stock Exchange (NYSE), and the National Association of Securities Dealers Automated Quotations (NASDAQ). Companies that do not qualify to have shares sold in one of these three exchanges are often found listed in one of the lesser exchanges, often known as the Over-the-Counter (OTC) market or on the Pink Sheets. These stocks, often referred to as penny stocks, represent companies that still offer opportunity and value, but are not traded on the major markets.

Companies also may be traded on foreign stock exchanges. Examples are the Tokyo Exchange (tse.or.jp), the Toronto Exchange (tmx.com), and the Jamaican Stock Exchange (jamstockex.com). Each exchange and country will have its own oversight group. Wikipedia is a reasonable resource to find a list of foreign exchanges at en.wikipedia.org/wiki/List_of_stock_exchanges.

Publicly traded companies operating in the U.S. are required by Federal law to register with the Securities and Exchange Commission (SEC) and submit filings quarterly and annually to the SEC. However, publicly owned companies that only operate within a particular state may file with their state's bureau of securities instead of the SEC. All of the state bureaus are part of the larger consortium, the

North America Securities Administrators Association (NASAA). Both the SEC and these state agencies monitor these companies for any irregularities or potential fraudulent behavior.

It is very easy to find out if your subject company is traded. Each traded company has a stock symbol, a short coded identifier such as EBA for Ebay or GE for General Electric. All major brokerage firms with a Web presence offer research on stock symbols and detailed overviews of the company's profits and operations. If you do not have a stock account, I recommend visiting the financial pages at either Yahoo (finance.yahoo.com) or Google (google.com/finance). Similar in offerings, both sites provide symbol look-ups, news on the company in question, and a plethora of corporate-structure details for free.

For various reasons, some companies will be delisted from a major exchange and listed on the OTC. Perhaps a company is delisted because it is acquired by another company, or merges with another company. But a firm may also be delisted if its stock price does not meet the exchange's minimum, or it fails to file proper papers or it has have solvency problems. Companies also can be demerged, decentralized, demutualized, or re-privatized.

As you examine the particular filings of the company you are investigating, a good idea is to keep a financial dictionary within arm's reach. Or, you may want to place a Web site like investopedia.com on your favorites list as a resource to define financial expressions.

Regulatory Sources: SEC, FINRA, and NFA

There are three primary regulatory agencies that oversee regulatory and compliance issues with publicly traded securities or with security dealers:

- Securities & Exchange Commission (SEC)
- Financial Industry Regulatory Authority (FINRA)
- National Futures Association (NFA).

The SEC is a Federal government agency. FINRA and NFA are self-regulatory bodies.

Each agency is an excellent resource for investigating compliance issues and enforcement actions. Chapter 6 examines in detail how to access the information from these agency databases when investigating compliance issues and sanctions. For the purposes of this chapter, we will examine EDGAR, the SEC's repository of filings from publicly owned companies.

EDGAR

EDGAR – the Electronic Data Gathering Analysis and Retrieval system – was established by the SEC to allow companies to make required filings to the SEC by direct transmission. Since May 6, 1996, all public domestic companies are required to file their filings electronically on EDGAR, except for filings made to the SEC's regional offices or those filings made on paper due to a hardship exemption.

EDGAR has an extensive repository of U.S. corporation information, most of which is available online. Companies must file the following reports with the SEC:

- 10-K: an annual financial report that includes audited year-end financial statements.

- 10-Q: a quarterly, un-audited report.

- 8K: report detailing significant or unscheduled corporate changes or events.

- Securities offerings, trading registrations, and the final prospectus.

The list above is not conclusive. There are other miscellaneous reports filed, including those dealing with security holdings by institutions and insiders. Access to these documents provides a wealth of information.

How to Access EDGAR Online

Search EDGAR at sec.gov/edgar/searchedgar/webusers.htm. A number of private vendors offer access to EDGAR records. LexisNexis acts as the data wholesaler or distributor on behalf of the government. LexisNexis sells data to information retailers, including its own Nexis service.

EDGAR's search features have expanded considerably. Companies can be searched by name or by filing specifics, such as only for the DEF14 reports (good for getting executive compensation information). Also searchable are Mutual Funds, historical findings and Variable Insurance Products back to February of 2006. EDGAR also offers full-text searching for the past four years of entries, which enables the investigator to search by keyword. Keyword searches allow you to search by personal name or company name. Results are "keyword-like," meaning if the person or company you are searching for is mentioned in a filing, the keyword will appear, even if it is ancillary. For example, sample searches in EDGAR for Barack Obama turned up close to 1,300 matches, Derek Jeter had seven matches, and Mickey Mouse turned up 72 matches. When searching on full names, be sure to use quotes around the name ("john doe").

A sample screen shot of EDGAR follows on the next page.

For more information on how to use the SEC and EDGAR for investigations see Chapter 6.

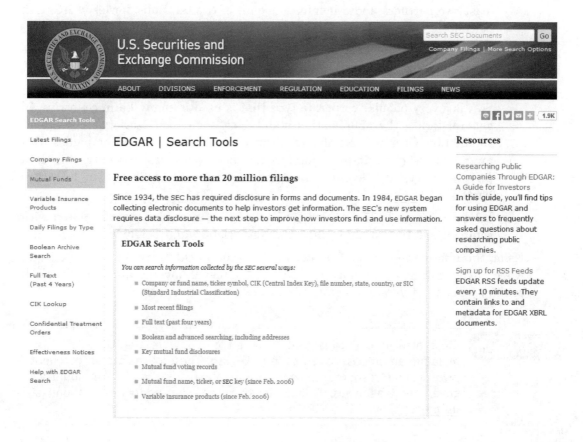

(source: sec.gov/edgar/searchedgar/webusers.htm)

Researching Foreign Country Company Designations

In the U.S., most companies are designated as Inc. or LLC. If you notice a U.S.-based company name with Ltd. at the end, then you would look for a foreign parent. Foreign designations can be confusing if you have not seen them in the course of your work. Eventually you get accustomed to seeing designations like GmbH, Ltd., and S.A.

Below are several examples of foreign company designations. An expanded list of 193 countries' foreign designations is graciously provided by Winthrop Corporation (CorporateInformation.com). See Chapter 13.

- Gesellschaft mit beschränkter Haftung, or GmbH, is German and literally translates to company with limited liability. GmbH indicates the company is incorporated, but not publicly traded. Aktiengesellschaft, or AG, is a loosely translated German term for publicly traded companies. A GmbH must have at least two partners and a nominal amount of capital. Subsidiaries of AGs can be GmbHs.

- Limited, denoted as Ltd., is commonly used in the United Kingdom and in the Commonwealth, in Japan, and in the United States. Ltd. indicates that the company is incorporated and that the owners have limited liability.

- S.A. is a very popular corporate type that is used in many Latin countries. In general terms, the abbreviation stands for "anonymous society/corporation." In addition, Greece, Luxembourg, France, and Belgium mark companies with an S.A. It is difficult to generalize all these countries; however, S.A. is a private entity, with a minimum capital ownership required of at least two parties.

- B.V., a common Dutch symbol for Besloten Vennootschap, can be found with companies in the Dutch Antilles, the Netherlands, and Belgium.

Using the information in the Chapter 13, you can quickly surmise where to begin when investigating a company that has an unusual incorporation mark. Each country will offer different amounts of information on each company.

AUTHOR TIP Most foreign countries that have an embassy in the U.S., will also maintain an embassy Web page in English. These pages are an excellent investigative resource to learn more about that particular country's government agencies. A links list to these Web addresses is found at usembassy.gov.

About Privately-Held Ownership and Investors

Privately-held ownership of a company means the firm has not sold ownership to the public. A privately-held company may be owned by the company's founders, management, or a group of private investors, or family members such as Mars, Inc., famous for its candy bars. Many small businesses may be held privately. Then there are sole proprietors, such as the local plumber, where there is one owner of record. But for the purpose of this section of the book, we are concerned with privately held entities that do not offer or trade its **company** stock to the general public on the stock market exchanges. Private companies have less reporting requirements to the government than public companies. The SEC does not require quarterly or yearly statements to insure the legitimacy and honesty of a company for its shareholders.

Sizable private companies may be involved with private investors known as venture capitalists, private equity investors, or even public companies. Note that a public company can have a private venture, and vice versa. In this instance, use EDGAR to find ownership or involvement.

It can be difficult, if not impossible, to find the terms of a private deal between two private entities, especially if they do not want the details disclosed. Perhaps you may find a press release that says a little more than, "ABC Company was purchased for an undisclosed amount by the DEX Firm."

To find financial information on private companies, evaluate their known assets and liabilities (see Chapter 7), as well as reviewing business and credit reports from vendors, such as Dun & Bradstreet (D&B), Standard & Poor's (S&P), and Experian.

Finding who owns the company is sometimes the most complicated question to answer. One or many persons or entities may be involved, and sometimes ownership is a matter of a one percent difference in shareholder value. Breaking down company ownership into small and large corporations helps when starting your research.

 If you are investigating the Board of Directors of a private company and you determine several of the directors are strictly financial types, with other positions at investment groups, this can be an indicator to other investigation tracks. For exmaple they very well may be angel investors or hedge managers who invested in the company you are investigating.

Identifying Small Companies

According to the U.S. Small Business Administration, "Small firms represent 99.7 percent of all employer firms."[12]

Given the vast number of companies considered small, there is a strong probability most investigations will involve small companies. Even though small companies can still be million dollar firms, their corporate structure is generally easier to assess than huge conglomerates. These companies tend to be private entities, and can be as small as the local pizzeria, and as large as a multi-million dollar, multi-state organization. Keeping subsidiaries out of this group, tracing the origin of ownership of a company should be as easy as obtaining its annual report from the Secretary of State's office. Unfortunately, not all states require ownership information to be on file, and only request the contact information for Service for Process, where legal papers should be sent in case the company is sued.

The first place to look for a small company is through the Secretary of State's business registration where the company is located. Follow up with a request for an actual photocopy of a report or in a special formation such as the TIFF[13] files. Florida supplies online, but not in the standard online formation such as a PDF or

---

[12] sba.gov/sites/default/files/FAQ_Sept_2012.pdf
[13] TIFF - Tagged Image File Format is a file format for storing images, including photographs and line art

HTML format. View the original filing as written and submitted to the state and not a converted document. You may very well find that the filer has crossed out some information, such as an address, an error you will not see in the online version.

The Proof is on the Paper

A large company contracted me to assist on an employee fraud issue. The subject employee was a real estate manager for the company's Midwest division in Michigan. He was having an affair with a young Chinese woman, who was of interest to the U.S. authorities. Beyond the original reason for launching the investigation, the company was also told that the couple was working together in real estate. If true, this would have been an employee violation of the non-compete contract the manager had signed. My task was to find out what he was doing outside of company business.

Both parties had created businesses, filed in the state of Michigan. His filing listed him as a corporate officer, and her filing listed her as a corporate officer. Unfortunately, they did not list each other in the same documents. After looking at the Web page that provided this information, I thought it would be interesting to see the actual documents. So, I ordered copies of the corporate registrations and waited patiently, as it took Michigan's Corporation Division a few weeks to send.

When the copies arrived, I noticed a few, very distinct and obvious clues. First, both applications were typed, using the same typewriter. (Who has a typewriter anymore?!) The typing was similar on each form, using the same indenting and spacing style. I was feeling like Sherlock Holmes making these odd, but important, discoveries, until I realized the most obvious clue of all. Both forms had her home address typed in the Service of Process section. But on his form, the typed information had an "X" through it, and she carefully had written his address next to it. I knew it was her handwriting because she had used the same cursive style in her own signature on her own form.

These facts would never have come to light without obtaining hard copies of the actual filing documents.

Business registrations, changes, and annual reports can be found at each state's Secretary of State Web site. A list of state link with free searching to this material is provided in Chapter 12. View these links and more at BRB Publications site at https://www.brbpublications.com/freesites/freesites.aspx. Another source for locating small business information is through a town's Chamber of Commerce such as worldchambers.com.

(source: <u>worldchambers.com</u>)

Small Company — Big Web Presence

Do not underestimate the value of news stories, press releases, and a company's Web site. The About Us section may accurately offer company history and ownership information. However, it is best to verify any company-produced literature.

Given that investigators always verify their leads, review the findings on the company's Web site that might offers clues about the company. Visiting the Web site will give you a sense of the company background.

Perhaps you may remember Peter Steiner's cartoon "On the Internet nobody knows you're a dog"[14] published in *The New Yorker* (pg 61 of July 5, 1993). The point is some very impressive looking Web sites are just fronts for small garage operations. At-home moms and dads, people working side jobs, and any number of individuals are doing business on the Internet by selling travel services, financial advice, or providing consulting on a variety of subject – some of which may or may not be illegitimate.

My first step is to locate the owner of the Web domain itself, meaning the "company.com" ownership, using a site like <u>Domaintools.com</u>. If you know the company, the results should match to a name or address that is familiar. However it is possible a Web hosting company may be listed. However, if you suspect the company you are searching is fraudulent and is operating as a shell company, don't be surprised to find the real people listed at this site.

Below is the search result of my company, <u>hetheringtongroup.com</u>, at Domaintools. As you can see, many usable facts are provided:

```
Domain Name: HETHERINGTONGROUP.COM
Registry Domain ID: NA
```

---

[14] en.wikipedia.org/wiki/On_the_Internet,_nobody_knows_you%27re_a_dog

```
Registrar WHOIS Server: whois.enom.com
Registrar URL: enom.com
Updated Date: 2014-04-17 01:50:54Z
Creation Date: 2005-05-16 22:27:06Z
Registrar Registration Expiration Date: 2015-05-16
    22:27:00Z
Registrar: ENOM, INC
Registrar Abuse Contact Phone: +1.4252744500
Domain Status: clientTransferProhibited
Registry Registrant ID:
Registrant Name: CYNTHIA HETHERINGTON
Registrant Organization: HETHERINGTON INFORMATION
    SERVICES, LLC
Registrant Street: PO BOX 134
Registrant City: HASKELL
Registrant State/Province: NEW JERSEY
Registrant Postal Code: 07420-0134
Registrant Country: US
```

Using the About Us Section to Your Advantage

When you view a Web site and you are skeptical as to the validity of the product or company, again a good starting point to weed out the truth is the About Us section which often reflects how the people who put up these sites are presenting themselves and their company.

The About Us section is meant to tout to readers how talented and capable the leaders of a company are in their respective roles. These biographies always discuss their history, talents, and education. Keep in mind there is a bias. Also, you get what you pay for, so verify all the information being provided on the About Us Web pages.

If that information is freely given, then fee-based services can only enhance the return for the investigator. For small and large companies, fee-based information services are rich resources for gathering data quickly about a company. Refer to the discussion on databases at the end of the chapter.

Now let's focus on the other end of the spectrum – the large company – to gain a perspective on the unique challenges and free-service offerings when researching information on large to mega-large companies.

Identifying the Large Company Structure

Large companies become complicated quickly. The corporate tree is just that; a complicated top-down view of a company's hierarchy of ownership relations. A tree provides a clear understanding about who is the ultimate parent of the company.

Publicly traded companies have their corporate structures written in their annual reports. However, this information is not easy to discern.

You would think Coca-Cola is the ultimate parent of Coke, the soda beverage. But is it? Is Coca-Cola Enterprises the ultimate parent? Tricky question, but important if you are working on a product-liability case, and need to know whom to track down for your client.

Chances are a canning company, contracted to can the soda for Coca-Cola as well as other companies, is liable. Yet, to find culpable parties, litigators will search for the deepest pockets. The canning company may be simply a contract firm, hired only to can a beverage. The firm may also be partially or completely owned by Coca-Cola Enterprises. There is never one single answer to the issue, and each matter must be researched thoroughly to understand the unique circumstances.

Fast-food service companies often go this route. You may never have heard of Yum! Brands, but its subsidiaries Kentucky Fried Chicken and Taco Bell are familiar to most Americans. Visit a Web site such as yumfranchises.com and see how many opportunities there are for partnership.

AUTHOR TIP Interestingly, for most of the large company investigations I have worked, the target company is actually a subsidiary that was five branches removed from the ultimate parent, which demonstrates another reason to focus on the tree.

Using Web sites for research is generally as effective for large companies as they are for the smaller ones. Be sure to search the actual company Web site's About Us section, as well as any Investor or Financial Web pages.

Finding the Parent

When the question is asked who owns whom?, I can recommend two valuable resources for finding the ultimate parent of a company:

1. The Directory of Corporate Affiliations (corporateaffiliations.com) is owned by LexisNexis. Per their Web page their coverage includes:

    *   Over 1 million global public and private company profiles

    *   Over 1,700,000 unique executives – including directors – and titles

    *   Detailed biographical information for more than 140,000 executives and directors

    *   Parent companies with an annual revenue of $1 million or greater

    *   Subsidiaries having no revenue qualifier

    *   Enhanced business descriptions

- Company brands with product descriptions
- Corporate hierarchies (corporate structure)
- Competitor listings
- Specific company news (90 day news file)
- Executive move alerts
- Merger & Acquisition news via MergerTrak™
- Outside service firm relationships (e.g., legal, audit, ad agencies, transfer agents)
- Unique permanent company numbering scheme

2. Who Owns Whom at https://solutions.dnb.com/wow is owned by Dun & Bradstreet. This international database covers the following industries since January 2006; "...manufacturing, retail trade, wholesale trade, agriculture, mining, construction, financial services, educational institutions, business services, professional services, public, private, and government-run companies."

Recognize Location Issues

"Location, Location, Location" is the mantra of many real estate investors. The same is true for many businesses. An investigator must keep in mind businesses will locate their headquarters, offices, plants, and warehouses in the precise location(s) that works best for their situation.

Perhaps a major, international law firm, wanting to impress and capture the attention of wealthy potential clients, will be located center stage in New York City, London, Hong Kong, Singapore, or other prestigious and expensive real estate locations. Some companies must locate near specific transportation resources, such as railroad yards, freeways, waterways, or airports, for ease of operation. Corporations, especially larger ones, may operate in more than one country. Some mega-companies, such as Coca-Cola and Microsoft, can claim more than 100 different locations. A customer-support team for a software company does not necessarily need downtown views of a seaport, nor does it necessarily need to be in the same country as the company's headquarters. Today, many firms outsource their tech support to locations in Third World countries, such as those found in Asia or in South America. Outsourcing to Poland is also in vogue. The trend allows companies to man their customer-service lines 24/7 with inexpensive labor.

Retail companies, looking for local clients, will be found in the middle of residential and business neighborhoods, where their neon signs and other forms of advertising will lure new customers.

Knowing where to investigate companies with more than one location, whether the company has two offices in two cities, or is a multinational firm with subsidiaries, branches, satellites, plants, and help desks located in multiple nations, is an important factor. A research starting point is to obtain business reports from vendors such as Kompass, Hoover's, SkyMinder, or Dun & Bradstreet, as covered at the end of this chapter. Each vendor should offer a view of the corporate structure, or, at the very least, the highest level of the company with its immediate subsidiaries.

A good starting point is to find the company's main corporate headquarters.

How to Locate the Company Headquarters

Multinational is the wave of business in this technically connected world of the 21st century. With the improvement of technology and advantages of cheaper labor, tax shelters, and weak environmental and labor laws in some countries, many American businesses move overseas to set up companies in foreign countries. Researching these company headquarters can sometimes be a little like playing a game. Where is the true location of a company's headquarters, and where does the CEO report to work? Or does he?

Use Annual Reports

A first-step is to locate a firm's annual reports. With a search of Google you can find many Web services that provide annual reports, such as annualreports.com.

Annual reports may often be found on the company's Web site or in SEC filings, if available. First, look to see if headquarter-friendly locations are shown. As mentioned previously, many businesses use the tax advantages of registering corporations in places such as Delaware, the Bahamas, the British Virgin Islands, and other offshore locations.

These locations are commonly not the true headquarters. For example, a search in the Dun & Bradstreet database for a specific location known as Road Town in the British Virgin Islands, returns thousands of companies, all registered in care of trust companies. Lexus Investment Group c/o Mission Trust Company is one example. Technically, there is nothing wrong with registering in offshore locations; doing so allows companies to take advantage of easier taxation, anonymity, and asset protection. However, if an investigator sees a British Virgin Islands address is listed as a company's headquarters, or comes across addresses in the Bahamas or another tropical resort country known more for tourism than industry, then the investigator should immediately consider that the company is registered here, but operating elsewhere.

Watch for Emerging Markets

A noticeable trend is when a company moves its headquarters to an area where emerging markets are connected to its product line. Dubai is now considered a prestigious location for wealthy enterprising companies. Many corporations in the petroleum, infrastructure, and manufacturing industries are establishing their headquarters, or a substantial presence, in Dubai to service the needs of their clients in the Middle East.

Firms serving the technology market may take a similar approach. In order to demonstrate commitment to their current clients and be near potentially new clients, technology firms often establish their headquarters in marketing facilities that are geographically close to their clients. These firms may maintain a paper headquarters somewhere else, perhaps in the British Virgin Islands, but physically maintain their headquarters in one of their main sales and marketing facilities in the U.S. This pattern is used by many technology companies created in the U.S., but are sending the majority of their IT work overseas to contractors, or subsidiaries in India, Pakistan, and other Asian countries.

Trying to discern which office location is the actual headquarters can be vexing, because of the nuances these corporations place upon themselves. For example, some Israeli technology companies have research and development divisions in one country, their founders and lead scientists in another country, and their headquarters in a U.S. location, such as the Silicon Valley in California. In this case, placing the headquarters in the U.S. provides a cost savings for the company, because the tax burden on companies in Israel is steep.

Use Media Sources

Using the media as a source is also a good investigative route to take. One Dun & Bradstreet business report might indicate the ultimate parent company, ABC, located in India, whereas a news article on the same company might have an executive claiming, "our parent company here in the U.S..." This certainly can cause confusion. Keep in mind that both statements may be true. You might be looking at the American division of a company, whose headquarters is in the U.S., and yet the parent company is actually the subsidiary of a larger group that operates overseas. An excellent example is the Tata family of businesses.

The Tetley Tea Example

Tata Tea is a rich and complicated company, larger than Coca-Cola. However, in the U.S., you would know it by one of its brand names, such as Tetley, and not by Tata Tea. Tetley is a subsidiary of Tata Tea Limited and Tetley Group U.K., and is known as Tata Tetley. In the U.S., two other subsidiaries are Tata Tea Inc. and Tata Coffee. Per their Web site:

> "The Tata Group comprises 96 operating companies in seven business sectors: information systems and communications; engineering; materials; services; energy; consumer products; and chemicals. The Group has operations in more than 54 countries across six continents, and its companies export products and services to 120 nations."

(source: tcsrd.org/about_us_TATAhistory.html)

Take a Test Drive

Since there are many industries that Tata is involved with, it is a company that is a perfect example for new investigators to use in practicing investigative research and analysis. Tata provides a great deal of information on its Web site, plus additional information can be found in vendor business and finance reports, legal sources, and through the media and other open sources.

Other great examples to use for practice searching and which have great depth and interesting backgrounds are Sir Richard Branson of the Virgin enterprises, Biz Stone, Twitter founder and vegan entrepreneur; Warren Buffet; Jimmy Buffet; and William Gates; they all have large and interesting portfolios.

Investigating the HQ Address

Once the headquarters is located, there are some additional steps to take. If the subject company is a large operation, then the headquarters could be in a prestigious location, such as a metropolitan city or center of commerce. Check your property-records resource to see if the company owns the building. If it does not, then you need to determine if the company only occupies a few floors of a skyscraper or shares the address with other businesses.

Watch for Tenants at Same Address

Be sure to check out who else is at the same address, since there may be some cooperative entities, partners, or business associates also located at the same address. This is a vital requirement if you are investigating a smaller company, such as an entity with only one address. The possibility exists that not only are there collusive parties in the same building, but they are also located in the same suite.

Examples of Searches

Let's say you did a search using D&B on the address 409 Washington Street, Hoboken, New Jersey. You might find 45 companies located in this single building, where you can conclude it is a multiple tenant facility, such as an apartment building or office building.

There are a number of excellent vendors who supply business reports. D&B, perhaps the largest database provider of company information worldwide, offers researchers and investigators the ability to search by address. Whether performing a large or small company research, a subscription to D&B is an immediate help.

Below is a sample screen shot.

By location		
Street number starting with [ ]	ending with [ ]	

Check for ○ Odd street numbers ○ Even street numbers ⊙ Both

*Street name: [   ]

*City/Town: [   ] *State: [———US States——— ▼] Zip code: [   ]

[Search]

(source: dnb.com)

Search engines such as Google can be helpful. Run the following address search on Google: 409 Washington Hoboken, but remove Street, Road, Avenue, or Court to in your query, and do not search using NJ or N.J. Even though you might receive more results than necessary, in this case, it is better to be overwhelmed with hits than miss a vital link. Another technique is to view the initial results and then repeat the search using some filters, such as street or road, which will help you whittle the results to a more useful list. When the address is located in Google Maps, look for the Street View offering to see if you can get a view of building itself. Look for the number of mailboxes or electric services on the side, if possible.

Search by a telephone number. Searching D&B or similar vendors is a good route to go, but so are search engines. When searching a phone number in Google or other search engines there are tricks to use - like leaving out the usual dashes, parenthesis, backslashes and other phone number separators. The search should look like this: "xxx xxx xxxx" or "212 555 1212." In most search engines, particularly Google, those marks are considered to be *stop symbols* that are automatically ignored by the engine. However, the space is respected. So, anything can occur between the 2 and the 5 and Google will return results. A search on the phone number "212 555 1212" returned more than 75,000 hits in Google. The actual number goes to Verizon 411 service.

When searching a land line, fax, or cell number search, investigators may find leads and links between companies. A common red flag to spot is when multiple companies are using the same phone number. While this can be a legitimate sign of a spin-offs or subsidiaries, it can also mean some fraudulent companies are piggy-backing off of the same address and phone number.

Do not discount the importance of searching a fax number. Fax numbers, because of the machine's physical location, are often used by multiple companies or entities.

For example, let's say your target or search is the ABC Company using the 409 Washington Street, Hoboken, N.J., with a phone number 201-555-1234 and a fax number 201-555-1233. The phone number and address may be authentic. However, when searching the address 409 Washington Hoboken, you might find six or more companies listed. Now, perform the search using the fax number and you might find three different company names that appear. Following back theses links, you might have located three companies, all with the same address and fax number, but each with a different phone number. You have uncovered the fact that there is some sort of cooperation of shared office space, which means potential collusion. Another avenue to explore is to see if these companies are using rented office space, which might be rented by the hour, month or week.

Your analysis/report should note:

> "ABC Company resides at 409 Washington Street in Hoboken, N.J. Also, the DEX Company and the XYZ Investment Group are located at this address and share the same fax number."

Parent Companies, Subsidiaries, Divisions, and Affiliates

A **parent** company is a company that operates and controls separately chartered businesses. The businesses beneath it are known as subsidiaries.

A **subsidiary** operates as a separate entity, but is controlled by the parent company that also wholly or partially (50% or more) owns it.

A **division** is a functional area of the company that specializes in services or product offerings.

An **affiliate** is a chartered business whose shares are owned by one or more companies, with each company owning less than 50%.

Subsidiaries—Who and Where Are They?

As mentioned above, a company owned in majority by another company is called a subsidiary. Subsidiary research requires you to determine who the parent company of this entity is. You should determine the parent company's percentage of ownership and who the shareholders are. Also, an investigator must be aware of the possibility that a subsidiary could be an acquired company. Maybe the company has continued with its own brand name and logo, but has not taken the parent's name. This it is not readily apparent that the firm is a subsidiary. And finally, be cognizant that the management of subsidiary companies usually has multiple roles in the larger company and perhaps in other subsidiaries as well. Here are two examples:

1. Although this example is a mock-up, the idea is very commonly found. Coca-Cola is the parent company and it manages the many Coke companies under the Coca-Cola banner. One of the subsidiaries is Coke Enterprises. Coke Enterprises manages the bottling and shipping of Coca-Cola products. Coke Productions is a division of Coca-Cola. It is a small production company that creates Coca-Cola commercials and ad design work. Coca-

Cola HBC Polska, a bottling plant in Poland, is partly owned by Coca-Cola and it is considered an affiliate.

2. When evaluating a company, especially an international one, it is not uncommon to see a long line of subsidiaries. For example follow this chain:

a. Groupo de Brazil (Brazil) Ultimate Parent

b. GDB Services Company (Brazil) Headquarters

c. GDB Services Telecom (Brazil) Subsidiary

d. GDB Telecom (Brazil) Subsidiary of Subsidiary

e. Brazil Telecom (NY, U.S.) Subsidiary of Subsidiary, U.S. Headquarters

f. Brazil Telco Corp (CO, U.S.) Final Subsidiary, actual operating company.

A good deal of information about subsidiary relationships can be located in the company's annual report, on its Web site, in the media, in press releases, and in corporate reports. The fee side of D&B and Hoover's does a great job of family hierarchies, as well.

Sometimes, subsidiaries can be discovered quite easily. Using Tata Tea Limited as an example, you find that the company is based in India and is the 100 percent shareholder/owner of Tata Tea Inc. (U.S.), located in Plant City, Florida. According to the financials link on the company's Web site, the majority shareholder, with 20 percent of the shares, is Tata Sons Limited. Look at the list below for the top ten shareholders in this corporation.

Top Ten Shareholders as of March 2013

Sr. No.	Name of Shareholder	Total holdings	%
1	Tata Sons Limited	14,28,54,570	23.10
2	Tata Chemicals Limited	4,31,75,140	6.98
4	Life Insurance Corporation of India	4,23,48,874	6.85
3	Tata Investment Corporation Ltd.	2,75,00,000	4.45
5	Bajaj Allianz Life Insurance Company Ltd.	1,76,01,155	2.85
6	Skagen Kon-Tiki Verdipapirfond	1,71,83,504	2.78
7	Government Pension Fund Global	89,76,940	1.45
8	Platinum Investment Management Limited A/c Platinum International Brands Fund	83,56,060	1.35
9	National Insurance Company Ltd.	64,45,780	1.04
10	Deutsche Bank Trust Company Americas	59,84,945	0.97

(tataglobalbeverages.com/docs/document-manager/tata-global-beverages-ltd-annual-report-2012-13)

One percent, or less, ownership of a company may seem insignificant. However, consider that to obtain the product VitaminWater in 2007, Coca-Cola acquired Glaceau for more than $4 billion. Further research shows that Tata Tea and Tata Group were 30 percent shareholders of Glaceau. This change of hands may be significant to a background investigation. An asset search of an individual (see Chapter 7) that uncovers even 1 percent ownership of a company in transition could mean the individual owns stock worth thousands or hundreds of thousands of dollars.

A key point is since subsidiaries do not necessarily have the same brand name or logo as the parent company, investigating subsidiaries will turn up an array of investigative leads to track.

Take, for example, the long fusion of Sirius and XM Radio. Seventeen months after the merger was proposed, the FCC gave permission to continue with the merger. Prior to this, they both had very unique and descriptive logos. Then in July of 2008 per the acquisition of XM Satellite Radio Holding, Inc. by Sirius Satellite Radio, the logo changed permanently.

Another pattern to watch for in a subsidiary investigation is when a subsidiary has its own senior management, but the parent company's board of advisors oversees the actions. Often the chief executive officer of a subsidiary is a vice president of the parent company. For example, Percy T. Siganporia was the managing director of Tata Tea. He also sat on the board of Eight O'Clock Coffee, another Tata-owned company.

Satellite Offices and Plants

Sometimes a business background investigation will necessitate research on a company's secondary sites. These satellite offices could house entire divisions of the company, or merely two employees in a rented office to give a local business presence for a company. The satellite office may be in a major metropolitan area, in the suburbs, or in another country, where the office houses a research and development team or a group in charge of a certain product line.

To find these secondary sites, a good place to start is the company's Web site, under Contact Us or a similar page. Another search resource is an online phone directory, such as yellowpages.com or superpages.com. If you search Google for additional sites, use the company name and the city name in the same search sequence.

Sometimes, an investigation of a subsidiary location will turn up interesting results.

Who is Answering the Phone?

A branch of a well-known insurance firm was located 40 miles from the nearest major city. That branch, actually a small office, had been located there for more than six years. In a consolidation effort to reduce costs, the parent company decided to close the branch and relocate the employees. Not long after the office closed, a group of individuals moved into the same space. This group of rogue individuals placed advertisements in small, foreign-language newspapers and advertised itself as the same company as the former tenant. The group successfully sold a number of insurance policies. However, after a few months without receiving their insurance documents, the policy owners became frustrated with the now-bogus branch office and began calling the corporate headquarters for assistance. Unfortunately, by that time the rogue individuals were long gone with the policy owners' money.

The concept behind this corporate identity theft was brilliant, because these individuals took the identity of an established company. Even if a suspicious customer had called the Better Business Bureau or Chamber of Commerce, he would have received glowing reports for that company. And if he obtained a D&B report, he would know the branch had been located there for six years. In this example, even the parent company had to check the location and records to make sure it had truly closed the branch!

Plants located outside of the corporate headquarters are easy to locate by using the same resource when looking for satellite offices. In addition, there are several excellent manufacturer directories to turn to, the most popular being the Thomas Register of Manufacturers (see thomasnet.com).

Searching ThomasNet can be done by product/brand name, company name, and product type. The level of detail provided for each company listing is very useful. An example follows.

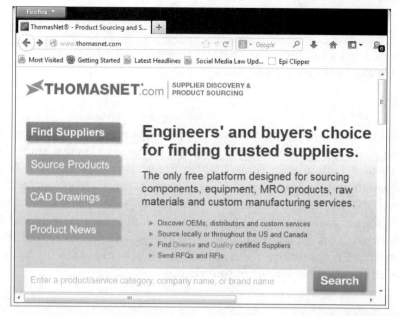

(source: <u>thomasnet.com</u>)

A search of bicycle locks turned up 20 matches, including Courage Industries. In the example below (also from <u>thomas.net</u>), you can see the details in the registry and find the company's home Web page.

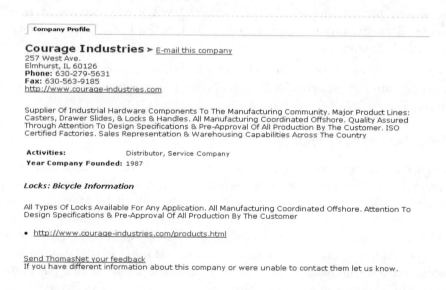

This resource is helpful, not only for looking up a specific plant or facility, but also it is incredibly useful when trying to locate potential suppliers a company might enlist for a project. For example, if your investigation involves a brewery opening a new plant in Arkansas, anticipate the brewery will be looking for aluminum-can manufacturers. In Arkansas, one manufacturer appeared; Ball Company in Springdale.

For additional searching tips within targeted industries, turn to Chapter 9 on Industry Focused Research.

Franchises

A franchise is an enterprise that sells or provides products or services, and is owned and supplied by a manufacturer, supplier, or parent. Typical franchise operations are fast-food restaurants, fitness clubs, financial-service entities, tanning salons, construction groups, hotels, and medical groups. A franchise contract, or agreement between the parties, is finalized with specific terms and conditions. Franchise ownership can be in almost any form of a business entity, including a subsidiary. There is no limit to what type of corporation can be doled out as a franchise opportunity. The pervasive theme to franchise is to maintain the brand and quality of service that the supplier or parent requires.

AUTHOR TIP A Dunkin' Donuts franchise in the Italian section of New York City can not offer zeppolles (Italian donut with no hole), since this would violate the brand the Dunkin' Donuts parent was trying to establish.

Of course, parent-company kitchens will often try new recipes in specific cities. Burger King tried its vegetarian burger first in the U.K., before it slowly made its way into U.S. stores.

The most common type of ownership in a franchise is a small investment group that owns 10 stores in a particular region of the country, versus a single owner/operator store.

The Ownership Chain in a Franchise

When a patron of a restaurant is served substandard food and decides to sue the company, the lawsuit must first establish the chain of ownership. A Taco Bell located in Harrisburg, Pennsylvania might be owned by Harrisburg Investment Group, which owns six Taco Bells, two Long John Silvers, and one Kentucky Fried Chicken. The plaintiff may insist on going to the top of Taco Bell's corporate ladder, but the litigating attorney will have to create an issue for the case to go that high. While not that complicated, considering the brand is owned and guaranteed by the corporate entity, suing a franchise can add a layer of individuals named in a lawsuit.

Sometimes finding who owns a particular franchise is easy as visiting the store, or hotel, or shop. There is usually a sign somewhere in the facility that states, "This Taco Bell is owned by..." And hotels usually post a sign by the lobby front door.

Obtaining a business report from one of the fee-based services mentioned at the end of this chapter is a good search resource. You may see the company name as a "doing business as" (DBA), with the true franchise owner's name as the company name. Also, search the particular state's business registration database for filings, usually held by the Secretary of State. Searching a franchise by address should produce two company names: one for the franchise and one for the franchise owner.

Once you obtain a franchise owner's name, begin looking for other franchises under that name. Lawsuits that may have occurred in the past also can lead to future investigations involving media attention.

Franchisers also have been known to form their own trade associations, which can be a great investigative resource. For example, The American Franchisee Association offers an interesting list of who's who in franchiser-specific associations at its Web site franchisee.org/supporters.htm.

Do not underestimate the type of company that can be franchised, such as major hotel chains, retailers, pharmacies, and gourmet restaurants. Franchisees are not all fast-food chains.

Non-Profit and Charitable Entities

Private foundations, charities, non-profits, churches, hospitals, schools, or publicly supported organizations are subject to special considerations when it comes to federal taxes. These entities file different forms with the IRS, and all must contribute detailed financial and member information, which can be a great asset for the online intelligence investigator.

Whether you are looking to reveal experts in the field, local interests to a region, or the financial participation of a particular foundation, these organizations can open a bevy of investigative leads. Finding out what organizations or affiliations a person belongs to can give you insight into the person's character. Categories can include religious, athletic, health, child focused, or specific-interest related. For example, there are two non-profit associations dedicated only to avocados.

Using Non-profits as Corporate Shells

Although many professionals will join organizations for networking purposes, some professionals realize having an opportunity to lend their name, time and finances to a group carries more weight than networking potential.

Often while doing a name search in an investigation, you may locate a foundation named after the subject. This may be a technique to divert assets into a non-profit status, thereby creating a tax shelter.

Given the choice to pay more taxes to the government or to give money to a charity of your choice, the obvious answer is to support your cause. What better way for a corporation to do this than to create a charity or foundation and support it directly?

Not every company that creates a foundation does so to avoid paying taxes, but a few do create these foundations to shelter money that would otherwise leave their coffers. As a foundation, they can appoint board members, directors, and management. Spending can be influenced by the parent organization, unless the bylaws of the foundation specifically state otherwise.

Finding Information About Non-Profits

Below are several recommended fee and free resources specifically geared to find information on non-profits, foundations, and the wealthy:

- GuideStar: guidestar.org
- The Foundation Center: foundationcenter.org
- NozaSearch: nozasearch.com

The information regarding officers and the financials in a non-profit organization is transparent on Form 990, an annual reporting return that certain federally tax-exempt organizations must file with the IRS. Form 990 provides information on the filing organization's mission, programs, and finances.

Reading through the Form 990 doesn't necessarily require a financial background, though it is helpful if you understand some of the basics of business management and the costs of running an organization. Where your degree in Forensic Accounting may be lacking, common sense should prevail. In the example that follows, you see the revenue and expenses spelled out. And though revenue has not changed drastically from one year to the next, the revenue less expenses has jumped almost 1.2 million dollars. I would want to find out where that money was being spent.

			Prior Year	Current Year
Revenue	8	Contributions and grants (Part VIII, line 1h)	47,448,042	45,494,199
	9	Program service revenue (Part VIII, line 2g)	75,858	448,610
	10	Investment income (Part VIII, column (A), lines 3, 4, and 7d)	312,151	266,917
	11	Other revenue (Part VIII, column (A), lines 5, 6d, 8c, 9c, 10c, and 11e)	-41,407	415,885
	12	Total revenue—add lines 8 through 11 (must equal Part VIII, column (A), line 12)	47,794,644	46,625,611
Expenses	13	Grants and similar amounts paid (Part IX, column (A), lines 1–3)		0
	14	Benefits paid to or for members (Part IX, column (A), line 4)		0
	15	Salaries, other compensation, employee benefits (Part IX, column (A), lines 5–10)	29,299,442	31,925,654
	16a	Professional fundraising fees (Part IX, column (A), line 11e)	177,141	183,694
	b	Total fundraising expenses (Part IX, column (D), line 25) ▶2,661,965		
	17	Other expenses (Part IX, column (A), lines 11a–11d, 11f–24f)	18,509,915	15,962,868
	18	Total expenses Add lines 13–17 (must equal Part IX, column (A), line 25)	47,986,498	48,072,216
	19	Revenue less expenses Subtract line 18 from line 12	-191,854	-1,446,605

In the example below you can see Part 8 of a random Form 990 taken from GuideStar. The names are blocked out to protect the identities, but I can mention that they all have the same last name as the foundation itself. They appear to be siblings and children of the corporate owner. In other words, what better way to take care of your children than to appoint them as trustees of your own foundation!

Form 990-PF (2005)   Page **6**

| Part VIII | Information About Officers, Directors, Trustees, Foundation Managers, Highly Paid Employees, and Contractors | | | | |

1 List all officers, directors, trustees, foundation managers and their compensation (see page 21 of the instructions).

(a) Name and address	(b) Title, and average hours per week devoted to position	(c) Compensation (If not paid, enter -0-)	(d) Contributions to employee benefit plans and deferred compensation	(e) Expense account, other allowances
██████████████████████	Trustee 40	400,000		
██████████████████████	Trustee 40	400,000		
██████████████████████	Trustee 40	400,000		

(source: guidestar.org)

Identifying and Researching Key Location Concerns

Each business location, whether the corporate headquarters, franchise, satellite office, or manufacturing plant is in the U.S. or abroad, will have unique regional concerns. These issues may be environmental or cultural in nature, or may have legal or sanction requirements.

Targeting Licenses and Permits

Company regional issues represent an investigation avenue for business research. Specific knowledge of state, county or town laws, governances, and local codes often come into play.

A simple example of how a very large, multinational company has to abide by small-town laws is when a communications company, like Verizon, decides to locate a retail store in a prominently historical neighborhood. It has to abide by the local codes for building design and signage, yet skillfully maintain its logo integrity without compromising the design requirements of the neighborhood.

There are many small-town laws, such as blue laws (no shopping on Sunday), liquor- licensing laws (bars closing for two hours), dry counties (no alcohol served), or environmental codes. Knowing the laws, codes, and issues that a company faces within the town and county of operation can be important to an investigation.

Not in My Bailiwick

An investigator called me for assistance on a case involving a traffic accident outside of San Diego. I thought it odd that a West Coast investigator would contact a New Jersey investigator for a California traffic accident. But nothing is normal or to be expected in this business.

Apparently the defendant was in a fender bender with a man who claimed he was mentally traumatized by the accident that occurred. There was no question about the accident itself. An automobile insurance claim was paid for the incident. However, a mental-trauma claim lawsuit was also filed against my client.

The basis of the claim was because the man had been reminded of the deaths of his wife and two daughters in New Jersey in the 1970s. His story was that on the Sunday following Thanksgiving, his wife took their children shopping to the Bergen Mall in Paramus, New Jersey. While exiting the mall parking lot, her car was struck by a semi-trailer truck, instantly killing his wife and children. Although this recent accident occurred in California almost thirty years later, he was unable to do anything else, but think of the loss of his entire family back in New Jersey.

Truly a sad story, but if not for my research, he might have gotten away with the blatant lie he told.

As the investigator was telling me the story, I stopped him when he mentioned the location and time. I said, "Wait a minute. Did you say the Bergen Mall on the Sunday after Thanksgiving?" He replied, "Yes." I responded that it wasn't possible for this accident to have occurred as the man asserted. The Bergen Mall is located in Bergen County, New Jersey, which has had a blue law for decades. The Bergen County Blue Law forbids the sale of non-necessary items, such as clothing, shoes, and other retail items commonly found at the mall.

Of course, to verify this statement I visited the Paramus public library. Using the said date, I scrolled through the newspapers to make sure I was not mistaken, and the county had not changed the law for one year, or even for one weekend. I looked for two major items:

- First, to read any mention of the accident. An accident that horrific would certainly have gained the attention of the local press.

- Second, I researched the week prior to Thanksgiving to insure there were no advertisements mentioning open hours on Sunday.

I found no mention of the accident plus the advertisements specifically stated the Sunday hours for stores in nearby Passaic and Hudson Counties, but indicated that the Bergen County stores were closed on the Sunday in question.

> After giving that vital detail to the investigator, I asked him to look further into the man's history. Not only during the supposed time of his family's accident he was incarcerated in a state prison, but also he was never married.

This story demonstrates three key investigative facts.

1. First, be **aware of the local laws and customs** of the region you are working in. If you are not familiar with them, call a local investigator in that area and ask about any issues that you should be aware. If you are not sure you want to discuss your case with the other investigator, then call the local library or city clerk's office. The California investigator followed up my research by calling the Paramus Police Department and talking with a captain, who had joined the force in the late 1970s.

2. The second issue is the **use of the local library for regional research**. Local newspapers are important for more reasons than I cover in the chapter on media. In this instance, I utilized the local press to get information that is not available in a database. Anything prior to 1980 is sketchy. And you will never see advertisements in media database searches outside of ProQuest databases, which highlight only very popular historical newspapers, like the *New York Times*. This kind of newspaper captures full-screen shots.

3. The third piece is to **check the obvious**. Check facts if you have a history of an individual who has mental lapses regarding time. In the previous story, it did not cost the West Coast investigator a lot of money to hire me to run to the library; however, he could have saved that budget and his own time, if he had spent more time interviewing the subject and uncovered the incongruent details of his story.

Be cognizant of other types of laws and different inspectors that could also be involved with your investigation. For example, if a company operates an air hanger, the Federal Aviation Administration (faa.gov) will have documentation and inspection records on that particular hanger or company. If your case involves media broadcasting, the Federal Communications Commission (fcc.gov) oversees licensing for radio, television, satellite, and all other communications in the U.S.

AUTHOR TIP **Check Government Sites**

There really is no limit on how involved federal, state, and local governments will become with a business. These venues are good places to use a little imagination when searching. When presented with a new company to investigate, ask yourself "Who in the government would care?" Chances are there is a license, permit, or inspection involved with the particular company. Visit the state's Web site, search the occupation in the generic search box for the state and see what types of links surface. If there are too many, then simply search the occupation + license (or) + permit.

Environmental Issues

Producers and manufacturers usually deal with oversight organizations involved to insure they are in compliance with environmental laws. County, state and federal boards all will have special interest in the pollution concerns of the community.

The federal government's Environmental Protection Agency (EPA) has regional offices throughout the U.S.

State environmental agencies will also use enforcement to protect property. The EPA Web site has a convenient link to these state agency pages at www2.epa.gov/home/state-and-territorial-environmental-agencies

(source: water.epa.gov/type/location/regions.cfm)

Counties and towns have health departments, with appointed health officers who act as regional guardians, are usually a part of the first response when a toxic spill occurs or a pandemic/epidemic begins. Locate the official county and town Web sites to find a link, or their actual contact information.

These agencies are important resources to use if you are trying to determine if the plant or factory you are investigating has followed regulations and passed inspections. Documents are often available for review; these document may offer a good deal of information about the plants and their managers.

Civic and Cultural Factors

Regionally located companies often become an integral part of the local community. You will find that large companies, with key offices, manufacturing plants, and operational facilities located outside of company headquarters, are usually involved with outreach efforts in the community. This involvement is good for business and demonstrates civic responsibility and respect for the communities. Communities will sometimes develop around a large plant facility. When a company decides to move its operations abroad or to another region, the town often collectively fails.

Key investigative leads may be found through the local economy supporting these companies. The plants and satellite offices are not only filled with people, but also with people who need to purchase goods and services. They hire local cleaning companies, eat in local restaurants, buy gas, and organize events, like holiday parties at local hotels. Local retail and hospitality venues are good places for interviewing employees and establishing dialog, when local feedback becomes necessary in an investigation.

While you will find the locals need the company in town to help their shops thrive, you may also find that some locals may hold some resentment for the employees, the company, or both. Outsiders often are not welcomed right away.

Local Investigative Resources

One excellent way to further determine how a community feels toward its local company is to read the local newspapers and interview the residents. Contact the local public library or visit it online to see what regional newspapers cover the neighborhoods. Factiva is one of the better sites for getting very small newspapers on its database. However one of the best resources for searching inside a community is by perusing through social media sites such as Yahoo Local, Yelp.com, TripAdviser.com, and other rating Web sites to get a flavor for an area. Certainly reviews of the businesses in the area tout where to eat and who to let service your car, but a sense of the community also shines through. Pride, relief, and stress bleed through media sites. Especially straightforward ones such as Facebook, Twitter, and Instagram where you do not need a specific topic or issue to discuss how you feel about the local police, mayor, or future events.

Also, remember to contact support organizations such as the chamber of commerce, VFW, rotary, etc. You can usually find people who like to talk about their community.

Dealing with Cultural Issues

Cultural issues can come as a surprise to many new investigators who are located overseas or working with foreign guests. With corporations becoming global so quickly, it is difficult to keep up with the cultural norms of guests or host countries.

Does a woman wear a headdress? Do you bow or shake the hand of your Asian client? Who eats first and do you eat everything on your plate, or leave just a little to show you are satisfied?

Pick a Card, Any Card

When playing host to Japanese software developers many years ago, I was given a half-day instruction on Japanese business etiquette. I clearly recall that I was supposed to stare at the visitor's business card, with reverence, for at least 15 seconds. That is a long time when you have six cards in front of you. However, I decided to maintain this practice, and find that I clearly remember a person by his business card now.

Although there are books with plenty of good information about dealing with other cultures, I have found that working with a consultant is the most efficient means to learn more about cultural issues. For example, visit globalimmersions.com. If this company's owner cannot help you, she will find someone who can.

Local Unions

Put three people on the payroll, and one will call himself a manager and the other two will be organizers. The labor movement, or as several bumper stickers profess, "The people who brought you the weekend," has left its mark on many companies.

(source: syracuse.com/news/index.ssf/2010/03/unions_protest_at_site_of_live.html)

Whether for good, bad, or indifferent, unions and organized parties are a necessary and apparent part of the workforce in the U.S. and abroad.

Investigators who specialize in strike forces tend to work from the security standpoint, a necessary and helpful function when a company is preparing to lay off entire divisions, because of financial cutbacks. When combining intelligence with security, it is beneficial to gain perspective on how the union operates, how the employees will be affected, and if the employees are planning any legal, physical, or verbal retaliation.

A 2004 Associated Press story told of a protest, organized by the Communication Workers of America, at the home of their company's CEO. The story originally contained the CEO's true home address, and was wired to more than 1,000 Associated Press affiliates globally until AP discovered the oops and redacted the address.

Unions have their own Web sites filled with news, updates, and rally information. These are working-class individuals, and not gang members, who normally use bargaining strategies and legal means to achieve their goals, and only strike as a last resort. However, some of these organized parties are well known for bullying contractors who have brought non-union help or scabs onto a job site. They also may try to coerce non-union shops into organizing. Anytime an investigator finds himself at a corporate location with management and unions involved, he should assume there will be two sides: an *us* and a *them*.

A source location for investigating union activity is blogs. Not your typical social media profile, but actual blogs that are linked to the union's Web site, like aflcio.org/blog. The quickest way to finding organizational blogs is to locate the parent organization's Web site. Most of the major unions also have Twitter handles, Facebook accounts and you will see their organizers and members on LinkedIn. In fact, Unions.org has a Facebook page (facebook.com/UnionVoice) which claims to connect sixteen thousand union members.

Recommended Online Database Services

Key factors to learning more about a company is to determine out who are the administration peopel, what types of financials can be obtained, how many locations there are, and what type of industry is involved.

There are numerous online services to research both large and small corporations. The larger the company, the easier it is to find and gather information on them. The tasking issues are discerning the volumes of data to decide what is valuable and current versus what is not. Researching the target company by using online database vendors is a must.

The remainder of this chapter is devoted to recommended services to turn to first when researching companies.

Dun & Bradstreet - D&B

Dun & Bradstreet (D&B) is the largest provider of business reports internationally, with more than 100 million companies in its database. Very small, one-man companies and very large, mega corporations are in its international collection. For investigators who conduct a lot of due diligence or find themselves looking into companies often, D&B is worth the starting subscription price of several thousand dollars. If the budget is not justified for the D&B price tag, consider Hoover's.com, D&B's subsidiary company with 80 million current companies outlined.

Though D&B can be expensive, there is a search option that can be done for free on their Web site, Dnb.com. Looking at the above screen shot, you will see their Company Search box. This search box extends to international searches. Therefore, look to see if your company is even listed.

AUTHOR TIP **Name Searching on D&B**
Search by the person's last name or full name, instead of the company name. This is especially handy for small companies. D&B will find the owner's name and cite it as "Also Trades As:" For example, I searched on "Cynthia Hetherington" in New Jersey and came up with:
HETHERINGTON INFORMATION SERVICES LLC
Also Trades As: CYNTHIA HETHERINGTON
1501 HAMBURG TPKE STE 302 WAYNE NJ

Key things to know about searching D&B reports include:

- For information that contributes to your report, use D&B reports as a lead, not the answer.
- The best part of the reports is not the financial information.
- The best parts of a report for investigators are:
  o Name of company and owner
  o Phone and fax
  o History of company and principals
  o Public filings.
- And the really best part of D&B is being able to search inside its database.

Below is my list of significant reasons that illustrate the need to use D&B:

- Fraudulent companies often share fax numbers, even though they generate new phone numbers for business. Always search the fax number.
- Searching by the principal's name will often show former company interests or current company interests.

- Dun & Bradstreet automatically does Soundex searching. The name Bill will generate William hits.

- Address searches will show other companies listed at the same address, including mail drops and suspicious addresses.

If you cannot afford D&B directly, or are not interested in subscribing to Hoover's, you can access their reports through one of D&B's resellers, such as Dialog, SkyMinder, LexisNexis and Bureau van Dijk. If you are a licensed investigator with LexisNexis Accurint or IRBSearch both resell D&B reports. However, keep in mind that direct service subscribers receive much better pricing.

Kompass.com

Kompass, which originated in Switzerland, is now present in 70 countries and includes over 4.5 million companies registered within its databases and product lines. Kompass offers a very reasonably priced collection of information on more than two million companies globally. With a subscription, you can locate the executives of companies; obtain addresses, corporate structures, names of key figures, company turnover information, company descriptions, product names and services, trade and brand names, and location of branches. Kompass offers free searches for the following topics:

- Region – Geographically locate all companies

- Products/Services – Type of product (i.e. clocks, telephones, hamburgers)

- Companies – Name of company

- Trade names – Name of product

- Executives – Search by person at the top

- Codes – NAICS, SIC and other government-related codes.

I searched the name Richard Branson in United Kingdom and discovered multiple choices to explore including Virgin Atlantic, Virgin Mobile Telecom Ltd and Virgin Media Inc.

Selecting Virgin Atlantic, the free results (see below) include the start date of the company, Web site address, physical address, number of employees and other basic information which will get my investigation started.

This is a considerable amount of information when you are starting from nothing. The address and phone numbers are leads that can be explored at google.com or other databases, such as D&B. Having a ballpark number of employees also is helpful.

ACTIVITY

Airline

GENERAL INFORMATION

Year Established:	1981
www :	http://www.virgin-atlantic.com
Registration no :	01600117
Type of company :	Headquarters

BRAND/TRADENAMES

IMPORT/EXPORT REGIONS

Import regions :

Export regions :

Asia-Pacific
Central Asia
Middle East
Africa
Central/East Europe
Western Europe
North America
Central America
South America

The current free version of Kompass provides enough information to rival expensive business reporting services. And in the past, when you had to buy credits to obtain any report, the cost would be as little as $3.00 per report.

SkyMinder.com

SkyMinder, located in Tampa, Florida and formerly an affiliate of CRIBIS S.p.A., is based in Bologna, Italy. SkyMinder is an incredible aggregator of other corporate business and credit reports. Consider the following:

- Used by more than 330 Italian banking and financial institutions and more than 14,000 Italian, European and U.S. companies.

- Supplies online credit and business information on more than 50 million companies in 230 countries.

- Only works with Internet Explorer version 5.0 and newer.

- One of the best places to buy inexpensive D&B header reports.

- Available data (per their Web page) includes: "...marketing data, line of business, incorporation details, shareholders/owners, executives, employees, office and facilities, business structure (headquarters, parent, branches, subsidiaries), rating, credit limit, payment information, financials, banking relationships and accountants, litigations, etc."

A complete source list for Skyminder is located on its Web site at skyminder.com/basic/ info_sources.asp. The source list indicates how often the data is updated for each of the 46 sources.

Sample Skyminder Search

A search for the popular Saudi family name Bugshan in the company section automatically seeks credit reports. The return offers 32 matches under Credit Info and ten matches under Company Info.

Bugshan Sweets & Tahina is not named in either corporate or credit results lists. However, the Abdullah Said Bugshan & Bros. listing at the top of the Company Info results page states that it is the headquarters. This could be the parent of Bugshan Sweets.

Below is sample of a free description provided for this company.

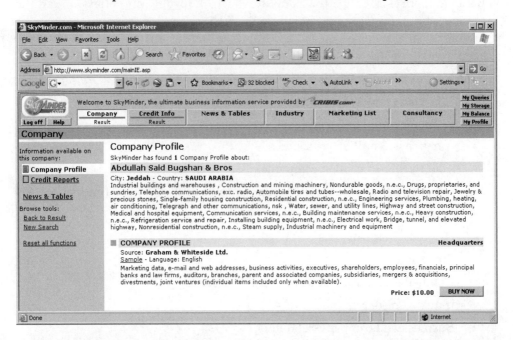

This listing may be the parent of the Sweets branch, considering it is naming just about every type of manufactured product from construction materials to sundries. The key here is to see what sort of reports skyminder.com is selling. In this case, Graham & Whiteside Ltd. has a document for sale that includes contact information, employee size, principals, banking and finance, and associated companies. For $10.00, that's a bargain.

The Graham & Whiteside report (if purchased) is phenomenal. The investigator can see industry specifics, banking information, the majority ownership (Saudi Wiemer & Trachte Ltd.), and a great amount of detail, which would cost hundreds of dollars from Dun & Bradstreet.

SkyMinder also resells credit reports, which are similar to business reports, but with more financial offerings, such as payment history, credit ratings and profit, loss and reported financials. These reports tend to be ordered on-the-fly, and a certain amount of time is taken to generate the documents. In other words, once the report is ordered, a local researcher actually conducts the investigation in that country and delivers the results within a week or more.

As an example of prices, credit reports for Abdullah Said Bugshan & Bros. are available from D&B at a price slightly over $200, at Asian CIS the fee is about $140. At RIME Information Bureau, CreditInfo Middle East Ltd., and ICP the fee ranges from $130 to more than $200, depending on how quickly you want the information.

Bureau van Dijk (BvDEP)

Because there is so much that Bureau van Dijk (bvdep.com) offers, it is difficult to catalog the many databases offered. With a unique name for each service, international databases, such as Mint and Osiris, are teamed up with country-specific services like Ruslana (Russia), Sabi (Spain) and Jade (Japan).

Mint is a global database that has information on more than 120 million companies.

Below are specs on the coverage of ORBIS:

- Europe 70 million companies
- Americas 40 million companies
- Asia Pacific 15 million companies
- Information on over 6.5 million patents linked to 585,000 companies.
- Directors and contacts
- Original filings/images
- Stock data
- Detailed corporate and ownership structures
- Industry research
- Business and company-related news
- M&A deals and rumors

The information is sourced from more than 40 different information providers, all experts in their regions or disciplines. With descriptive information and company financials, ORBIS contains extensive detail on items such as news, market research, ratings and country reports, scanned reports, ownership and mergers and acquisitions data.

ORBIS provides several different company reports to choose from. You can view a summary report, a report that automatically compares a company to its peers or view more detailed reports that are taken from BvDEP's specialist products. For listed companies, banks and insurance companies, plus major, private companies, more detailed information is available.

Searching ORBIS can be done in basic or advanced modes. The advanced mode, as seen in this screen shot below, offers searches by company names, locations, board member and executive names, specific financials, mergers and acquisitions deals, etc.

Once a name is searched, a page with the number of results is offered. You can pay to look at all the results or choose a free preview to see if you are close to the results you wanted.

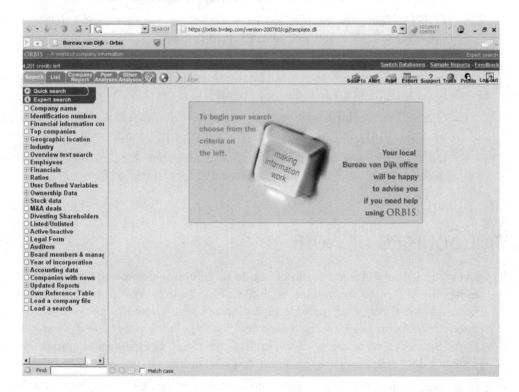

(source: bvdinfo.com/en-us/products/company-information/international/mint-global)

A search for Bugshan in this service returned only one match in Germany. But reviewing the offerings, there are 65,000 companies listed in East and Central Asia. The Bugshan corporate name is well known, so the result of one match is surprising. With this service, as with any service, once you have questionable or no results call customer service and ask the representative to check your findings. Customer-service representatives should be experts in their own database products and it is to the investigator's advantage to tap into that intellect. Bureau van Dijk has thousands of subscribers and its representatives will assist in the research. In this case, the researcher verifies that there are no Bugshan reports of value in ORBIS, and either recommends searching in another Bureau database, or offers to create a report that can take several days to generate and deliver.

The other Bureau databases can be examined by viewing their brochures online at bvdinfo.com/en-us/our-products. Other unique database services of Bureau van Dijk include:

- ZEPHYR – A worldwide database of detailed information on rumored, announced or completed financial deals; it includes approximately 80,000 new deals a year.

- CAMEO / TRACE – Search for and verify any individual's name and address, anywhere in the United Kingdom, using the Electoral Roll.

- FAME – Company accounts, ratios, activities, ownership and management of the largest 2.4 million British and Irish companies, and summary information for an additional 950,000 smaller businesses.

- JADE – Company accounts, financial ratios, activities and management of more than 380,000 Japanese companies.

- ODIN – Standardized annual accounts, financial ratios, activities and ownership information for 700,000 companies in Scandinavia.

- QIN – Company accounts and financial ratios for 300,000 companies in mainland China in both standardized and local detailed formats.

Other Sources of Note

Everything you will need does not reside in an online database. Corporate research, especially of foreign companies, will often require expertise from that country. Hire licensed (when required) private investigators who know the laws, limitations, and public records for their country. Be very clear about what need and what you do not want. Sad but true in many cases, investigators will break laws to gain information. This not only reflects poorly on them, but also on the company who hired them.

If a large company hires the rogue investigator, the company can be held responsible for these offenses. In this country, a firm can be cited for breaking certain federal and state laws, such as the Fair Credit Reporting Act (ftc.gov/os/statutes/031224fcra.pdf) or the Economic Espionage Act (fbi.gov/about-us/investigate/counterintelligence/economic-espionage), or other laws or statutes.

Places to find assistance in these matters are libraries, associations, personal Web sites, and embassies.

Domestic and Foreign Libraries

When searching for local information on a company, the local librarian probably will be able to offer at least some directory information and even as much as a personal clipping file on the firm itself. To find these librarians, simply search google.com and type the words public library +<town name state> (i.e. public library Springfield Illinois).

When searching for foreign companies, not only will the librarian overseas offer all the regional information she can find, but also she will search using her own language and in her own databases. I recommend you contact an American university within that country to find the most cooperative librarian available.

Associations

Check association Web sites that are akin to the company being researched. The association may have some historical pages, or share insight into its members. *The Encyclopedia of Associations* (Thomson Gale) is offered through Proquest.com and LexisNexis. It is also a very common resource found in the reference collection of most public libraries.

A list of U.S. national trade associations with connections to public records or using public records is found in Chapter 12.

Personal Histories

Look for personal histories, biographies, tear sheets and resumes of the lead professionals at the particular company being investigated. A personal history may reveal an interesting perspective as to why a particular company started. An example is the following statement from Anita Roddick, founder of the Body Shop.

> "It wasn't only economic necessity [a woman's struggle to earn a living for herself and two young daughters] that inspired the birth of The Body Shop. My early travels had given me a wealth of experience. I had spent time in farming and fishing communities with pre-industrial peoples, and been exposed to body rituals of women from all over the world. Also the frugality that my mother exercised during the war years made me question retail conventions. Why waste a container when you can refill it? And why buy more of something than you can use? We behaved as she did in the Second World War, we reused everything, we refilled everything and we recycled all we could. The foundation of The Body Shop's environmental activism was born out of ideas like these."

Before fully understanding Ms. Roddick's personal history, one might think of this multi-national company as just another product manufacturer, and not for its unique approach to green business and female empowerment that this corporation embraces.

Foreign Press and Foreign Embassies

When researching a foreign company, do not neglect contacting a business-affairs correspondent in the country of the company being investigated. Be prepared to have a lot of patience waiting for the information to be delivered. A list of U.S. embassy locations abroad is found at usembassy.gov.

Also do not hesitate to contact a librarian overseas and request that he or she conduct a brief search through a local regional news index for your company. Patience and a great deal of appreciation should be given to these individuals who agree to assist. In the meantime check two very large, general news databases that cover an extensive amount of foreign press check at factiva.com and lexis.com. In addition, dialog.com is another resource offering specialized media database material.

Social Media and Business Due Diligence

Companies are run by people. In an investigation on companies, when possible, research the involved company individuals' personal social media profiles for useful information (see Chapter 4 of this book). For your investigation, also research specific businesses on such company social media Web sites as Indeed (indeed.com), Vault (vault.com), and GlassDoor (glassdoor.com) for information. From these sites, you might find the rants and raves of disgruntled former (and not so former) employees, complaining about management, wages, and hours.

The following is a rant review of the interview process for a well-known U.S.-based company.

> "It was unorganized and the recruiter was very unprofessional and lax in communication. She didn't call for the first interview at the time she was scheduled to. She called a few hours later and acted like it was nothing and did not even apologize or explain why she did not call and was not available for our scheduled call. By the time she got her stuff together, I had already got 2 other offers and accepted one of them. I really wanted to work here, but after the bad experience with the recruiter it left a bad impression. Also, she would never get back to me for weeks. This was the worst interview experience I've ever had."

One such impression shouldn't guide your entire investigation; however, the revelation does leave room for speculation as to what other cylinders the company is misfiring. If you see a great deal of this type of complaining on business social media Web sites, then that might be an indicator of poor corporate culture.

Chatrooms and message forums for all manner of industries can offer up more places to find online social content. Some industries have very busy online forums where employees like to vent anonymously – or somewhat anonymously. The pharmaceutical and medical sales industry has its Cafepharma (cafepharma.com); pilots of regional, fractional, and other jet carrier services have their Airline Pilot Central Forums (airlinepilotforums.com); the cellular phone sales industry has its Howard Forums (howardforums.com).

It is possible that most any industry has a chat forum. If you don't see your industry listed above, go to your favorite search engine and search on your industry's name and the word forum. For example, searching on "construction and forum" will most likely bring up Contractor Talk (contractortalk.com) in your search results.

Business Information Everywhere and Not a Drop to Spare

Investigators need to be comfortable using free online resources such as social media reviews, fee-based reports from business services, and corporate reporting agencies. No one is ever an expert in all areas, but the investigator's task is to be expert at finding the information and determining the value it holds for his case. If you are working on a case that involves an industry that is not in your bailiwick, then locate a professional in that field for advice. Or perhaps you yourself start self-studying the field to gain some insight and understanding as to what it's all about so you know what you are looking at in your research. In the construction industry, for example, you may note a lag in communications during the summer, but a lot of postings in the winter. Common sense tells you that in the snowbelt states winter is the industry's slow season, which gives construction people more free time and thus more apt to be using online chat forums.

In this chapter, we have done a fairly close reading of the various online information resources to use, and touched briefly on the business industries themselves. Be aware, too, that information databases grow and change as well. Keep on top of what new information services are being offered for professional industries as well as social media sites that discuss the professional personnel reorganizing within corporate entities.

Trade associations, such as Certified Fraud Examiners (acfe.org) and ASIS International (asisonline.org), host annual conferences with continuing education opportunities including training in information and investigations products. Pay attention to the vendors who present at such conferences; their database products are often closely aligned with the subject matter of the conference. Two more associations to mention, which are strictly business research oriented, and work very closely with the vendor community for this market are; the Association of Independent Information Professionals (aiip.org) and the Special Libraries Association (slg.org). While not strictly investigations-oriented, both these associations can offer interesting professional resources – some of which you might never have heard of but could be surprisingly useful.

As mentioned, a list of national trade associations whose members deal with public records is provided in Chapter 12.

Ch 6:

Court Records, Regulatory Sanctions, and Enforcement Boards

You see, in this world there's two kinds of people, my friend: Those with loaded guns and those who dig. You dig.

—Clint Eastwood (from the movie *The Good, the Bad and the Ugly*)

Due Diligence Meets the Good, the Bad, and the Ugly

One purpose of a due diligence investigation is to locate any negative or problematic information relating to the target of the investigation. Or perhaps locating data to ultimately clear the target of any accusations or supposition that fraud or wrong doing has occurred. Essentially, investigators are asked to dig up the dirt, so to speak, and dirt sometimes surfaces in the form of legal filings, sanctions against the company or person, or regulatory notices. In most cases, we do not find the level of evil and harm that you often see in television crime shows. However, investigations may uncover nefarious activities that can be quite substantial, such as corruption, racketeering, fraud, breaking international treaties, or other similar legal problems.

This chapter examines the various investigative trails that develop because of involvement with, or violation of, government regulatory issues. These trails of investigation are grouped into six segments:

1. Local, State, and Federal Court Records
2. Licensing Boards and Disciplinary Actions
3. Financial Crimes
4. Publicly Traded Companies and Security Dealers Compliance Actions
5. Government Watch Lists
6. Sanctions, Terrorists, and Other Law Enforcement Sources

AUTHOR TIP

It Depends

Finding companies or people on regulatory watch lists does not necessarily mean they are suspected of crimes or should be avoided completely. Investigators must examine and understand the circumstances, especially when very large companies are involved. An act or violation could be the responsibility of but one section of a company. Also, at first look a violation may appear to be major, but upon further examination it may be merely a minor issue meriting a fine and wrist-slap from the courts.

Searching Court Records

Since court records are one of the most widely sought types of public record in the U.S., we will take a strong look at these records. Key areas of focus are criminal cases, civil actions, and sources of various disciplinary actions. Researching court records is complicated because of the extensive diversity of the courts and their record keeping systems. Courts exist at four levels: federal, state, county (or parish), and local municipalities, and all four levels can be found within the same county!

Each state's court system is created by statutes or constitution to enforce state civil and criminal laws. Sometimes the terms "state court" and "county court" can be a source of confusion because state trial courts are located at county courthouses. In general, the phrase "state courts" refers to the courts belonging to the state court systems; and the phrase "county courts" refers to those courts administrated by county authority.

Courts at the municipal or town level typically are not managed by the state's court administration. They are be managed by the local city, town or village government whose laws they enforce. Sometimes these courts are called justice courts.

Keep in mind in several state nuances on the names of the jurisdictions. In Louisiana the word Parish is equivalent to what is a county in another state.

Alaska is organized by Boroughs. In Colorado, Missouri, and Virginia, a city may have the same jurisdictional authority as a county.

The State Court Structure

An investigator needs to be familiar with basic court structures and procedures. The general structure of all state court systems has four tiers:

1. Appellate courts
2. Intermediate appellate courts
3. General jurisdiction trial courts
4. Limited jurisdiction trial courts

The two highest levels, **appellate** and **intermediate appellate** courts, only hear cases on appeal from the trial courts. Opinions of these appellate courts are of particular interest to attorneys seeking legal precedents for newer cases. However, opinions can be useful to record searchers because they summarize facts about the case that will not show on an index or docket.

General jurisdiction trial courts oversee a full range of civil and criminal litigation, usually handling felonies and higher dollar civil cases. The general jurisdiction courts often serve as the appellate courts for cases appealed from limited jurisdiction courts and even from the local courts. Many court researchers refer to general jurisdiction courts as upper courts.

Limited jurisdiction trial courts come in several varieties. Many limited jurisdiction courts handle smaller civil claims (such as $15,000 or less), misdemeanors, and pretrial hearings for felonies. Localized municipal or town courts are also referred to as courts of limited jurisdiction. Many court researchers refer to limited jurisdiction courts as lower courts.

Some states, Iowa for instance, have consolidated each county's general and limited courts into one court location holding all records. Other states, Maryland for example, have very distinct differences between upper and lower courts. In these states if an investigator is performing a county search, each court must be separately searched.

Some courts – sometimes called special jurisdiction courts – have general jurisdiction but are limited to one type of litigation. An example is the Court of Claims in New York which only processes liability cases against the state.

How Courts Maintain Records

Each case is assigned a number and case record information is indexed by this number. Courts also, usually, cross reference the case number index to the names of the parties involved. Therefore, to find specific case file documents, you to know to the applicable case number or else you must perform a name search to find the case number. Be aware that case numbering procedures are not necessarily consistent throughout a state's court system. One county may assign numbers by location or district while another may use a number system based on the judge assigned to the case.

The Docket Sheet – A Key Information Resource

Information from cover sheets and from documents filed as a case goes forward is recorded on the docket sheet. The docket sheet, sometimes called a register of actions, is a running summary of a case history. Each action, such as motions, briefs, exhibits, etc., is recorded in chronological order. While docket sheets differ somewhat in format from court to court, the basic information contained on a docket sheet is consistent. Docket sheets will contain:

- Name of court, including location (division) and the judge assigned
- Case number and case name
- Names of all plaintiffs and defendants/debtors
- Names and addresses of attorneys for the plaintiff or debtor
- Nature and cause (e.g., statute) of action
- Date and summary of all materials and motions filed in a case
- Case outcome (disposition)
- Most courts enter the docket data into a computer system. Within a state or judicial district, the courts may be linked together via a single computer system.

AUTHOR TIP **What is Really Found Online**
The primary search of court records is a search of the docket index. When someone tells you "I can view xxx county court records online," this person is most likely talking about viewing an index summary of records and not about viewing the actual case file document pages.

Docket information from cases closed before the advent of computerization may not be in the computer system. And some court and counties still are non-computerized. So a case record index can be electronic, but also can exist on-site on card files, in books, on microfiche, etc. Also, a record index can be organized in a variety of ways, for example by name, by year, by case or file number, or by name and year. Depending on the court and on how many years back a search is needed, multiple indices may need to be searched.

The Case Disposition

The term "disposition" refers to the final outcome of a case, such as if a party is determined to be guilty in a criminal matter. Or if a judgment is awarded ina civil matter

In certain situations, a judge can order the case file sealed or removed – expunged – from the public repository. Examples include if a defendant enters a diversion program (drug or family counseling), or a defendant makes restitution as part of a plea bargain; these cases may not be searchable. The only way to gain direct access to these types of case filings is through a subpoena. However, savvy researchers and investigators will sometimes search news media sources if need be.

Searching Hint: Watch for Divisions and Name Variations

The structure of the court system and the names used for courts often vary widely from state-to-state. Civil and criminal records may be handled by different divisions within a court or sometimes by completely different courts with different names. For example, in Tennessee the Chancery Court oversees civil cases but criminal cases are tried in Circuit Courts, except in districts with separate Criminal Courts as established by the state legislature. In Iowa the District Court is the highest trial court whereas in Michigan the District Court is a limited jurisdiction court.

About Municipal, Town, and Village Courts

Localized courts preside over city or town misdemeanors, infractions, and ordinance violations at the city, town or township level. Sometimes these courts may be known as justice courts. Notable is the state of New York where nearly 1,100+ Town and Village Justice Courts handle misdemeanors, local ordinance violations, and traffic violations including DWIs.

In most states there is a distinction between state-supported courts and the local courts in terms of management, funding, and sharing of web pages.

The Types of Court Cases Found Online

Below is a list of possible court cases and records found at the state or local level. Note that bankruptcies are not found on this list because bankruptcy cases are filed at the federal level.

Civil Actions – Actions for money damages usually greater than $5,000. Also, some states have designated dollar amount thresholds for upper or lower (limited) civil courts. Most civil litigation involves torts or contract.

Small Claims – Actions for minor money damages, generally under $5,000, no juries involved.

Criminal Felonies – Generally defined as crimes punishable by one year or more of jail time. There can be multiple levels or classes.

Criminal Misdemeanors – Generally defined as minor infractions with a fine and less than one year of jail time. Misdemeanors also have multiple levels or classes.

Probate – Estate matters, settling the estate of a deceased person, resolving claims and distributing the decedent's property.

Eviction Actions – Landlord/tenant actions, can also known as an unlawful detainer, forcible detainer, summary possession, or repossession.

Domestic Relations – Also known as Family Law, with authority over family disputes, divorces, dissolutions, child support or custody cases.

Juvenile – Authority over cases involving individuals under a specified age, usually 18 years but sometimes 21.

Traffic – May also have authority over municipal ordinances.

Specialty Courts – These courts address one area or have specifically defined powers, such as matters involving water, equity in fiduciary questions, tort, contracts, tax, etc.

Facts on Searching Criminal Records

The information that could be disclosed on a criminal record or docket index includes the arrest record, criminal charges, fines, sentencing, and incarceration information.

The first step in criminal record searching is determining where to search. A county courthouse search is the most accurate and least complicated search, but not always the most practical. There are over 6,000 courts in the U.S. that hold felony or significant (non-traffic related) misdemeanor records. For those of you who think everything is online, know that 32 percent of these courts do not provide online access to a searchable record index; and far less offer online access to actual case files.[15]

Once You Find the Case

Once a criminal (or civil) matter is located it is important to understand and report clearly what the citation, docket sheet or case file states. As mentioned, the docket sheet will give you dates, parties and some idea as to the conclusion or disposition. However, it may be necessary to send a public record retriever on site to the court to make and send you photocopies of file documents. These large files can take hours or longer to review, but are worth the time.

The details within the case files (especially civil business matters) will indicate many interesting details, such as associates that you have been trying to match up, perhaps brought in to testify as a witness. The appended case files also can help you locate assets.

Use of Identifiers and Redaction

Identifiers – such as the date of birth, a middle initial, address, and even part of Social Security number – are important to an investigator's record searching. A subject's identifiers must be matched to a case record to verify if a case record

---

[15] From *The Sourcebook to Public Records Information* by BRB Publications, Inc.

belongs to the subject. If the docket contains all or part of the OB or part of a SSN a positive match is likely. However, if the subject has a common name and no identifiers are shown on the docket index, then further research is required.

Thus, the display of identifiers is an important safeguard for both the requesting party and the subject of the search. A misidentification can cause harm which can be decreased substantially if other identifiers can be used to match the individual to the record.

The federal, state, and local agencies maintaining court record systems make substantial efforts to protect the public from identity theft and limit the disclosure of certain personal information such as Social Security numbers, phone numbers, and addresses. As a result, many agencies redact or hide certain identifiers within the case documents or the record index. Often though, the redaction will not apply to the entire DOBs. Many government jurisdictions realize at least part of the DOB is necessary to determine the proper identity of someone who has a common name. Plenty of news stories exist about people denied jobs because a background check reported erroneous information pertaining to someone else with the same name. The balance of privacy interests versus public jeopardy goes well beyond the purposes of this book. However, the key point here is to know that the redaction process can significantly alter court record searching procedures.

Online Access to Statewide Judicial Systems

The states' judicial Web sites are good places to find decisions and opinions from the states' supreme courts and appellate courts. These web pages also provide plenty of good information about the states' court structure and the locations of the courts.

Many states also offer a statewide online access system to the county level court records. Some of these systems are commercial fee-based, some are free. The value of these systems depends (1) which particular courts are included in their online system, (2) what types of cases are included or not included, and (3) what personal identifiers are presented.

The article below provides an overview of these systems and a series of record searching tips to keep in mind when utilizing these online systems.

Court Records on Statewide Judicial Systems

By Michael Sankey

Every state has a judicial branch that oversees that state's trial and appellate court system. The name of the agency will vary, but it is often known as the Administration Office of the Courts (AOC) or the Office of Court Administration (OCA).

The online court records obtainable from this venue are widespread, often free, and overall very worthwhile. Knowing about these agencies and their online services is important because thru the AOC there are more counties and courts online when compared to the individual county-based systems. Consider these overall statistics about state judicial systems and the state courts at the county level:

- 28 States Offer Online Access to Both Civil and Criminal Records
- 3 State Offer Access to Only Online Civil Records
- 2 State Offer Access to Only Online Criminal Records
- 18 State Have Online Access to Neither

These Systems are Not Created Equal: Learn the State-by-State Variations

Online researchers must be aware that there are many nuances to these searches. The value of a statewide court search will vary considerably by state. Consider these evaluation points:

- Is the site free or a pay site? While some of the free search sites are good, the old adage *you pay for what you get* will certainly apply here.
- Is the search a statewide search vs. a single county search? And are all counties/courts on the system?
- Is the throughput date posted and is there uniformity? For example, one county may have cases dating back for seven years, while another county may have only two years of history.
- Are Identifiers shown? The lack of identifiers to properly identify a subject varies widely from state-to-state. A lack of identifiers is especially apparent on the free access search systems.
- And perhaps the most important evaluation point: Is an online search equivalent to searching onsite?

The level of your due diligence and need for accuracy will determine if the online site you are using is truly a primary site, or if it is a supplemental search site. Of course this is true for ANY online site for ANY type of public record.

Searching Federal Court Records

Federal court records involve federal constitutional law or interstate commerce. The task of locating the right court is seemingly simplified by the nature of the federal system.

- All civil and criminal cases are heard by the U.S. District Courts.
- All bankruptcy cases are heard by the U.S. Bankruptcy Courts.

- The location of the court assigned a case is often dependent upon the plaintiff's county of domicile.

Searching records at the federal court system can be one of the easiest or one of the most frustrating experiences that record searchers may encounter. Although the federal court system offers advanced electronic search capabilities, at times it is practically impossible to properly identify a subject. This is because few, if any, identifiers are displayed within the case files and record dockets.

Cases and Court Locations

At one time, all cases were assigned to a specific district or division based on the county of origination. Although this is still true in most states, computerized tracking of dockets has led to a more flexible approach to case assignment. For example, rather than blindly assigning all cases originating from one county to designated court location, districts in Michigan, Minnesota and Connecticut use random numbers and other methods to logically balance caseloads among their judges, regardless of the location. This trend seemingly confuses the case search process. But finding cases has become significantly easier with the availability of Case Management/ Electronic Case Files (CM/ECF) and the PACER Case Locator (see descriptions to follow). Most case files created prior to 1999 were maintained in paper format only. Since 2006, all cases are now filed electronically through CM/ECF.

Case information and images of documents are available the individual federal courts for a timeframe determined by that court and then are forwarded to a designated Federal Records Center (FRC), found at archives.gov/frc. Older case files may be ordered from the court which in turn obtains the needed documents directly from the FRC.

Electronic Access to Federal Court Records

The two important acronyms associated with federal court case information are CM/ECF and PACER.

Case Management/Electronic Case Files (CM/ECF)

CM/ECF is the case management system for the Federal Judiciary used by all bankruptcy, district, and appellate courts. The CM/ECF system allows attorneys to file and manage cases documents electronically and offers expanded search and reporting capabilities.

A significant fact affecting record researchers is the CM/ECF Rules of Procedure that require filers redact certain personal identifying information. This means filings cannot include Social Security or taxpayer-identification numbers, full dates of birth, names of minor children, financial account numbers, and in criminal cases, home addresses, from their filings.

For further information on CM/ECF, visit pacer.gov/cmecf/index.html.

PACER and the PACER Case Locator

PACER. an acronym for **P**ublic **A**ccess to **E**lectronic **C**ourt **R**ecords, is the electronic service that allows the public to obtain case and docket information from the U.S. District, Bankruptcy, and Appellate courts. The site is pacer.gov.

To search for records, you must know the individual court where the case was filed or held. Therefore, a researcher will likely need to use the PACER Case Locator – a national index for U.S. District, Bankruptcy, and Appellate courts. Using the Case Locator, a researcher can determine whether or not a party is involved in federal litigation and, if so, the court location.

The information gathered from the PACER system is a matter of public record and may be reproduced without permission. Essentially each court maintains its own database of case information and decides what to make available on PACER. PACER normally provides the following information:

- A listing of all parties and participants including judges, attorneys, trustees
- A compilation of case related information such as cause of action, nature of suit, dollar demand
- A chronology of dates of case events entered in the case record
- A claims registry
- A listing of new cases each day in the bankruptcy courts
- Appellate court opinions
- Judgments or case status
- Types of case documents filed for certain districts.

PACER Fees

There are fees to use PACER. Electronic access to any case document, docket sheet, or case specific report is $0.10 per page, not to exceed the fee for thirty pages. The fee to access an audio file of a court hearing via PACER: $2.40 per audio file. If an account holder does not accrue charges of more than $15.00 in a quarterly billing cycle there is no fee charged.

Bankruptcy Records and the Voice Case Information System (McVCIS)

McVCIS (Multi-Court Voice Case Information System) is a means of accessing information regarding open bankruptcy cases. Information is available 24/7 by using a touch-tone telephone. An automated voice response system will read a limited amount of bankruptcy case information directly from the court's database in response to Touch-Tone telephone inquiries. The advantage? There is no charge. Individual names are entered last name first with as much of the first name as you wish to include. For example, Joe B. Cool could be entered as COOLJ or COOLJOE. Do not enter the middle initial. Business names are entered as they are written, without blanks.

Note at one time each Bankruptcy Court had its own telephone number (VCIS). But now all Bankruptcy Courts provide access through one centralized phone number at 866-222-8019 and the service is now referred to as McVCIS, which stands for Multi-Court Voice Case Information System.

Federal Court Record Searching Hints

The best way to search federal court records is to make use of CM/ECF, PACER, and McVCIS. If you have trouble finding the location of a current case (there can be multiple Divisions within a District), then also check the web page of the court for the assigned counties for each Division. A Federal Court Locator is at uscourts.gov/court_locator.aspx.

As mentioned, one of the biggest problems when searching federal court records is the lack of identifiers. As mentioned, very few identifiers are entered in the CM/ECF system. A handful of courts will include the last four digits of the SSN, or they may provide the birth month and year of birth, but not the day. Federal courts have a well deserved reputation of no longer providing the means to accurately identify a subject of a search.

What to Do When Record Search Results Do Not Include Identifiers

This is a struggle and a tough problem to solve, especially if a researcher is dealing with a common name. Below are several ideas to help verify a subject's identity.

- **View Case Files** - Review the documents found in the case files for any hints of identification.

- **Call an Attorney Involved in the Case** - The docket will list the attorney (or prosecuting attorney) involved in a case. Sometime the people will help you determine the identity of a subject.

- **Check Incarceration Records** - Searching prison records is an alternative means for identity verification. Search the Bureau of Prisons at bop.gov.

- **Check the News Media** - Some record searchers have been successful in confirming an identity by using news media sources such as newspapers and the Web. Even blogs may help.

State Criminal Record Repositories

Criminal court records are eventually submitted to a central repository controlled by a state agency such as the State Police or Department of Public Safety. This location is often designated as the state's official repository.

There is a huge difference regarding record access procedures between the state repositories and the courts. Records maintained by the court are generally open to the public, but a number of state criminal record repositories do not open their criminal records to the public. Of those states that will release records to the public, many require the submission of fingerprints and/or signed release forms.

For example, per the *Public Record Research System* from BRB Publications, only 27 states release criminal records (name search) to the general public without consent of the subject, 17 states require a signed release from the subject, and 6 states require submission of fingerprints.

Check out CriminalRecord Sources.com to locate free database availability.

The article below provides in interesting overview of the reliability of the record centers.

Facts about Accuracy and Completeness at State Criminal Record Repositories
By Michael Sankey

Employers and state occupation licensing agencies depend on state criminal record repositories as a primary resource when performing criminal record background checks. However these entities may not realize that a search of these databases may not be as accurate and complete as assumed, regardless if fingerprints are submitted.

There are three key reasons why the completeness, consistency, and accuracy of state criminal record repositories could be suspect:

1. Timeliness of Receiving Arrest and Disposition Data

2. Timeliness of Entering Arrest and Disposition Data into the Repository

3. Inability to Match Dispositions with Existing Arrest Records

The basis for these concerns is actually supported by facts provided by the U.S. Department of Justice (DOJ). Every two years the DOJ's Bureau of Justice Statistics releases an extensive Survey of State Criminal Record Repositories. The most recent Survey, released January 2014 (based on statistics complied as of Dec 31, 2012), is a 118-page document with 39 data tables. See https://www.ncjrs.gov/pdffiles1/bjs/grants/244563.pdf.

Below are some eye-catching facts taken directly from this Survey:

*   13 states report 20% or more of all dispositions received could NOT be linked to the arrest/charge information in the state criminal record database. 14 states don't know how many dispositions they have that cannot be linked.

*   17 states have over 1.8 million unprocessed or partially processed court dispositions, ranging from 200 in Wyoming to 633,100 in Utah.

*   17 state reports there is at least a 60 day backlog between the time a felony case is decided and when the record is entered in the criminal history database. 12 states do not know how long the delay is.

See criminalrecordsources.com/documents/CrimReposit.pdf for a two page article with additional details regarding this Survey.

Incarceration Records

The records of inmates held (or formerly held) in state prisons and federal prisons, and in local jails can be a valuable investigative resource. Local level jail records are often a mix of persons with misdemeanor and traffic sentences. Online accessibility varies widely by jurisdiction.

Federal Prison System

The Federal Bureau of Prisons web page offers a searchable Inmate Locator and a Facility Locator at bop.gov. The Inmate Locator contains records on inmates incarcerated or released from 1982 to present.

State Prison Systems

Each state has a government agency that manages the corrections departments and prisons. These state agencies consider the inmate records to be public and will process information requests. Most states offer an inmate locator Web page. The level of information available varies widely from state to state. Some states provide historical records and information on parolees. Be sure to check these facts if using a search of these resources in an investigative reports.

A list of all free online searchable state sites appears in Chapter 12.

Vendor Resources

The web pages of several private companies are great resources to information and find links and searchable inmate locators to state prison systems.

An excellent website devoted to information about prisons and corrections facilities "...with the most comprehensive database of vendor intelligence in corrections..." is the Corrections Connection (corrections.com).

VINELink.com, by Appriss Inc., is the online resource of VINE (Victim Information and Notification Everyday), the National Victim Notification Network. The primary objective of this site is to help crime victims obtain timely and reliable information about criminal cases and the custody status of offenders. From the map page a user can search for offenders in practically every state in the U.S. by name or identification number.

Several private companies are great resources to find links and searchable inmate locators to state prison systems. Check theinmatelocator.com and inmatesplus.com.

Also most of the free public record links lists sites (such brbpublications.com and http://publicrecords.searchsystems.net) offer a wealth of searching links.

Sexual Offender Registries

Sexual offenses include aggravated sexual assault, sexual assault, aggravated criminal sexual contact, endangering the welfare of a child by engaging in sexual conduct, kidnapping, and false imprisonment. Under Megan's Law (the Sexual Offender Act of 1994, ojp.gov/smart/legislation.htm), sex offenders are classified in one of three levels or tiers based on the severity of their crime as follows: Tier 3 (high); Tier 2 (moderate); and Tier 1 (low).

Sex offenders must notify authorities of their whereabouts or when moving into a community.

The state agency that oversees the criminal record repository, often the same agency that administrates the Sexual Offender Registry (SOR), offers a free search of registered sexual offenders who are living within the particular state. These free search state web pages are shown in Chapter 12.

The creation of the National Sexual Offender Registry (nsopr.gov) is the result of coordinated effort by the Department of Justice and the state agencies hosting public sexual offender registries. The website has a national query to obtain information about sex offenders through a number of search options including name, Zip Code, county, and city or town. The site also has an excellent, detailed overview of each state's SOR policies and procedures.

State Sex-Offender Registers searches can also be performed using vendors such as IRBsearch, CLEAR, TLO, TracersInfo and LexisNexis to name a few.

Outside of the United States, you will have to check on the laws of that country to see if criminal histories are available, and if they require a signed release.

So-Called National Criminal Record Databases

There is no such thing as a national criminal record database. Yes the FBI has a national database. But it is not searchable by the public, it is incomplete (does not have all records), and it is inaccurate (does not contain final dispositions for all court records).

However, a number of vendors have aggregated criminal record and criminal record-related data from courts, state agencies, etc. into proprietary databases and offer search services to investigators and to the general public. Some of these vendors are easy to spot on the Web. While these databases are quite useful, they are certainly not complete.

The following copyrighted text appears in *The Safe Hiring Manual*, written by Lester S. Rosen and published by Facts on Demand Press. Mr. Rosen's material provides an excellent overview, primarily from the viewpoint of an employer, about this topic. His analysis is very pertinent for anyone using these tools and we sincerely thank him for allowing us display his text in this book.

The Good and Bad When Using Vendor Databases of Criminal Records
By Lester S. Rosen

A tool widely touted to employers is a "national database search" of criminal records. A number of vendors advertise they have, or have access to, a national database of criminal record information. These services typically talk about having millions of records from all states. Unfortunately, this form of advertising can create an impression in an employer's mind that they are getting the real thing — access to the nation's criminal records. Nothing could be further from the truth.

These databases are compiled from a number of various state repositories, sexual offender registries, correctional, and county sources. There are a number of reasons why this database information may not be accurate or complete. It is critical to understand that these multi-state database searches represent a research tool only, and under no circumstances are they a substitute for a hands-on search at the county level.

Users of these databases must proceed with caution. Just because a person's name appears in one of these databases it does not mean the subject is a criminal. On the other hand, if a person's name does not appear, this likewise should not be taken as conclusive that the person is not a criminal. In other words, these databases can result in "false negatives" or "false positives"; and an over-reliance can cause one to develop a false sense of security.

Database Value and Limitation Issues

These database searches are of value because they cover a much larger geographical area than traditional county-level searches. By casting a much wider net, a researcher may pick up information that might be missed. The firms that sell database information can show test names of subjects that were 'cleared' by a traditional county search, but criminal records were found in other counties through their searchable databases. In fact, it could be argued that failure to utilize such a database demonstrates a failure to exercise due diligence given the widespread coverage and low price.

But overall, the best use of these databases is as a secondary or supplemental research tool, or 'lead generator' which tells a researcher where else to look.

The compiled data typically comes from a mix of state repositories, correctional institutions, courts, and any number of other county agencies that are willing to make their data public, or to sell data to private database brokers that accumulate large 'data dumps' of information.

The limitations of searching a private database are the inherent issues about completeness, name variations, timeliness, and legal compliance.

Completeness and Accuracy Issues

The various databases that vendors collect may not be the equivalent of a true all-encompassing multi-state database.

- First, the databases may not contain complete records from all jurisdictions – not all state court record systems contain updated records from all counties. The various databases that vendors collect are not the equivalent of a true all-encompassing multi-state database. First, the databases may not contain complete records from all jurisdictions — not all state court record systems contain updated records from all counties. In California, for example, a limited number of counties allow their data to be used, and even those counties do not provide data of birth. Since most firms need to use both name and date of birth to find names, there are very few hits from California. If the date of birth was not used in the search, then there would be too many names returned to deal with. New York is another example. These databases only contain New York corrections records of people who have been to prison and can only be obtained by going through an official New York statewide search offered by the New York AOC for a large fee. So, when Texas is added into the mix as discussed earlier with its problems, then the three of the largest states—California, New York, and Texas—will represent insufficient coverage.

- Second, for reporting purposes, the records actually reported may be incomplete or lack sufficient detail about the offense or the subject.

- Third, some databases contain only felonies or contain only offenses where a state corrections unit is involved.

- Fourth, the database may not carry subsequent information or other matter that could render the results not reportable, or result in a state law violation concerning criminal records use. For example, in states that provide for deferred adjudication, once a consumer goes back to court and gets the record corrected, the database firm may still be reporting the old data. There is typically not a mechanism for a data broker to correct any one individual's record. Because of the issues with database as to completeness and accuracy, another issue is a false sense of security. Databases can have both false positives and false negatives. This is another reason why employers should be very cautionary.

- Finally, there are some states where a date of birth is not in the court records made public. Since databases match records by date of birth, searching when no DOB exists is of little value since no "hits" will be reported. In those situations, it is necessary to run a search in just the state in question and then individually review each name match. That can be tedious, especially if a common name is being searched.

The result is a crazy quilt patchwork of data from various sources and lack of reliability. These databases are more accurately described as multi-jurisdictional databases.

Name and Date of Birth Match Issues

Besides the possibility of lacking identifiers as described above, an electronic search of a vendor's database may not be able to recognize variations in a subject name, which a person may potentially notice if manually looking at the index. The applicant may have been arrested under a different first name or some variation of first and middle name. A female applicant may have a record under a previous name. Some database vendors have attempted to resolve this problem with a wild card first name search (i.e. instead of Robert, use Rob* so that any variations of ROB will come up). However, there are still too many different first and middle name variations. There is also the chance of name confusion for names where a combination of mother and father's name is used. In addition, some vendors require the use of date of birth in order to prevent too many records from being returned. If an applicant uses a different date of birth, it can cause errors.

The issue comes down to technically how broad or how narrow the database provider sets the search parameters. If a database sets the search parameters on a narrow basis, so it only locates records based upon exact date of birth and last name, then the number of records located not related to the applicant would be reduced. In other words, there will be less false positives. However, it can also lead to records being missed, either because of name variations or because some states do not provide date of birth in the records.   That can lead to 'false negatives.' Conversely, if the parameters are set broadly to avoid missing relevant records, then there is a greater likelihood of finding criminal records relating to the applicant, but at the same time, there are likely to be a number of records that do not belong to the applicant. That can happen for example in a state where no date of birth is provided, and the database is run on a 'name match only' basis.

Timeliness Issues

Records in a vendor's database may be stale to some extent. The government agency selling the data often offers the data on a monthly basis. Even after a vendor receives new data, there can be lag time before the new data is downloaded into the vendor database. Generally the most current offenses are the ones less likely to come up in a database search.

Legal Compliance Issues

When there is a hit, an employer must be concerned about legal compliance. If an employer uses a commercial database via the Internet, the employer must have an understanding of the proper use of criminal records in that state. If the employer acts on face value results without any additional due diligence research, potentially the applicant could sue the employer if the record was not about them.

If a screening firm locates a criminal hit, then the screening firm has an obligation under the FCRA Section 613 (a)(2) to send researchers to the court to pull the actual court records...[sections omitted]... So, unless an industry is controlled by a federal or state regulation, there are no national standards and few state standards for conducting criminal record checks by private employers (beyond FCRA)...[sections omitted]....The best approach for an employer is to insist that a CRA always confirm the details of a database search by going to the courthouse to review the actual records.

———

Searching Civil Litigation and Civil Judgments

Civil litigation is a matter between two private parties. However some criminal cases turn into civil matters (as in the OJ Simpson Trial), and some civil matters turn into criminal trials (as in many financial fraud cases).

Civil cases can be tried, mediated or dismissed. Civil matters include bankruptcy, contract failures, real estate disputes, property, insurance and liability claims. Tort cases can be thought of as *do no harm* lawsuits. Product liability, neglect, and trespass are all examples of tort cases. These files are found in federal and state court systems, using the same sources federal and state research. However, when finding a product liability case, registered as a tort, be sure to check for class action lawsuit, which can be located in classaction.org or

When searching a company for civil filings an investigator needs to be sure to look closely under the company name, their subsidiaries and the principals. Also be aware that the company may have changed names even a large company will change its name to avoid being identified with its unscrupulous past.

Conduct a business search prior to legal search so you know all the names to look under, and not just the one you commonly know. The ABC Company may be the popular name, and is a good search idea to use, but the legal name – the one taken to court – could be ABC Group. If you do not look for ABC Group, the legal history may be missed.

Civil court records can be found form state and local courts in the same manner as described above in the Criminal Records section. There is one additional resource that is worthy of mention. Stanford University has a terrific open source, free, class action lawsuit database, as shown below.

Naming the chief principals of a company is also popular in lawsuits. Individual claims against the company will want to draw in all the parties responsible for their grievance.

A lawsuit against ABC Company may name 5 defendants, such as this example below—

> Mark Johnson vs. ABC Group, et. al.
>
> Defendants:
>
> - ABC Group
> - ABC Company, Subsidiary
> - Robert Smith, Chief Employment Officer
> - Michael Colfax, Chief Finance Officer
> - John Roberts, General Counsel

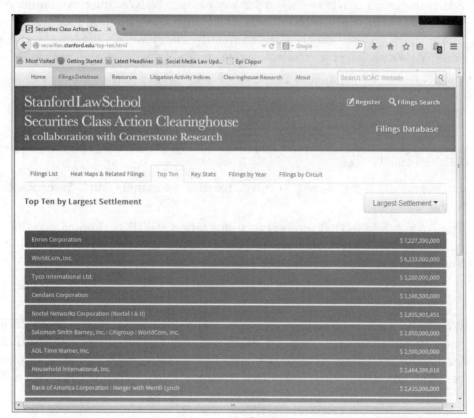

(Source: securities.stanford.edu/top-ten.html)

Unique but Unfamiliar Court Systems

The NYC Taxi Court

Taxi Court is a very unique court system, an almost underground version of traffic court, stationed in New York City. It is run by the NYC Tax and Limousine Commission - nyc.gov/html/tlc/html/home/home.shtml. There will not be a business reason to search Taxi Court, but the court is mentioned here is an example of how odd the legal system sometimes can be. For example, check out the Water Court in Colorado (courts.state.co.us/Courts/Water/Index.cfm).

Tribal Courts

Tribal Courts represent a unique legal system that works within the separate sovereignty of the Indian nations within the United States. The impact on using these courts in business investigations is considerable within the gaming industry. The key point here is that case information in tribal courts is NOT found in any level within the rest of the courts in the U.S.

Searching tribal courts is a must for any obvious Native American name. Also any particular cases which may be brought against any gambling facilities or casinos. These court systems encapsulate criminal, civil, summary judgments and similar cases. Below are several excellent sources to find tribal courts:

- National Tribal Justice Resource Center: naicja.org/training/ntjrc
- Tribal Court Clearinghouse: tribal-institute.org
- A listing of Tribal Courts is also provided by versuslaw.com

International Courts

International legal issues involve treaties, tribunals and recognized global authorities.

The World Intellectual Property Organization, (WIPO), formed by the United Nations in 1967, is a recognized authority with jurisdiction on intellectual property. The WIPO mandate from Member States is:

"...to promote the protection of IP throughout the world through cooperation among states and in collaboration with other international organizations."[16]

WIPO offers several database searches available at wipo.int for patent, trademark and copyright property. Web site domain names will often end up in WIPO courts for dispute mediation. As in the example of T.A. Hari (see story below), the case was based on an International recognized trademark, so eventually the case was tried in the internationally recognized WIPO court.

---

[16] wipo.int/about-wipo/en/what_is_wipo.html

The United Nations also is involved with sanctions and embargos through the Security Council.

What's In a Name?

Several years ago I was called to investigate an individual with a unique name. His last name combined with first and middle initial spelled out matched a famous designer label. For example, T.A. Hari, when spelled together, would look like Tahari – which is a noted women's clothier label. T.A. Hari registered the domain name tahari.com and used it for his own purposes, which were not related to the clothing industry. Tahari, the clothier, sent him a cease and desist letter for the use of their trademark. Mr. Hari offered to settle for a few thousand dollars, but the clothier felt it was their trademark and they had a right to take it back.

The dispute went to ICANN for resolution. T.A. Hari was judged to be using his own name with permissible purpose. Since the name was his own, he had the rights to it. The court informed him as long as he did not use the name to resell clothes, or for the clothier market, it would not be an intrusion on the Tahari trademark.

Another example of an international court is the International Criminal Court (ICC). This independent, permanent court tries persons accused of serious crimes of international concern, such as use of genocide, crimes against humanity, and war crimes. The ICC was formed per a treaty, which now represents 104 countries. Visit icc-cpi.int.

There are other court systems as well, including military and tribunal. Think about jurisdiction when investigating a case. Remember to check for all the parties first, if there are name variations, or if the company is a subsidiary of a larger firm. Look for the principals behind the company, as well as any guarantors (investors) that also can be named as a party. Once you know the players involved, first consider the location of the individual, if in the United States or abroad. Second, find out what sort of legal jurisdiction would be involved, if criminal or civil, or in a unique court perhaps on the International level or something local like a tribal court.

Searching Motor Vehicle Offenses

Motor vehicle checks are commonly used in background investigations and pre-employment searches. Much can be learned about an individual by obtaining their motor vehicle history. Traffic-related violations are tried in local courts and the records of convictions are forwarded to a central state repository (the DMV). The record retrieval industry often refers to driving records as MVRs.

Typical information found on an MVR, besides traffic infractions, includes full name, address, physical description, and date of birth. The license type, restrictions and/or endorsements can provide background data on an individual. If a person received many tickets, lost a license, has DUI indictments, then he or she could be just as reckless with a company car. If other issues surface, such as driving while suspended or repeated DUI offenses, may indicate poor judgment or bad decisions.

The Federal Driver's Privacy Protection Act (DPPA) regulates the policy of what personal information found in state motor vehicle records can be released to the public. Per DPPA, to determine who may receive a record containing personal information, states must differentiate between requesters with a permissible use (14 are designated in DPPA) versus requests from casual requesters with a non-permissible use. For example, a state DMV may choose to sell a record to a casual requester. However, the record can report personal information (address, etc.), only if the subject has given written consent. Otherwise this personal information in the report is cloaked unless the requester has a permissible use and the state chooses to release the information.

Below are four of the DPPA permissible uses directly tied to private investigators and when they are considered to have a permissible to receive personal information:

"(3) For use in the normal course of business by a legitimate business or its agents, employees, or contractors, but only-

(A) to verify the accuracy of personal information submitted by the individual to the business or its agents, employees, or contractors; and

(B) if such information as so submitted is not correct or is no longer correct, to obtain the correct information, but only for the purposes of preventing fraud by, pursuing legal remedies against, or recovering on a debt or security interest against, the individual.

(4) For use in connection with any civil, criminal, administrative, or arbitral proceeding in any Federal, State, or local court or agency or before any self-regulatory body, including the service of process, investigation in anticipation of litigation, and the execution or enforcement of judgments and orders, or pursuant to an order of a Federal, State, or local court.

(6) For use by any insurer or insurance support organization, or by a self-insured entity, or its agents, employees, or contractors, in connection with claims investigation activities, antifraud activities, rating or underwriting.

(8) For use by any licensed private investigative agency or licensed security service for any purpose permitted under this subsection."

Of course, it is up to the individual states to adopt these permissible uses or be more restrictive if they wish. Not all states adopted all 14 permissible uses.

There is a great site explaining driving records and state fees, plus a copy of DPPA. See MVRDecoder.com.

Licensing Boards and Disciplinary Actions

Occupational Licensing Boards

There are literally thousands of government licensing authorities or boards that oversee and regulate the occupation of an individual or type of industry for a business. Certain licensing categories are more regulated than others. For example a food service company will have more licensing and permits than a bookstore. That does not mean the bookstore is free from government bureaucracy requiring the store abide by town ordinances, county and state law. While some industries manage to self-regulate, and majority are over sighted by government agencies.

Searching for licenses and permits is a windfall opportunity for an investigator. Sometimes the only place you will find a true admission of business ownership, asset holders, or just get the right contact information is from a license registration.

A good rule to go by when determining if a professional is licensed is to consider the consumer. A perfect example is anything that deals with touching the body or hands on physical work, will be a licensed occupation. For example, manicurists, beauticians, massage therapists; doctors and dentists are all licensed in every state.

Florida's Department of Regulation and Business is a great example of the occupations that states will license. In Florida, everything appears to have a license authority, so if your subject has any affiliation with the State, be sure to check for a license there. You will find good information, even on a regional basis. For example, a recent check of *body wrappers* in Miami-Dade County located 68 licensed individuals. A licensing board may be willing to release part or all of the following—

- Field of Certification
- Status of License/Certificate
- Date License/Certificate Issued or Expires
- Current or Most Recent Employer
- Address of Subject
- Complaints, Violations or Disciplinary Actions

The New Hygienist

I recently helped a female dental hygienist moved to a suburb of Dallas and found a job at a local dentist's office. She was the only hygienist on staff, as the dentist claimed to have recently lost a long-time employee.

> Within the first month the dentist sexually assaulted her. The case evolved to her word against his so we needed to find past employees to interview and perhaps corroborate the story. Using the county Web site, we located a list of all the registered hygienists in the county, and then with a map, we called them starting with those closest to his office.
>
> Within four phone calls, we found a woman who did work at his office, but only for a short period of time. When I explained why I was calling, she gave us the name of a colleague who worked with her at the same location and had told that the dentist was fondling her. I then called this person who was very cooperative and provided information, which my client used to win the case.

Disciplinary Actions

Probably the most widely searched fields of occupational licensing are in the medical and legal industries. The licensing boards for these professions usually maintain disciplinary databases that are quite resourceful.

Below is an example of a search of disciplinary actions on three nurses from the state of New York. Note: The last name and license number have been changed, but the reported facts are taken straight from the Office of Professional Management at op.nysed.gov. Notice that two out of three received probation in lieu of having their license suspended, regardless of unethical and dangerous mishandling of their patients.

```
Kathleen T. Clive, Goldens Bridge, NY

Profession: Registered Professional Nurse; Lic. No.
126692; Cal. No. 13831

Regents Action Date: April 15, 1994

Action: Application to surrender license granted.

Summary: Licensee could not successfully defend
against charges of documenting nine sessions with
patients that she did not perform.
```

```
Charles O'Shea, Wyandanch, NY

Profession: Registered Professional Nurse; Lic. No.
291296; Cal. No. 10667

Regents Action Date: April 28, 1995

Action: 3 year suspension, execution of last 24 months
of suspension stayed, probation for last 24 months.

Summary: Licensee was found guilty of charges of
having placed a patient in a tub of running water,
failing to insure that the temperature of the water
```

```
was safe, and having placed the patient in such a
manner that the patient's head was in close proximity
to the metal spigot, the patient thereafter being
diagnosed with first and second degree burns which
caused his death.
```

———

```
Rosemary P. Ratchet, Valley Stream, NY

Profession: Registered Professional Nurse; Lic. No.
237207; Cal. No. 12614

Regents Action Date: April 28, 1995

Action: Suspension until successfully completes a
course of treatment - upon termination of suspension,
probation 2 years.

Summary: Licensee was found guilty of charges of
practicing the profession while her ability to
practice was impaired by alcohol and drugs, involving
respondent practicing the profession under the
influence of wine and Valium while on duty.
```

More Searching Tips for Licensing and Disciplinary Actions

As mentioned in the last chapter, there are approximately 8,700 state licensing boards in the U.S. and nearly 5,000 offer online searching to some information about licensees.

To find these services or find the ones not online, there are several options:

- Visit usa.gov and look for the state and license type
- Visit brbpublications.com/freeresources/pubrecsitesOccStates.aspx
- Visit the state home page (i.e. in.gov for Indiana) and do a search.

If you are having a hard time researching a subject's special profession, there could be several reasons. Perhaps the state may not require licensing for a particular profession. In Idaho for example, private investigators are not required to be licensed by the state. Or, maybe your subject's profession is certified, but does not require licensing. Many groups self-certify, and some companies even do self-certification, such as a physical fitness club for trainers. But there may be a third reason which can be a red flag in an investigation – your subject may be purposely avoiding the licensing required in the state. This could signify the subject is avoiding paying taxes, or is a felon and ineligible to be licensed, or practicing but does not meet the qualifications of the state to obtain the license.

Another vexing problem is to figure out which profession is the right one to search. Perhaps your subject works in a hospital, but per the list of Florida Health licenses found at <u>doh.state.fl.us</u>, there are a possible 142 health vocations, from Anesthesiologist Assistants to Veterinary Prescription Drug Wholesaler.

Start by calling the office in the off hours of the person you are investigating. The title may be in the voicemail box. i.e. "Hello you have reached Roger, Director of Radiology for Farmers Hospital." Fortunately some states, like Florida, let you conduct an ALL search at once, so you do not have determine if your subject is an EMS Service Provider ALS or an EMS Service Provider BLS.

Once you get a sense of what type of title this person holds, numerous state Web sites can be scanned. You may still need to contact the licensing authority. More information is found on file than online. Usually the licensing agent has the training, schooling, contact information, and other details on file.

Another fact is many industries require businesses to be licensed. Examples include manufacturing, contractors, automotive, hospitality, liquor, gaming, etc. Most of these industry workers are regulated by state. Check with the same state agency resources to find the proper authority regulating the industry in question. Follow the same searching procedures as searching individual professionals to determine if your subject is properly licensed or not, or has disciplinary actions.

Another way to verify or establish a contact for a subject is to check with trade associations. An industry association can be regional or national in scope, similar to the profession of private investigators. These organizations support networking, educational programs, legislative development, and consumer protection.

Licensing Boards Are Always Good Lead Sources

Searching for a person or about a person, by license, is one of the few ways you can find an "Average Joe" who does not show up in news stories, press releases, or on the company Web site. He is normally going back and forth to work with a big sense of obscurity. Using government oversight boards is a great information equalizer.

No matter the profession, if your subject has done something terrible to merit disciplinary action, chances are the incident appeared in the news, or was prosecuted by a state or district attorney. There could also have been a fine, or public notice. Make sure to research the news and legal filings for this person and their company.

Legal research is not complete until you combine the legal records with the disciplinary actions and investigate all the possible excluded parties and regulatory sanctioned lists. These lists are formed by international groups, national agencies, and law enforcement bodies which have found persons or companies in violation of the associated states' laws.

Investigating Financial Crimes

Financial crime is not limited to bank robbers and charlatans. Today's criminal may be found sitting behind a glossy boardroom table or on the Internet. The task of monitoring financial misdeeds falls to SEC, FINRA, and state securities bureaus which will be outlined in detail later. These organizations protect the investor from modern day thieves who manage to steal millions through stocks and securities.

Let's examine some of the most common types of financial fraud that you may come across during investigations. Keep in mind many of these practices are legal by themselves, such as backdating and short selling. But the abuse of them through manipulative tactics can make them illegal. Company executives, like Martha Stewart (Martha Stewart Omnimedia Publications) and Kenneth Lay (Enron) professed their innocence throughout their trials, claiming they were conducting legitimate stock maneuvers and taking advantage of loopholes. Since these cases, the SEC has created an oversight commission and has supported compliance laws in order to protect investors from those committing crimes connected to securities.

Ponzi Scheme

In the early 1900's Charles Ponzi popularized this fraudulent investment scheme, which has since been immortalized by Bernard Madoff. Essentially the initial investors are guaranteed very high returns with little risk. However the money used to pay these returns are actually funded directly by the newer investors, and so on, until the number of investors runs out, and the whole scam falls apart.

Manipulation

The SEC defines the word manipulation as:

"Manipulation is the intentional conduct designed to deceive investors by controlling or artificially affecting the market for a security. Manipulation can involve a number of techniques to affect the supply of, or demand for, a stock. They include spreading false or misleading information about a company, improperly limiting the number of publicly-available shares, or rigging quotes, prices or trades to create a false or deceptive picture of the demand for a security. Those who engage in manipulation are subject to various civil and criminal sanctions." [17]

Investment message boards, such as found on Yahoo.com, are well known to investigators for spreading rumors about a company giving the impression that the company is in trouble, which leads real investors to sell their shares, thereby deflating the security and driving the price of the security down.

---

[17] sec.gov/answers/tmanipul.htm

Backdating Stocks

Backdating is dating any document earlier than the one on which the document was originally drawn up. Steve Jobs of Apple and Martha Stewart were both accused of backdating their stock options. They would backdate the options to land on the date when the stock was at its lowest value, allowing them the highest return when it is sold. In small terms, if a company is trying to attract a talented executive to their employ, they may offer him stocks. To get the best deal for him, they may backdate them to a date when the value of the stock was at its lowest. The tactic to protect them, and keep this legal, would be to clear this first with the board of shareholders and to compensate any fees associated to offer. The technique becomes illegal when only the executive who is signing off on the document knows about the backdating.

Extra Extra

SEC Charges Former General Counsel of RFI-Thames And ABC Company Inc. For Fraudulent Stock Option Backdating

ABC Company Settles Fraud Charges Brought by Commission

FOR IMMEDIATE RELEASE

2007-123

Washington, D.C., August 28, 20xx - The Securities and Exchange Commission today filed fraud charges against a Bay Area attorney for her role in illegally backdating stock option grants. The Commission charged Abby B. Cherry with routinely backdating option grants from 1997 to 2003, first as General Counsel of RFI-Thames Corporation and then as General Counsel of ABC Company, Inc. The Commission alleges that Cherry's misconduct caused the two companies to conceal hundreds of millions of dollars in stock option compensation expenses relating to undisclosed in-the-money options provided to company executives and employees.

Insider Trading

Insider trading is the act of buying and selling stocks with the foreknowledge of critical information not yet been released to the public. For example, a pharmaceutical CEO's son finds out through conversations with his father that the company is on the verge of receiving approval from FDA on a new type of diet drug. The son then buys large quantities of stock at what will be a reduced stock price, prior to the press release. Once the press release about the FDA approval is published, the stock prices soar as everyone tries to get in early on the new purchase. His foreknowledge is insider information and therefore he utilized that information illegally in purchasing the stocks.

Short Selling

Most long-term investors are "Going Long" meaning they purchase stocks with the hope of gaining wealth as the price of the security increases. But a Short Seller borrows on a stock and sells hoping the price will decrease. Wikipedia.org offers several examples of short selling. The example below is of a profitable trade

"Shares in C & Company currently trade at $10 per share.

1. A short seller investor borrows 100 shares of C & Company and immediately sells them for a total of $1,000.

2. Subsequently, the price of the shares falls to $8 per share.

3. Short seller now buys 100 shares of C & Company for $800.

4. Short seller returns the shares to the lender, who must accept the return of the same number of shares as was lent despite the fact that the market value of the shares has decreased.

5. Short seller retains as profit the $200 difference (minus borrowing fees) between the price at which he sold the shares he borrowed and the lower price at which he was able to purchase the shares he returned."

(source: wikipedia.org/wiki/Shorting)

And all of this is completely legal; shorting becomes illegal when it gets Naked. Naked Shorting is when you are selling stocks you do not even own.

An article found on Motley Fool (fool.com - a great resource for financial news on the Web) by Stephen D. Simpson, CFA titled *Manipulation and the Individual Investor*[18] states—

"In regular shorting, the seller (or the seller's broker, rather) must locate the shares to be shorted, borrow them, and sell them. Can't find any shares to borrow and short? Well, you can't short the stock. Unless you want to try a naked short, that is.

In a naked short, you just short the stock -- you don't make any attempt at actually locating the shares or borrowing them. Now, in theory there is a 13-day window in which those shares must be delivered. But brokerage houses have been known to hand off transactions to other houses and keep them moving around in such a way that they never settle.

If the bird actually does come home to roost after 13 days and no shares have been delivered, the broker has to buy those shares back. But if the manipulators succeeded in their attempt to push the stock down, that buyback can still be at a price that gives the wrongdoer a profit. Neat little scam, huh?"

---

[18] fool.com/investing/high-growth/2005/05/31/manipulation-and-the-individual-investor.aspx

In this way, the Naked Shorter has moved the stock, profited and has never actually borrowed it or against it to begin.

Pump and Dump Schemes

Pump and dump schemes are illegal manipulation of stock prices based on fraudulent claims. Companies promise advances in science, bigger returns, cures for diseases, technology that exceeds all standards, and in return investors clamor to get behind the latest and greatest company. Then the company fails to deliver their products, the demand for new capital wanes and the company is stock is dumped.

Pump and dump schemes were very common during the tech bubble years, when companies would continually prophesize their emerging products, promoting them beyond their real ability. Reading their press releases would inspire investors to get in young and fast. Venture capitalists and everyday people were all jumping on the bandwagon, putting money into false promises. Once the promotion stopped, or the fraudulent truths were discovered, the demand was removed, causing a collapse in the price of the investment, leaving many investors out of pocket. Key indicators in a pump and dump scheme are monthly, or regular, press releases making outlandish claims but no support. The indicator is how the company is funded. Are they completely funded by venture capital, or do they produce some sort of other service or product that can support them? Finally, use common sense, too good to be true inventions probably are.

Not So Smart

My client was concerned that a competitor was outranking his Smart Cards[19] in the market. The time frame was the mid-1990's when Smart Cards were still a hot item, with a lot of development yet to come. This competitor claimed to build gigabyte cards that were indestructible. My client obviously was concerned that the current standard of megabyte cards were going to be surpassed, and being a top scientist and business professional in the industry, he was stumped as to how the competitor beat him to market.

This investigation immediately was suspect, because the competitor was only discussing the release of his Smart Cards. The competitor actually did not have a product in place. When all the news articles were retrieved, I noticed that at the middle of every month this company placed its press release, discussing all sorts of improvements and relationships. Like clockwork each month one could read about how this company improved compression ratios, aligned themselves with a laminating company which

---

[19] Smart Cards, similar to credit cards, contain data which is used for a specific purpose. A room key pass, or identity badge is an example of a Smart Card.

had ballistics grade plastic to coat these cards in, and recent new investors to impress even the savviest of Wall Street tycoons. This ongoing pump of new information into the news generated a lot of buzz, and investors were hungry to buy shares and make investments in the company.

While researching the news, I focused on the management. They came from Canada, recently settling into the Silicon Valley, California area. I started looking for past companies in Canada where these executives may have worked previously. I found a mention of the Toronto Stock Exchange delisting a company the CEO worked for. This company was producing portable medical testing units that could scan for viruses such as HIV, without the need for electricity – a sort of finger-prick analysis. While researching this company I discovered the same mantra of monthly articles professing major accomplishments every month, until one day they stopped. As it turned out, Canadian authorities suspected the claims as fraudulent. The CEO and others were investigated. The Canadian company remains open today, but the stock is close to worthless and many investors were left without reprise.

This same CEO was doing the same pump and dump here in the U.S. with his Smart Card scam. For our client's sake, we knew the claimed technology did not exist and we exposed the fraudulent person to the SEC for further review.

Taking it Online

Pump and dumps, and misinformation campaigns can also be generated online. Online chat boards found on Yahoo.com and Ragingbull.com are famous for getting insider news. The anonymity of the identities of the posters shields them from being exposed talking about fights in the boardrooms, product releases, marketing schemes, etc. Companies need to monitor their own message boards for any truths or half-truths. It is not uncommon for a former employee, or current disgruntled employee, to post proprietary information in these chat forums.

A prime example is the case of Dendrite vs. John Doe, Dendrite, a Morristown, N.J. based provider of products and services for the pharmaceutical and consumer package goods industries. Dendrite went after several anonymous people who were posting defamatory information on the Yahoo Dendrite message board. Each poster was independent of the other, but all were suspected employees of the company. In at least two of the cases the court ruled that Yahoo did not have to expose the identity of the posters, claiming first amendment rights, and in the second case, no harm occurred. But according to court papers, Dendrite said John Doe No. 3 made a series of posts on a Yahoo bulletin board specifically devoted to the company's financial matters. "The company alleged that negative comments by several posters about Dendrite and its management constituted breaches of contract, defamatory statements and misappropriated trade secrets." [20]

The misappropriation of trade secrets is what opens the individual to criminal misconduct.

Individuals posting on the Internet, through blogs, message boards, social media and in forums, do not realize they truly are not invisible. While they think they are sharing insider secrets, opinions, and bad feelings about their supervisor, they do not realize investigators and corporate security are also monitoring the boards for any intellectual property loss.

Undercover

The best tactic is to prepare a proactive approach by becoming involved before information starts flowing. As a contributor you are monitoring the news, participating in the exchange of information, bantering back and forth with the other investors, and gaining trust.

The captioned image to follow is from Martha Stewart's company Omnimedia Publishing. This company's message board attracts a good deal of attention, and is excellent for new investigators to follow as a training exercise by doing the following. Every day for a week visit this message board (or pick another company message board of interest to you). As you check every day, you become familiar with who the frequent posters are, their biases, and the language they use to communicate with one another. When you are only observing it is known as lurking. Once you feel comfortable with the banter, start contributing small unimportant tidbits or opinions. This makes you active and seen by the other message board posters, and helps establish some credibility (like going undercover on the Internet). Hopefully you can continue to do this for your client before any issues arise on your identity. Thus when something of value to your case is posted, you are already inside on the message board and can ask some key questions without coming across as suspicious. Also notice the time the person is writing. Middle of the night? This might mean he or she works odd hours.   Middle of the day? He or she might not be employed.

---

[20] Bartlett, Michael. (July 11, 2001). *New Jersey Court Upholds Anonymity On Net Bulletin Board - Dendrite International.* Newsbytes News Network

(source: <u>messages.finance.yahoo.com/mb/MSO</u>)

There are many topical, random boards that you can access once you have created a profile in Yahoo. Again, this is to establish that you have some history in message boards and are not some Johnny Come Lately creating suspicion when you pipe up about a sensitive topic. If you do intercede on a new board, then at least when the other posters check out your profile they will see some history. The statement you open with is… "Hello I've been lurking on this board for a few months and…"

With so many types of financial fraud, continuing education is necessary to understand and investigate in this arena.

Two resources for continuing education regarding financial investigations are first read the white paper titled, *Short Selling, Death Spiral Convertibles, and the Profitability of Stock Manipulation* written by John D. Finnerty, Professor of Finance, Fordham University Graduate School of Business (March 2005)[21]. The second is to visit the Web site for the Association of Certified Fraud Examiners (<u>acfe.org</u>) and check their Fraud Resource Center for articles on various financial frauds as well as class offerings and industry news.

---

[21] <u>sec.gov/rules/petitions/4-500/jdfinnerty050505.pdf</u>

Publicly Traded Companies and Securities Dealers

As mentioned in Chapter 5, there are three primary agencies that oversee regulatory and compliance issues with publicly traded securities or with security dealers:

- Securities and Exchange Commission (SEC)
- Financial Industry Regulatory Authority (FINRA)[22]
- National Futures Association (NFA).

The SEC is a federal government agency. FINRA and NFA are self-regulatory bodies.

Another important entity, profiled later in this chapter, is the North American Securities Administrators Association (NASAA).

Each agency is an excellent resource for investigating compliance issues and enforcement actions. In summary, each organization monitors public companies and brokers for impropriety; it also oversees securities dealers, brokerage firms, and compliance requirements. Each has the authority to investigate and enforce regulatory actions.

The types of investigations are pump and dump schemes, stock manipulation, backdating of stocks, short selling, and insider trading, as described earlier.

The Securities and Exchange Commission (SEC)

The SEC is the primary overseer and regulator of the U.S. securities markets. According to the SEC's Web site (sec.gov), "The mission of the U.S. Securities and Exchange Commission is to protect investors, maintain fair, orderly, and efficient markets, and facilitate capital formation... "

The SEC oversees the key participants in the securities world, including securities exchanges, securities brokers and dealers, investment advisors, and mutual funds. Here, the SEC is concerned primarily with promoting the disclosure of important market-related information, maintaining fair dealing, and protecting against fraud.

Part of the SEC function is the enforcement of civil actions against individuals and companies that violate securities laws. Typical infractions include insider trading, accounting fraud, and providing false or misleading information about securities and the companies that issue them. For more information, visit sec.gov/litigation.shtml.

---

[22] Formerly the National Association of Securities Dealers – NASD

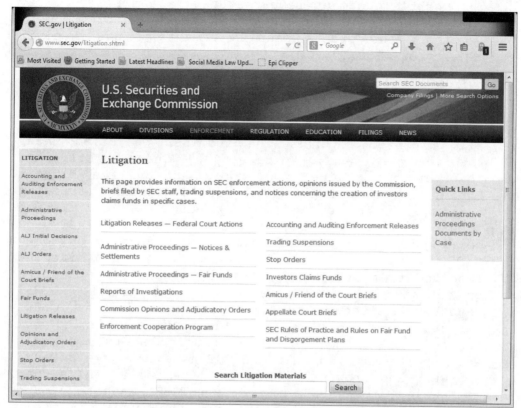

(source: sec.gov/litigation.shtml)

These news releases concerning stock fraud and misappropriation of securities are issued daily. A sample release is shown below.

U.S. SECURITIES AND EXCHANGE COMMISSION

Litigation Release No. 23090 / September 22, 2014

Securities and Exchange Commission v. Trendon T. Shavers and Bitcoin Savings and Trust, Civil Action No. Civil Action No. 4:13-CV-416

Final Judgment Entered Against Trendon T. Shavers, A/K/A/ "Pirateat40" - Operator of Bitcoin Ponzi Scheme Ordered to Pay More Than $40 Million in Disgorgement and Penalties

The Securities and Exchange Commission announced that, on September 18, 2014, a United States District Court in Sherman, Texas entered final judgment against Trendon T. Shavers and Bitcoin Savings and Trust ("BTCST"), the online entity Shavers created and used to operate his Ponzi scheme, and through which he defrauded investors out of more than 700,000 bitcoins. The Court's judgment requires Shavers and BTCST to pay more than $40 million in disgorgement and prejudgment interest, and orders each Defendant to pay a civil penalty of $150,000.

The Commission established, and the Court found, that from February 2011 through August 2012, Shavers offered and sold investments in BTCST over the internet. Shavers solicited all investments, and paid all purported returns, in bitcoins. Operating under the internet name, "pirateat40," Shavers solicited investors in online chat rooms and on the Bitcoin Forum, an online forum dedicated to Bitcoin, promising them up to 7% returns weekly based on his claimed trading of bitcoin against the U.S. dollar, including selling bitcoins to individuals who wanted to buy them "off the radar." In reality, Shavers used new bitcoins received from BTCST investors to pay purported returns on outstanding BTCST investments, and diverted BTCST investors' bitcoins for his personal use. The Court further found that, even as he publicly denied the Ponzi scheme on the Bitcoin Forum, Shavers knowingly and intentionally operated BTCST as a sham and a Ponzi scheme, and repeatedly made materially false and misleading representations to BTCST investors and potential investors concerning the use of their bitcoins, how he would generate the promised returns, and the safety of their investments.

The Court's judgment permanently enjoins Shavers and BTCST from future violations of Sections 5 and 17(a) of the Securities Act of 1933, and Section 10(b) of the Securities Exchange Act of 1934 and Rule 10b-5 thereunder; orders them to disgorge, on a joint and several basis, $39,638,569, plus $1,766,098 prejudgment interest thereon, for a total of $40,404,667; and orders Shavers and BTCST each to pay a $150,000 penalty.

(source: http://sec.gov/litigation/litreleases/2014/lr23090.htm)

Financial Industry Regulatory Authority (FINRA)

According to FINRA's Web site (finra.org)—

"The Financial Industry Regulatory Authority (FINRA) is the largest non-governmental regulator for all securities firms doing business in the United States. All told, FINRA oversees nearly 5,100 brokerage firms, about 173,000 branch offices and more than 665,000 registered securities representatives.

Created in July 2007 through the consolidation of NASD and the member regulation, enforcement, and arbitration functions of the New York Stock Exchange, FINRA is dedicated to investor protection and market integrity through effective and efficient regulation and complementary compliance and technology-based services."

FINRA is important to investigators as a resource to check on brokers. The Web site allows name searching of an individual or a brokerage firm. This is a key resource when investigating any type of investment advisor. If the advisor or broker is registered in FINRA, the user can download an eight-page Adobe Acrobat PDF file that outlines the subject's history, including his employment history. Brokerage firms also are searchable for any disciplinary actions taken against a company, or brokers who are involved with arbitration awards, disciplinary and regulatory events.

National Futures Association (NFA)

Per the NFA's Web site (https://www.nfa.futures.org)—

"National Futures Association (NFA) is the self-regulatory organization for the U.S. derivatives industry, including on-exchange traded futures, retail off-exchange foreign currency (forex) and OTC derivatives (swaps). NFA has developed and enforced rules, provided programs and offered services that safeguard market integrity, protect investors and help our Members meet their regulatory responsibilities and has done so for more than 30 years."

Searching the futures database is very straightforward, with basic searches using an individual's name or a firm's name. Results give any arbitration or regulatory action filed against the individual or firm, if listed with the NFA.

In summary, each organization monitors public companies and brokers for impropriety, and oversees securities dealers, brokerage firms, and compliance requirements. Each has the authority to investigate and enforce regulatory actions.

A screen image from NFA is shown on the following page.

Background Affiliation Status Information Center

Welcome to the National Futures Association's **Background Affiliation Status Information Center (BASIC)**. Whether you are an investor thinking about opening a futures account or an NFA Member contemplating a new business relationship, BASIC can be a valuable resource for you.

BASIC contains Commodity Futures Trading Commission (CFTC) registration and NFA membership information and futures-related regulatory and non-regulatory actions contributed by NFA, the CFTC and the U.S. futures exchanges.

Information regarding IBs, CPOs and CTAs and APs of FCMs, IBs, CPOs and CTAs
Generally, any firm and individual that conducts futures or certain swaps business with the public must be registered with the CFTC. However, the CFTC's Division of Swap Dealer and Intermediary Oversight issued No-Action letters on October 11, 2012, December 21, 2012, and December 28, 2012, that allow certain firms to conduct futures or swaps business while their applications are pending so long as they have filed their applications by December 31, 2012, and that allow certain APs to conduct futures or swaps business if they file applications by March 31, 2013. If you are doing futures or swaps business with a firm or individual that is not currently registered, you should contact that firm or individual to confirm that you are dealing with a firm or individual eligible to conduct this business under one of the no-action letters.

Information regarding CFTC No-Action letters for certain pooled investment vehicle types
NFA Bylaw 1101 requires NFA Members to conduct business with only those firms and individuals that are registered with the CFTC and Members of NFA, unless they qualify for specific CFTC exemptions. Recently, however, the CFTC's Division of Swap Dealer and Intermediary Oversight issued several No-Action letters which provide relief from CPO registration for CPOs that operate specific types of pooled investment vehicles.

Please be advised that some claims for relief will not appear in NFA's BASIC System immediately after being filed. If you are doing business with a CPO claiming relief under these No-Action letters, you should request a copy of such claim for your records.

The system may occasionally be unavailable due to system maintenance.
Use of these search tools indicates you have accepted the Terms and Conditions of Use

Search by **NFA ID** Number	Search by **Firm Name**
NFA ID [ ] GO	**Firm name** [ ] GO
Enter an NFA ID Number.	Search for information associated with a firm only.
Search by **Individual** Name	Search by **Pool Name**
Last Name* [ ] GO	**Pool name** [ ] GO
First Name [ ]	Search for information associated with a commodity pool only.
This search may return both individuals and firms. ***Required Field**	

efficient and innovative regulatory programs that   Site Index | Contact NFA | News Center | FAQs | Career Opportunities | Industry Links | Home

(source: nfa.futures.org/%5C/basicnet/Welcome.aspx

North American Securities Administrators Association (NASAA)

Another excellent resource that merits attention is the North American Securities Administrators Association (NASAA). With members from the 50 states, the District of Columbia, Puerto Rico, the U.S. Virgin Islands, Canada, and Mexico, NASAA is devoted to investor protection.

NASAA members license firms and their agents, investigate violations of state and provincial law, file enforcement actions when appropriate, and educate the public about investment fraud.

NASAA members also participate in multi-state enforcement actions and information sharing. The NASAA Web site (nasaa.org) contains links to individual state, provincial, and territorial jurisdictions for securities laws, rules and regulations.

Central Registration Depository (CRD)

An important collaborative effort of NASAA, FINRA, and the SEC was their joint development of the Central Registration Depository (CRD). State securities regulators for NASAA, FINRA and the SEC realized that it was inefficient for each regulator to have their own filing systems to license broker-dealers and their agents, so they created the CRD for this purpose. The CRD reports are available through state regulatory authorities. A list of which can be located at the NASAA Web site.

Quick Scrambling

A longtime client called one day with the name of a company to investigate. The client was clear about the company name and asked me to conduct a due diligence investigation. I dutifully wrote the company name and started the project. After pulling together a large report, highlighting all the key information concerning litigation, media, business filings, financials, and key principals, I reported my findings to the client.

The next day the client called and explained that he only wanted to locate the company's factory locations in South America, and was not interested in all the minutiae of details I had pulled together for his report. I asked him if he had checked the company's Web site. On the site was a Web page, under the Locations tab, with all the contact information for each of the factories.

Not all was lost though. In my research, I discovered media stories that mentioned there were talks of this company acquiring one of its competitors. The client was quite happy to receive that information.

The story demonstrates a common occurrence in investigations. The investigator does a great job, but the client still is not impressed. Here is where the customer-service angle comes in. Always follow up with the client and ask him what he thought of your work. This is often times avoided, because it can be very difficult to hear criticism.

 Business personalities, business types, and foreign entities – whether they are small, private companies or large, multinational, publicly traded corporations – will present unique challenges to the investigator. This is especially true for those new to the corporate world. Always remember there is someone smarter than you out there, so do not be afraid to reach out and ask questions. Also join associations and attend seminars that offer business and investigations training. Consider enrolling in community-college business classes. One semester in International Business 101 will broaden your horizons and give you a better understanding of the corporate world. And you might meet fellow constituents or future clients.

Key Federal Sanctions and Watch List Sites

The U.S. Excluded Parties List

While the above legal entities are useful when researching the legal history and filings of a company, there are many other sites with searchable information on companies cited for compliance problems or have regulatory violations that block them from doing business with the government.

One of the most important is the Excluded Parties List System (EPLS) housed by SAM.gov. EPLS contains information on individuals and firms excluded by over 85 federal government agencies from receiving federal contracts or federally approved subcontracts, and certain types of federal financial and non-financial assistance and benefits. Note that individual agencies are responsible for the timely reporting, maintenance, and accuracy of their data. When reviewing this list, you realize the government generates this information from a variety of agencies that you may not be aware of, such as the Appalachian Regional Commission.

Searching the EPLS

You can search for the company-excluded parties on the EPLS via sam.gov. Easily search the list by full names, partial names, or even multiple names, by Social Security numbers, and by federal employment identification numbers. Information shown may include names, addresses, DUNS numbers, Social Security numbers, employer identification numbers or other taxpayer identification numbers, if available and deemed appropriate and permissible to publish by the agency taking the action. An important point in sams.gov, because it also includes entity records from CCR/FedReg and ORCA, is to note:

> "...that when matches are found, there may be instances where an Individual or Firm has the same or similar name as your search request but is actually a different party. Therefore, it is important that you verify a potential match with the debarring agency identified in the record information."

The search example below shows the search box and a partial result search using "abc ...". (The names have been changed.)

(source: sam.gov/portal/SAM)

(source: sam.gov/portal/SAM)

Note that that the agencies reporting to the EPLS also may have their own excluded party databases searchable on their Web sites. An example is the Department of Health and Human Services. Locating independent lists from EPLS is easy. Search google.com using the agency name and add excluded (e.g. Department of Health and Human Services excluded).

The Department of Health and Human Services has an Office of Investigative General, with an excluded parties list at exclusions.oig.hhs.gov. Search by personal or company name. Results for individuals return the addresses, names, and dates of birth, as well as a box to verify the Social Security numbers, if you have them. Companies' results return the addresses, points of contact, and a box to verify federal employee identification numbers.

Each state and practice will have its own excluded parties list. For example, in New Jersey, the Bureau of Securities (njconsumeraffairs.gov/bos/bosdisc.htm), part of the Division of Consumer Affairs, has a listing of enforcement actions taken against persons involved in securities fraud. Check with brbpublications.com for a listing of each state's consumer affairs, or similar, agency and see what is available online. A phone call may be necessary, since not every agency has published its material on the Internet.

The next section is a combination of excerpts from *The Manual to Online Public Records* by Facts on Demand Press and from data appearing on web pages belonging to BRB Publications.

More on Federal Agency Sanctions and Watch Lists

Import, Export Databases

This section examines specific watch lists from the Commerce Department, Labor Department, State Department, and Treasury Department. A downloadable file at export.gov/ecr/eg_main_023148.asp has six export screening lists from these Departments consolidated into one spreadsheet relevant to import/export transactions. The purpose is as an aide to industry in conducting electronic screens of potential parties to regulated transactions.

Below are details for each of these 6 databases, sorted by the originating agency.

Three Lists from the Commerce Department, Bureau of Industry and Security (BIS)

1. Denied Persons List

The Denied Persons List contains Individuals and entities that have been denied export privileges. The list is meant to prevent the illegal export of dual-use items before they occur, and to investigate and assist in the prosecution of violators of the Export Administration Regulations.

2. Unverified List

This list of parties whom BIS has been unable to verify in some manner in prior transaction, includes names and countries of foreign persons who in the past were parties to a transaction with respect to which BIS could not conduct a pre-license check ('PLC') or a post-shipment verification ('PSV') for reasons outside of the U.S. Government's control.

3. Entity List

The Entity List is a list of parties whose presence in a transaction can trigger a license requirement under the Export Administration Regulations. The original purpose was to inform the public of entities whose activities imposed a risk of diverting exported and re-exported items into programs related to weapons of mass destruction. Now the list includes those with any license requirements imposed on the transaction by other provisions of the Export Administration Regulations. The list specifies the license requirements that apply to each listed party.

Two Lists from the Department of State:

4. Nonproliferation Sanctions List

This shows parties who have been sanctioned under various statutes per the Bureau of International Security. Note webpage is updated as appropriate, but the Federal Register is the only official and complete listing of nonproliferation sanctions determinations.

5. AECA Debarred List

Per the Directorate of Defense Trade Controls, this displays entities and individuals prohibited from participating directly or indirectly in the export of defense articles, including technical data and defense services. Pursuant to the Arms Export Control Act (AECA) and the International Traffic in Arms Regulations (ITAR), the AECA Debarred List includes persons convicted in court of violating or conspiring to violate the AECA and subject to statutory debarment or persons established to have violated the AECA in an administrative proceeding and subject to administrative debarment.

One List from the Department of the Treasury:

6. Specially Designated Nationals List

Per the Office of Foreign Assets Control, the Specially Designated Nationals List shows parties who may be prohibited from export transactions based on OFAC regulations.

The rest of this section is presented in alphabetical order by agency name.

FDA – Food & Drug Administration

The FDA regulates scientific studies designed to develop evidence to support the safety and effectiveness of investigational drugs (human and animal), biological products, and medical devices. Physicians and other qualified experts ('clinical investigators') who conduct these studies are required to comply with applicable statutes and regulations intended to ensure the integrity of clinical data on which product approvals are based and, for investigations involving human subjects, to help protect the rights, safety, and welfare of these subjects.

FDA Enforcement Report Index – Recalls, Market Withdrawals, and Safety Alerts

The FDA Enforcement Report, published weekly, contains information on actions taken in connection with agency regulatory activities. Data includes Recalls and Field Corrections, Injunctions, Seizures, Indictments, Prosecutions, and

Dispositions. A record of Enforcement Reports going back 8 years is found at the agency's web page at fda.gov/safety/recalls/enforcementreports.

Visit www.fda.gov/Safety/Recalls/default.htm for the most significant recalls, market withdrawals and safety alerts of products; all listed are based on the extent of distribution and the degree of health risk

Debarment List

See fda.gov/ICECI/EnforcementActions/FDADebarmentList/default.htm. These individuals and entities that are prohibited from introducing any type of food, drug, cosmetics or associated devices into interstate commerce.

Disqualified or Restricted Clinical Investigator List

A disqualified or totally restricted clinical investigator is not eligible to receive investigational drugs, biologics, or devices. Some clinical investigators have agreed to certain restrictions with respect to their conduct of clinical investigations. See fda.gov/ICECI/EnforcementActions/ucm321308.htm

Human Health Services, Department of

Excluded Individuals/Entities (LEIE)

The LEIE maintained by the Office of Inspector General (OIG) for the Department of Human Health Services is a list of currently excluded parties. The exclusions are based on convictions for program-related fraud and patient abuse, licensing board actions, and default on Health Education Assistance Loans. The searchable database is found at exclusions.oig.hhs.gov. A downloadable version is at https://oig.hhs.gov/exclusions/exclusions_list.asp.

Justice Department

There are a number of Divisions within the Justice Department that maintain news articles, stories, records lists, and most wanted lists that can be very useful for research and investigation purposes.

Bureau of Alcohol, Tobacco, Firearms and Explosives

Below are two online resources:

- Federal Firearms License Validator: https://www.atfonline.gov/fflezcheck
- ATF Most Wanted List: atf.gov/most-wanted

Bureau of Investigation (FBI)

The FBI's Most Wanted Site at fbi.gov/wanted/wanted_by_the_fbi contains numerous lists to search, including kidnappings, missing persons, unknown bank robbers, and others.

Drug Enforcement Administration (DEA)

Search DEA fugitives at justice.gov/dea/fugitives.shtml by major metro areas. Also, major international fugitives and captured fugitives are found here.

Labor Department: Labor and Labor Unions

The Office of Labor-Management Standards (OLMS) in the U.S. Department of Labor is the Federal agency responsible for administering and enforcing most provisions of the Labor-Management Reporting and Disclosure Act of 1959, as amended (LMRDA). OLMS does not have jurisdiction over unions representing solely state, county, or municipal employees. OLMS responsibilities include:

- Public Disclosure of Reports
- Compliance Audits
- Investigations
- Education and Compliance Assistance

The OLMS Internet Public Disclosure Room web page enables users to view and print reports filed by unions, union officers and employees, employers, and labor relations consultants. See dol.gov/olms/regs/compliance/rrlo/lmrda.htm

Occupational Safety & Health Administration (OSHA)

The purpose of the Occupational Safety & Health Administration (OSHA) is to insure employee safety and health in the U.S. by setting and enforcing standards in the workplace. OSHA partners with the states for inspections and enforcements, along with education programs, technical assistance and consultation programs.

There are a number of searchable databases at OSHA (https://www.osha.gov). For example, search by establishment name for information on over 3 million inspections conducted since 1972 at see https://www.osha.gov/oshstats/index.html. You can also search by the North American Industry Classification Code (NAIC) or the Standard Industrial Classification Code (SIC).

Another useful search is of the Accident Investigation database at https://www.osha.gov/pls/imis/accidentsearch.html. This database contains abstracts dating back to 1984 and injury data dating back to 1972.

State Department

ITAR Debarred List

A list compiled by the State Department of parties who are barred by the International Traffic in Arms Regulations (ITAR) (22 CFR §127.7) from participating directly or indirectly in the export of defense articles, including technical data or in the furnishing of defense services for which a license or approval is required, is found at pmddtc.state.gov/compliance/debar.html.

Nonproliferation Sanctions Lists

The State Department maintains lists of parties that that engage in proliferation activities and have been sanctioned under various statutes and legal authority. See state.gov/t/isn/c15231.htm.

Treasury Department

Specifically Designated Nationals (SDN) List

The U.S. Department of the Treasury, Office of Foreign Assets Control (OFAC) publishes a list of individuals and companies owned or controlled by, or acting for or on behalf of, targeted foreign countries, terrorists, international narcotics traffickers, and those engaged in activities related to the proliferation of weapons of mass destruction.

See treasury.gov/resource-center/sanctions/SDN-List/Pages/default.aspx.

Federal Contractor & Vendor Eligibility Sites

An avenue of public record data sometimes overlooked is the licensing of individual and businesses to do business for the U.S. government. Below are two resources from this agency.

1. Central Contractor Registration (CCR)

The Central Contractor Registration (CCR) registers all companies and individuals that sell services and products to, or apply for assistance from, the federal government. The 450,000+ registrants at CRR are searchable online using a DUNS number, company name, or other criteria.

CCR is now provided by the System for Award Management (SAM), which is combining federal procurement systems and the Catalog of Federal Domestic Assistance into one new system. See https://www.sam.gov/portal/public/SAM.

2. Online Representations and Certifications Application (ORCA)

The ORCA system allows contractors to enter company data regarding certification needed on federal contracts. This is a publicly accessible database, but it does require the subject's DUNS number.

ORCA is provided by the System for Award Management (SAM) as described above.

More on OFAC

Office of Foreign Assets Control (OFAC), U.S. (<u>treasury.gov/about/organizational-structure/offices/Pages/Office-of-Foreign-Assets-Control.aspx</u>)

OFAC, and its predecessor, the Office of Foreign Funds Control, have been around since World War 2 following the German invasion of Norway in 1940. The enforcement list as developed by U.S. Department of Treasury consists of individuals and organizations that are suspected of being connected with terrorist and organized crime activities. The screen shot below is from OFAC.

More on Law Enforcement Resources and Most Wanted Lists

Law enforcement agencies usually display a wanted list on a Web site, in press releases, or on wanted tear sheets. Many applicable federal agencies and international bodies (and state law enforcement agencies) have a Web site with a most wanted list. The more popular agencies are listed below.

- U.S. Federal Bureau of Investigation (<u>fbi.gov/wanted.htm</u>)
- U.S. Bureau of Alcohol, Tobacco, Firearms and Explosives (<u>atf.gov/content/ATF-most-wanted</u>)
- U.S. Drug Enforcement Administration (<u>usdoj.gov/dea/fugitives/fuglist.htm</u>)

Note: The next section examines selected foreign list locations. Check Chapter 13 for a composite list of key foreign regulatory bodies and law enforcement entities.

United Nations Security Council Committee

The United Nations Security Council (UNSC) decides which countries and organizations to sanction. Sanctioning these entities indicates that a company is blacklisted. An embargo can be imposed because of the subject's involvement with known terrorists. The embargo prohibits any future arms deals, technical training, or technology transference. (See un.org/sc/committees)

The UNSC Resolutions can be viewed per resolution in PDF format. All countries tied to the UNSC follow this list, a good place to begin. The following country-sanction committees (not a complete list) also abide by the UNSC resolutions

- Hong Kong Monetary Authority
- Commission de Surveillance du Secteur Financier, Luxembourg
- De Nederlandsche Bank, Netherlands
- Department of Foreign Affairs and Trade, Australia
- Monetary Authority of Singapore
- Office of the Superintendent of Financial Institutions, Canada
- Reserve Bank of Australia

England - HM Treasury

The HM Treasury lists include those persons whose assets have been frozen in the U.K. The lists of sanctioned persons and organizations are in downloadable format and can be viewed online. A list of investment ban targets designated by the European Union under legislation relating to current financial sanctions regimes is available. See https://gov.uk/government/publications/financial-sanctions-consolidated-list-of-targets.

European Union Financial Sanctions

The European Union (EU) Financial Sanctions list includes the European Banking Federation, the European Savings Banks Group, the European Association of Cooperative Banks, and the European Association of Public Banks (the EU Credit Sector Federations). See eeas.europa.eu/cfsp/sanctions/consol-list/index_en.htm.

Databases Specializing in International Searches

Several services are available for a fee. One is Thomson Reuters Accelus which combined rivals Complinet and WorldChek into one global risk source. Another service is from LexisNexis WorldCompliance, which has been available for many years. The risk coverage they monitor is on specific individuals, essentially making a global criminal record database. Topics covered:

- Arms Trafficking & WMD
- Drug Trafficking

- Enforcement
- Fraud
- Global Sanction List
- Money Laundering
- Politically Exposed People
- Terrorism
- Wanted Individuals

Social Media Sites, Non-Official but Often Telling

Social media sites are often a great place to begin looking for any regulatory, statutory or illegal activity. Believe it or not, there are criminals who claim to have stolen money, raped innocent people or have used illegal drugs and even having murdered people and blatantly flaunt it on their social media profile.

Twitter Gone Terribly Wrong

During a training session with the California Highway Patrol (aka CHIPS) in San Diego on Advanced Internet Investigations Techniques, the most unlikely image came up. While we were looking at Twitter, the class searched for the keywords, CHIPS + hiring. Instantly we were treated to a post by a young woman who wrote, "Thank god for weed! Just left the 4th interview for the CHIPS hiring process, man I'm stressed out." She then proceeds to post pictures of herself smoking what appeared to be a marijuana cigarette while driving.

I suspect she did not get the job.

In Summary

While the value of litigation research and compliance review is paramount to your work as an investigator, risk-based due diligence requires a deeper level of review and scrutiny regarding regulatory and enforcement activity. Risk-based due diligence also means staying abreast of the various resources and services reviewed in this chapter because these products and associated laws do change. The task of keeping up with these changes is part of what defines the professionalism found in quality due diligence investigators.

Ch 7:

Asset and Lien Searching

*If a rich man is proud of his wealth, he should not be
praised until it is known how he employs it.*

—Socrates

Online due diligence is especially useful for asset investigations, helping the investigator to locate and then determine the value of a person, a company, possessions, or an event. Whether a law suit is about to be filed, a company is being considered for purchase, or a judgment needs to be collected, online investigative due diligence plays an important role in revealing where those assets and liens may be, and what, if any, value can be assessed.

An asset is anything of economic value. The International Accounting Standards Board (ifrs.org) defines an asset as:

"…a resource controlled by the enterprise as a result of past events and from which future economic benefits are expected to flow to the enterprise."

Locating the assets of a business can be quite complicated because assets can be held in a variety of formats. Some assets are out in the **open**, easily found in public records. Some assets are **intangible**, lacking a physical presence, and may prove difficult to determine a value. Some assets are **hidden**, cleverly intentional to disguise wealth, or difficult to find due to government financial protection laws.

Finding liens is an important part of a business asset search. To an investigator, assets and liens often go hand-in-hand since either display wealth, or lack of it. Liens are usually recorded as public record, and as any investigator knows, finding liens will lead to finding assets, or to other liens which could lead to other assets.

This chapter will examine the reasons why a business asset search is performed, where to look for assets and liens, some searching techniques to use, and some first-hand applications of a search.

Six Reasons for a Business Asset Search

Before launching an asset search, find out why your client wants the search performed. Knowing the specific intent of the search will help focus the investigation, will keep you on target to find what you are looking for, and will insure you perform your investigation in a legal manner.

Here are six reasons why a business asset search might be performed:

1. Pre-assess Before Filing a Lawsuit

Suppose a client of yours has not paid you for your services. Prior to filing a lawsuit against the offending client to recover money owed, you need to research and locate the party's assets. If an asset search reveals the debtor has nothing of real value, or has run out of funds and can no longer sustain his own business, it is likely that the outstanding debt may never be collected. You want to know early on if filing a lawsuit against the debtor is worthwhile or a waste of everyone's time – if there are no assets to be had, then there is no point to filing a lawsuit to gain them.

Beware when conducting an asset investigation prior to a lawsuit, the Gramm, Leach, Bliley Act[23] and the Fair Credit Reporting Act[24] can restrict the investigator, because in some cases he cannot obtain credit histories, bank statements, or financial reports without the authorization of the party or debtor.

2. Collecting on a Judgment

Finding assets of a debtor party will require an asset search. If a judgment from a lawsuit has been issued, the creditor may place a lien on the assets identified in the lawsuit or, preferably, collect on the judgment.

Even lawsuits can have liens placed on them. For example, a physician can place a lien on a pending lawsuit that involves an injury to his client. If a carpenter is hurt while working on the job and sees a doctor, but the carpenter does not have the insurance or funds to pay the doctor, then the doctor can place a lien on the carpenter's pending injury lawsuit against his employer. When the case closes and the money is awarded, the attorney is paid first, the physician second, and the injured carpenter last.

3. Locating a Project's Funding Party or Mysterious New Investor

Tracking down the silent partner in a business deal, or the money behind the mission, or the true owner of a company will each require an asset search.

Who are silent partners? They can be the lead investor in the company, or a family member funding a relative's seemingly-smart business idea, or large hedge fund investors, or private money from foreign investors, or fronts for shell companies.

---

[23] See ftc.gov/privacy/glbact/glbsub1.htm

[24] A copy of the Fair Credit Reporting Act can be located on the Federal Trade Commission Web site at ftc.gov/os/statutes/031224fcra.pdf

4. Finding Prior Ownership

There are different kinds of prior ownership that would require an asset search, property, historical property, and products among them.

Purchasing property from another party will require an asset search of prior ownership for liens against the property, to insure bad debt isn't being bought.

Or perhaps a company has purchased property and wants to make sure the land is clean, has no toxic waste sites on its land – for the Environmental Protection Agency (EPA) requires the current landowner pick up the tab for such a clean-up; millions of dollars in unanticipated costs for the purchasing company. And so the purchasing company will conduct a geographic survey of the property before the sale, to discover if the land is clean, or to discover where to send the clean-up bill if the land is not clean.

Asset searches can also be performed on products – especially old products. Perhaps a workman's tool fails in performance and results in an injury. In order to file a lawsuit, an investigator will need to perform an asset search to locate the manufacturer of the failed tool.

5. Employment Purposes

A company may want to tie an asset search into its pre-employment screening of applicants destined for key positions in upper management. If a company is going to place a high level of fiscal responsibility on a new hire, the company want to be sure that new hire is financially secure. An individual's financial history can be an indicator of his fiscal responsibility. Indicators of a troubled worker will appear in a credit report, as collection-agency notices, bankruptcies, and severely late payments to vendors.

6. Investment Opportunity or New Business Venture.

When an entity is considering a business relationship with another entity, it is prudent to establish the strengths of that particular company or individual. Researching and assessing a corporation's financial strength is not much different from an individual's financial check. Corporate financial reports are published by D&B and Experian. They offer their own indicators as to a corporation's financial strength, based on the payment history submitted by vendors, annual sales and revenue reported, and risk indicators determined by the industry.

Investigating the financial strength of a company can be quantified by a **SWOT Analysis** (see Chapter3). **Strength, weakness, opportunity,** and **threat** are the indicators devised by observing and analyzing how a company fairs by itself, in its market, and in comparison to similar companies.

For example a shoe manufacturer may demonstrate *strength* (particularly in cash flow) because of paying vendor invoices within 30 days, opposed to 120 days. A *weakness* can be noted if a company reports only $1.2 million in sales, when other shoe manufacturers of similar size are reporting $4 million and more. But if the end product is good, there is ***opportunity*** of acquisition. In other words, the company has the talent in place, but is not reaching the channels and market to the fullest extent. Finally, a ***threat*** can be seen if the shoe manufacturer has filed for bankruptcy, has been delisted, or has demonstrated poor financial health, such as extended credit problems.

When looking for the money behind a person or a company, start with a public records search. Researching properties, liens, automobiles, and other such tangible goods will help create a financial profile of the person. If an individual is deliberately hiding property from either the government, as in a lien, or from a potential lawsuit, he will often register the deed in someone else's name.

Liens and Security Interests

Before examining the different asset categories and searching techniques, let's review the types of liens that are researched in a business background investigation.

With or Without Consent

Liens are secured on assets either by choice or not by choice. Examples of liens placed with the consent of the asset holder include mortgages or loans on balance sheet items such as equipment or accounts receivable. Liens placed without the consent of an asset holder include tax liens, mechanic's liens, and liens filed on assets as the result of judgments issued by courts.

Uniform Commercial Code (UCC) Filings

Uniform Commercial Code (UCC) filings are referenced a good deal in this chapter because a UCC is essentially a statement of business ownership of possessions. A UCC is a document that cites a business loan. That loan could be for new equipment, new property, or the acquisition of other assets. The filing will state the debtor, the creditor, the contact information, and what has been placed as collateral. Examples are computers and machinery, communication systems, air compressors and conditioners, and even non-tangible goods.

A UCC recording allows potential lenders to be notified that certain assets of a debtor are already used to secure a loan or lease. Therefore, examining UCC filings is an excellent way to find bank accounts, security interests, financiers, and other similar assets.

Where to Find Old UCC Filings

A significant change in UCC filing took effect in July 2001. Prior to that date UCC documents were recorded one one of 4,200+ recording locations such as centralized state agency or at a local recording office.

Revised Article 9 of the Code mandated effective July 2001 that all UCC documents were to be filed and recorded at a state level agency, with the exception of real estate filings such as farm-related real estate which still can be filled.

However, there was a caveat – any existing UCC filings if previously filed locally could be renewed or extended at the local level, instead of being renewed at the state level.

Although there are significant variations among state statutes, the state level is now the best starting place to uncover UCC liens filed against an individual or business, but it is not the only place to search. Strict due diligence may require a local search also, depending on the state.

Non-Consensual Liens

Judgments

If a business fails to pay an attorney, a contractor, an engineer, etc., these parties have a right to file suit in court against the business. If the court finds in favor of the plaintiff, a judgment is issued. These judgments are generally found in the state court system at the county level, and liens will be recorded against assets (if any) of the defendant.

Federal and State Tax Liens

Another typical non-consensual lien is one placed by a government agency for non-payment of taxes. The lines could be triggered by non-payment of income tax, sales tax, or even property tax, depending on the jurisdiction.

Essentially there are 4 categories: federal tax liens on businesses, federal tax liens on individuals, state tax liens on businesses, and state tax liens on individuals. Normally – but not always – the state agency that maintains UCC records also maintains tax liens on businesses. Tax liens filed against individuals are frequently maintained at separate locations from those liens filed against businesses. For example, a number of states require liens filed against businesses to be filed at a central state location (i.e., Secretary of State's office) and liens against individuals to be filed at the county level (i.e., Recorder, or Register of Deeds, or Clerk of Court, etc.). Typically, tax liens on real property will be found where real property deeds are recorded, with few exceptions.

Unsatisfied state and federal tax liens may be renewed if prescribed by individual state statutes. However, once satisfied, the time the record will remain in the repository before removal varies by jurisdiction.

More on Investigating Liens

Do not be surprised if a search for liens and UCCs turns up an odd, tax lien in a state where your subject company is not located. A big company based in New York City might show a tax lien in Utah. This fact should be followed up by more research, because it could mean there is a second , unknown location for that company.

If a lien has been placed by a private authority, and not a federal or state tax entity, then there may be a collection issue. For example, the creditor party wins in lawsuit, but now has to wait for payment. So the business assets, personal home, property, or vehicles may be named in the judgment. Investigators will use these judgments, UCCs, and lien notices to help identify assets that are being outlined in the filings. Collecting on judgments is a unique talent that combines legal know-how with investigative ability. The judgment collector is well versed in the state laws and understands the involved ramifications. One such association, the California Association of Judgment Collectors (cajp.org), provides beginners with continuing-education training on judgment collection.

Types of Assets Held by a Business

As mentioned, an asset can be **liquid** (cash or easily converted to cash), **intangible** (hard to find or evaluate), or **hidden** (tucked way so no one can find them). Typical assets controlled by a business include—

- **Real Property**
- **Personal Property**
- **Investments and Trusts (Financial Assets)**
- **Intellectual Property**
- **Subsidiaries and Spin-offs**

We will examine each asset type and gives examples on how to search and investigate.

Real Property

Real property refers to real estate. For many individuals, the first sign of wealth is taking on incredible debt, like a mortgage. In most instances, a family owns at least one home and maybe more. There are plenty of baby boomers with extensive investment money who have purchased summer homes, investment properties, or second homes for their extended families. They may also own undeveloped property, farmland, or open-space land

Businesses also own property, manufacturing plants, and office spaces. They may use all or part of the property for themselves, or rent several floors to other interests.

Where to Search

Researching these property deeds or assessment records is easy with the right sources. Property records are recorded and maintained by the county or parish or city in which that property resides. These local county[25] records are open to the public. Most of the populous counties usually found on the Internet through a variety of free and fee sources. Once again, the Web page at brbpublications.com is a good starting place to locate county-by-county records. On the fee side, search LexisNexis, Westlaw, Accurint, IRBsearch, LocatePlus, and ChoicePoint.

A key point here is there are many counties that do not share these public records online. These counties may maintain their records in an electronic index and have decided not to supply online service, or the records may be maintained in card files or microfiche. When this instance occurs, contact the county recorder's office and ask about the cost and turnaround time for a search within that county, or hire a local record retriever for an on-site search.

Finding a Stalker via Property Records

Although not directly related to business investigation, I received a call one afternoon from a concerned investigator in Washington. Apparently, her new client was being stalked by someone who had an inordinate amount of information on her, including the client's nursing-school schedule, her visits to the library and her interests in kayaking and water sports. In fact, the stalker knew about her family's summer lodge deep in the mountains of Washington. He even went so far as to email her, saying that he would "love to visit you next time you and your brother go away to the lodge;" and then he gave the lodge's address.

Talk about frightening! The investigator hired me to trace the email and to coordinate with law enforcement on the technical issues. In the due course of the investigation, I located the vacation- property record. But a database search was not available online. Hence, the stalker knew about the property either from hearsay or by following her.

The stalker was eventually identified and it was learned he obtained the lodge's address by simply following her. And for the curious, he was also a nursing student. When I tracked the emails, I found that he was sending them to her from the same campus she attended.

---

[25] There are over 3,600 locations in the U.S. where property records can be recorded. When referring to county-level recorder, the author is also including reference to parish, city, and town locations where documents can be recorded.

Personal Property

This category includes transportation vehicles, and business equipment such as computer and machinery. Personal assets are classified as personal property. Big companies will own some or all of these assets.

Motor Vehicles and Vessels

The company car takes you to the company jet, and then you are flown to the company yacht for an important meeting. The company car might be something as simple as a fleet of work vans for a local contractor, or as imposing as limousines with their own dedicated drivers. Of course not every company will own an airplane but it certainly should be checked. There is also the possibility that a company may not own its own airplane, but may participate in fractional jet service. And small-business men may own vessels such as luxury, weekend crafts or imposing yachts.

Motor vehicle searches usually depend on which state you are searching. Motor vehicle records that contain personal information, like an address or physical characteristics are not public record. However and as covered in a previous chapter, if you have permissible purpose, and if the state chooses to accept all provisions of the Driver's Privacy Protection Act (DPPA)[26], you can look up title and registration records. For example, a look-up by plate number will give current owner information, or doing a name search can lead to vehicles registered or titled under that name. A permissible purpose includes enforcement of a judgment, an existing court case, or an investigation involving anticipated litigation. Of course it is up to the individual state to decide to adopt these allowable permissible uses.

You will find that many of the state agencies that oversee vehicle records also oversee vessel records, so the same DPPA restrictions apply. However, a number of states have a different agency regulate and hold vessel records. These agencies usually oversee wildlife and outdoor activities, including the issuance of hunting and fishing licenses. The good news for investigators is that many of these agencies do not follow DPPA and records may be open. An excellent reference book to find which states consider vessel records open is *The MVR Access and Decoder Digest* (see MVRDecoder.com).

Many of the state agencies that oversee vehicle records offer online access to record indices and sometime even to record images. Generally a subscription is required. This is a good way to find records for current and historical automobiles and vessels. If you do not see any cars registered to the individual, check the spouse's, or child's name.

---

[26] *Prohibition On Release And Use Of Certain Personal Information From State Motor Vehicle Records* is located at gpo.gov/fdsys/granule/USCODE-2011-title18/USCODE-2011-title18-partI-chap123-sec2721/content-detail.html

A great search technique that potentially offers more leads to assets is to conduct the search offline. Send a surveillance investigator to the home and workplace of the individual you are searching, or to the subject company's location, to see if there is a car or a fleet of vehicles. You can look up the plate numbers by state and get the owner's information as described above. In this way, if the individual has registered the vehicle under another name, or company name, this new lead may be the avenue to follow for other assets.

Vessels and watercraft that weigh more than five tons are registered with the U.S. Coast Guard, see st.nmfs.noaa.gov/st1/CoastGuard. Another handy location to search for larger vessels, or to search by lien or title, is the Coast Guard's National Vessel Documentation Center, found at uscg.mil/hq/cg5/nvdc.

For the very wealthy, if you are searching for yachts or luxury liners, it is very possible that the vessels have been registered in a foreign country, such as Bermuda. When checking for these large vessels as floating corporations, scan the business databases by the boat name. Also, search the Web with the boat name and any other indicators that you may have. It is possible that the company is selling or buying the boat, and is showing off photos of it online, with all of its statistics.

Finally, the vessel may be named in a UCC filing, and will have an insurance policy. Make sure to obtain all the UCC records for the company and individual.

Aircraft

The International Civil Aviation Organization (icao.int) maintains aircraft registration standards for participating countries. Each aircraft (over a certain weight) must be registered with a national aviation registration number. Different countries have different registration schemes. For example, the U.S. uses an N followed by 1 to 5 additional characters.

The following text about searching aircraft is an excerpt from *The Manual to Online Records* (2013) by Facts on Demand Press.

Government Record Sources

Besides regulations and policies, the Federal Aviation Administration (FAA) site at faa.gov provides a myriad of data about aircraft including registration and ownership, airports, air traffic, training and testing. The FAA site is the also the main government information center regarding certification for pilots and airmen. One may find current flight delay information nationwide and accident incident data here at the site.

The Federal National Transportation Safety Board (NTSB) maintains an aviation accident database from 1962 forward about civil aviation accidents and selected incidents within the U.S., its territories and possessions, and in international waters. Six different queries are available. Preliminary reports are posted within days; final reports may take months before posted. Some information prior to 1993 is sketchy. See ntsb.gov/aviationquery/index.aspx.

See   wwwapps2.tc.gc.ca/saf-sec-sur/2/CCARCS/aspscripts/en/menu.asp   for   the Canadian government site to search Canadian Civil Aircraft Register and aircraft information [Editor's note: wwwapps2 above is not a typo.]

For information of foreign countries, the International Civil Aviation Organization (icao.int) maintains aircraft registration standards for participating countries.

Private Record Sources

Leading private information resource centers for searching hundreds of indexed categories including news, reference data, flights, pilot certifications, and regulatory overviews include these sites:

- Landings.com is an excellent news and overall reference resource.
- Jane's   Transportation   News   and   Reference   site   at ihs.com/products/janes/transport/index.aspx is well known for its aviation related content. IHS, a global information supplier, acquired Jane's Information Group in June 2007.
- ARGUS International services include charter operator ratings and due diligence program, market intelligence data and research services, and aviation consulting. See aviationresearch.com.

———

Computers and Machinery

Several assets may be overlooked because they seem like everyday objects, such as computers or construction or farm equipment. However, like automobiles these are assets of value, depending on their depreciation and age.

Uniform Commercial Code filings (UCCs) will often list the major assets of a company because they are used as security for loans. Each state has a division of its Secretary of State office that handles UCC records, and records or at least the index can be searched directly from that agency's Web page. Finding these sites is easy using the public record database sources already mentioned. A list of free searchable state sites for finding UCC filings is in Chapter 12.

Also, there are excellent public record vendor Web-site services like knowx.com, TracersInfo.com,and TLO.com handy for viewing UCC filings.

Financial Investments and Trusts

Financial assets are stocks, international stocks, currencies and commodities, bonds, and mutual funds. These financial assets are often considered the *golden egg* since they are can be more valuable than physical assets like cars or machinery. If you are judgment searching, use some of your database sources and if necessary legal process (process serving) to find bank accounts and 401K plans. However without a judgment in hand, there is little in the way beyond gum shoe tactics to finding these accounts. Depending on the state and city laws, trash pickups are still a viable way to find bank accounts. One hint I can offer is to pick up garbage when companies' boards are meeting and approving quarterly reports. These voluminous printed quarterlies usually get thrown out in whole. However this is not the method of choice, and privacy laws are tightening up even on trash runs. The following technical approaches make it easier, if not cleaner, to locate assets.

Searching for Investments and Other Financial Assets

If you own more than five percent of a stock, it is public record and can be searched in Nexis and through SEC filings. However, most individuals own less than fiver percent of a company. One aspect to locating investments is to search legal filings. If the individual filed for a divorce, the assets listed in the divorce decree will offer a page-by-page account of all assets, including 401K retirement plans, stock options, and other key investment information. Trusts can be located by address. Search the individual's home address in a public-record database, and if trust accounts are registered to that location, you will see them. Without legal process, nothing further can be obtained about them other than an indication of assets being stored under the trust.

Another trust finder is D&B. Searching the free side of D&B is quite effective in tracking trusts under family names.

There are some excellent **industry news resources** that are incredible sources for venture capital and private equity research and alerts. These resources are on the high end of quality and offerings. Their subscription prices match the information they give allowing you to search by investor, find company reports, and help you understand what the status of funding is within a company.

- VentureSource, by Dow Jones, covers news in the venture-capital market for the US, and is a subscription service. venturesource.com

- Thomson Financial focuses on Canadian capital markets with its VCReporter service; found at thomsonone.com.

- Another great, but expensive, source is Standard & Poor's Capital IQ. Capital IQ offers almost 10,000 profiles on private, capital firms worldwide. Information on companies, co-investors, individuals' biographies, and corporate portfolios can be found here. See capitaliq.com.

- Mergermarket Ltd., owned by the *Financial Times*, offers intelligence, reporting, tracking, and alerting for any merger moves or equity shifts. See mergermarket.com.

- To keep abreast of these markets without spending the entire database budget on one service, go to edgar-online.com, secinfo.com, or sec.gov.

If you are involved in a judgment collections case, there are additional sources available like MicroBilt's eFunds Debit Report Collections (microbilt.com/efunds_debit.asp).

A sample report is shown below.

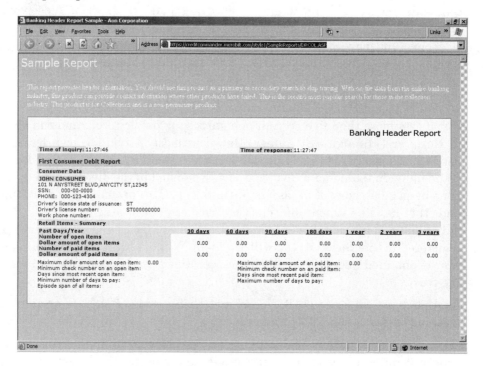

(Source: https://creditcommander.microbilt.com/style1/SampleReports/DRCOL.ASP)

Intellectual Property

If an investigator only focuses on cash in hand or capital investments, there is a significant area that gets missed. These are untenable assets referred to as **intellectual property**.

While flying back to Newark, New Jersey from Southern California, where I had spent some quality time training members of the California District Attorneys Association (CDAA), I reflected on what had transpired. The training was the conclusion of a three-day continuing education for prosecutors, paralegals, police officers, and detectives. The topic was asset forfeiture. If the topic had been about breaching, accident reconstruction, or weapons tactics, I would not have been invited as the closing-session speaker.

These CDAA professionals track down the finances of fraudulent individuals and their companies which can include drug traffickers, corporate raiders, and terrorists. The audience was a unique mix, from tattooed, sunglasses-wearing, thuggish-looking narc officers to librarian-looking soccer moms. Appearances, notwithstanding, they did have a keen sense of looking under mattresses or into family member accounts and other likely or unlikely places to track the assets of their subjects.

This audience also was equipped with resources not available to private investigators, such as access to a district attorney's office, the support of a full legal team, Experian credit reports, and subpoena power. With compliance of the Fair Credit Reporting Act in mind, private detectives spend hours agonizing over creating solutions to obtain credit information, bank reports, and financial details.

Searching for Intellectual Property

Imagine your target is the focus of an asset check for a divorce or pre-judgment claim. He has a house, a car, and a moderate income as a software developer with a small research firm, and a very modest 401K retirement plan in place. That is a pretty dry asset list, but it is not uncommon. Most individuals do not hoard stashes of cash in the Cayman Islands or secretly warehouse garages full of vintage cars in Dubai.

The key phrase above is software developer. The subject may be attached to patents for software, or ideas, registered in the U.S. This intangible asset maybe more valuable than a shipping yard full of Mercedes-Benz vehicles. This asset could be the next operating system idea for YouTube or a security patch for the destructive program Trojan horse. Your subject could be the next Bill Gates, and you are summing up your report with his most valuable asset equaling a 2004 Ford Taurus.

If your investigation is focused on identified new opportunities for a client, using intellectual property is a great way start an investigation track. Serious investors, market leaders, and competitive intelligence professionals are aware of the edge that is created by getting the right information first. Researchers who specialize in certain markets subscribe to patent-alert services that keep them posted on new developments and patent applications from particular companies in certain sciences and fields. Nefarious individuals wishing to launder money look for good investments, perhaps by putting their trafficked money into something that results in laundered money with a profit.

Sources for Finding Intellectual Property

The **United States Patent and Trademark Office** uspto.gov/main/patents.htm is the ultimate source. If you can spend some time learning to correctly search within the Web site, you will get the best results. Remember, when you are searching for a company, refer to it as assignee. Separately, search the assignee or the town, if small or unique, (skip New York and Los Angeles), and search for the inventor by last name. Other reliable sources include—

- freepatentsonline.com – Indexes the full page, but does not give the full results.

- google.com/patents – Does not index the full page.

If you specialize in patent research, work with an attorney who specializes in intellectual property or visit uspto.gov on a regular basis. Also, it pays to work with the professional tools, such as Thomson Derwent, that can be accessed through Proquest Dialog products. Derwent is well known amongst patent researchers as the go to source, according to the Proquest site:

> "ProQuest Dialog further leads the industry with the largest collection of prior art available in a single, integrated resource – optimizing patent and non-patent literature research with scientific, technical, and medical databases, full-text dissertations, global news, and trade press."[27]

Trademarks and Marks

A trademark, a type of intellectual property, typically comprises a name, word, phrase, logo, symbol, design, image, or a combination of these elements. It is used by an individual, business organization, or other legal entity to uniquely identify the source of its products and/or services to consumers, and to distinguish its products and/or services from those of other entities.

Simply put, if it is original, distinctive, and something you think others may value, then register it as a trademark.

One notable case of trademark infringement was the iPhone debacle. Years ago, CISCO registered the term iPhone. Later, Apple began naming its products that started with an "i." Its newest creation is the iPhone. This prompted trademark infringement lawsuits between CISCO and Apple, since CISCO owned the term first. Obviously, the lawsuits were resolved, but the story illustrates the important point of placing a trade mark your products and services.

Even more unusual was Harley-Davidson's bid to trademark the unique roar made by its motorcycle mufflers—

> THE MARK CONSISTS OF THE EXHAUST SOUND OF APPLICANT'S MOTORCYCLES, PRODUCED BY V-TWIN, COMMON CRANKPIN MOTORCYCLE ENGINES WHEN THE GOODS ARE IN USE.

Harley-Davidson Trademark Registration, U.S. Patent & Trademark Office, February 1, 1994.[28]

Since trademarks are a distinct form of intellectual property, you can visit the same Web sites and sources as patent searching.

---

[27] proquest.com/products-services/ProQuest-Dialog-Patents-Collection.html
[28] lectlaw.com/files/inp14.htm

Foreign Research for Patents, Trademarks and Other Intellectual Assets

Foreign research can be done country by country as well. The **World Intellectual Property Organization** (wipo.int) is one organization that oversees patent laws, litigation, and intellectual-property issues.

Also, to check European patents, visit the **European Patent Office** (EPO) Web sites at worldwide.espacenet.com or epo.org. These sites offer some free searches and a subscriber-only section. Searches can be done in English, as well as the language of origin.

According to the EPO's Patent Information Centres Directory:

"What are PATLIB centres?

PATLIB stands for PATent LIBrary. The PATLIB centres were created to provide users with local access to patent information and related issues. The centres have qualified and experienced staff who offer practical assistance on a variety of Intellectual Property Rights (IPR).

Working in the language of the country concerned, they are familiar with the needs and requirements of local industry, agriculture and trade, and are able to provide valuable information services, especially to small and medium-sized enterprises, private inventors and academics.

As the number of PATLIB centres has grown, the range of services has been expanded to include, for example, trademarks, designs and copyright. Many of the centres have diversified still further to provide an even greater breadth and depth of services.

What is the PATLIB network?

A joint creation of the national patent offices of the EPO member states and their regional patent information centres, the PATLIB network is made up of patent information centres located throughout Europe. It was set up with the aim of improving communication and co-operation between individual centres and promoting patent information awareness and the provision of services to the public. There are currently more than 320 centres altogether, although this number is constantly growing."

Non-Conventional Marks and Ownership Identifications

There is also a range of non-conventional identifiers that, when examined, can lead to other forms of intellectual properties. Some of these non-conventional identifying marks are ISBN, UPC, and domain names.

Visit a U.S. Patent and Trademarks page at uspto.gov/main/profiles/otherid.htm. This informative page lists 36 identifiers. Many identifiers, like ZIP Codes, SSN, EIN, etc., are commonly used investigators. But there are some rather obscure identifiers that may be able to assist an investigation into assets. Some of these include:

- Bar Codes
- UPC – Universal product Codes (check out uc-council.org)
- ISBN - International Standard Book Number - for the publishing industry
- NAICS - North American Industry Classification Codes

Web Domains

Trademarks also can be searched in the form of Web domains. A big issue is using trademarked names as domain names. For example, I registered the domain name virtuallibrarian.com more than 15 years ago. Another librarian wrote me and said that I was violating her ownership of that domain name since she owned virtual-librarian.com. Neither of us had actually registered the trademark ownership or mark ownership with the upsto.gov. However, when I checked on who had registered the domain name first, I found that I had exceeded her by at least three months. When I emailed that fact to her, she backed off, knowing that I had first-use rights of "virtual librarian" as a domain name on the Internet, and thereby making the mark mine.

The Web site icann.org is the authority that oversees the disputes of domain name usage. There are many companies and individuals who have registered hundreds of key expressions, business names, or similar names to themselves, regardless of their actual needs or uses. These entities are called cyber-squatters. Like leeches on an organism, they squat on these domain names and hold them hostage until a company either disputes the issue with legal process, through the Internet Corporation for Assigned Names and Numbers (ICANN), or pays off the squatter. Considering that international cases can be very expensive, it is often cheaper to just pay off the squatter.

Copyright Issues

The U.S. Copyright Office, part of the Library of Congress, is the source for copyright ownership, publication, transfers and derivative works. Searches can be performed from the Copyright Office site at copyright.gov/records.

Generally, the reason to search copyright records is to find the current owner of a copyright. However, you can search to find if an older work is now in the public domain. Each of these reasons requires a search of different Copyright Office records.

To determine the copyright ownership of a work, search the catalog for records of registered books, music, art, and periodicals.

The Certificate of Registration indicates who originally registered the work. But just as important are Assignments which occur when copyright ownership is transferred.

Search copyright information
Works registered and documents recorded by the U.S. Copyright Office since January 1, 1978.

|| Online Records ||

Search the Catalog
Search records of registered books, music, art, and periodicals, and other works. Includes copyright ownership documents.

Search **Vessel Hull** registrations

About the Catalog

View Tutorial

|| Other Services ||

Find records prior to January 1, 1978

How to Register a Copyright

How to Record a Document

How to Get Copies of Copyright Office Records & Deposits

Search the Catalog of Copyright Entries

View Tutorial

(source: copyright.gov/records)

Subsidiaries and Spin-offs

Subsidiaries sometimes may be the most valuable part of a business. Imagine if a very successful company starts to see a troublesome market and needs to consider preserving for future investment opportunities. It spins off the assets as separate subsidiaries, and then lets them leave the corporate nest altogether, with the full intention of recouping these businesses at a later date.

Preposterous? No.

Consider that during the technology swing of the late 1990s, most "e" companies survived completely on venture capital, and did not generate revenue. They eventually folded and many individuals lost investment money, jobs, and interest in investing in technology stocks.

What happened to all that new technology? Did it just get left on the desktop? No, the intellectual property was moved to a subsidiary or spin-off company, and is probably in the technology we use today, e.g. Web 2.0.

Where to Search

Spin-offs and the creation of subsidiaries are newsworthy events that can be expensive and time consuming. They also can alter the legal and accounting lines of the parent company. But as the saying goes, any publicity is good publicity. When a subsidiary is created the parent company will generally send a press release through PR Newswire (prnewswire.com) or the Associated Press (ap.org) announcing the change.

Eventually corporate record database vendors, such as D&B and Hoover's, will recognize and document the new subsidiary within the family tree section of these reports. You can also look into *Who owns Whom*, and other corporate database sources to see who is recognized as the parent company, or ultimate parent.

Finally, if the company is a publicly traded they have to list their assets, including subsidiaries, in their in their quarterly and annual reports, files with the Securities and Exchange Commission (SEC.gov) in the EDGAR database.

How to Search for Hidden Assets

Using the Five W's

Locating hidden assets is important for fraud investigations, locating special interest monies (i.e. funding for organized crime and terrorism). Hiding assets from ex-spouses, business partners, debtors or others who are there to collect on open liens and judgments is common practice. The investigator's challenge in finding assets will take them through the five W's.

1. With Whom

Individuals will hide their money under aliases, or with relatives, friends, and partners.

2. Where

For cash accounts, which are nearly impossible to locate, funds could be stashed away in their home, or in a safe deposit box. Money can be kept in offshore and foreign accounts.

3. When Paid Ahead

Money could be reserved in overpayments to life insurance policy, credit cards, federal tax payments, or mortgage payments.

4. As What

Cash could be turned into expensive physical assets as such automobiles, boats, planes, jewelry, and art. The asset can then be relocated to a brother, spouse, friend or other party to hold onto while being investigated.

5. Why Not For a Rainy Day

Keeping cash liquid for easy access could result in money being found as traveler's checks, savings bonds, money markets, or checking accounts filed under a different Social Security number (a subsidiary corporate FEIN which is now defunct, or perhaps a child's SS #).

Use your creative thinking skills when looking for these assets; the following tips will help.

Search Tactics

Some tactics for tracking hidden properties when the address is unknown:

- Search under the spouse name.
- Search under the father, mother, or sibling name.
- Search under the business name.
- Search by trust name. (Usually the last name of the family)

Some tactics for tracking hidden properties when the address is known:

- Run the address and find the last owner. Contact that entity and request to see the sale documents. The attorney of note and purchaser should be two key pieces within that mountain of paperwork.
- Search the address in business databases. It can be an office location, and not a real home address.

For example, when I researched a senior executive, I found that all his mail went to his office. Searching deeper, I noticed that his residential address was the same as his office. Finally, it dawned on me that he owned the building, a high-rise structure with most floors dedicated to business and the penthouse floor devoted to him personally.

Another key point on searching properties is the interaction you will have with individuals while researching them. Several of the fee-based resources will flag suspicious addresses when they match business post offices (UPS Store/MailBoxes Etc.), prison addresses, campuses, or similar, shared locations.

Little used, but very effective, D&B allows you to run an address search. If the subject is running a fraudulent operation from any of those shared addresses, or actually has more than one business running out of his suite or office address, it will list all the businesses registered there. Other recommended sources for similar searches are the public-record databases mentioned earlier.

A Few Words on Other Assets

Assets are something that can be taken, possessed, sold and bartered over. But while you are investigating assets, keep in mind to look for a bigger picture – what the assets mean to the individual or the company. If you are not sure what I mean by this, walk into any old established bar and look above the cash register. You will most likely see the first currency that they received, framed and signed. That first dollar carries more emotional weight to the owner than the entire register to the owner. If it is still not clear, ask a woman who has been married for 30+ years what is her favorite piece of jewelry. She will most likely tell you about jewelry her children gave her, any anniversary or sentimental pieces, or her wedding ring.

Companies do not have the same sense of loyalty or emotion attached to the assets, unless the asset is their brand name or patented technology. In some cases, companies realize their greatest asset is in the intellectual capacity of their employees. Years ago, large firms like IBM used to refer to their employees as family and would never consider reducing staff in order to maintain profitability. Today, companies are now faced with foreign markets and improved technology from competitors. Holding onto a dinosaur staff is no longer an option. The expression family was changed to team. Which can be translated into ... you make the cut, or you don't. But the fact is, the team can still be a company asset.

The point of this is that **not all assets are material, or property based.** When researching a company, check the staff size and see if it has changed in the last few years. Massive hiring and firing will give an indicator as to the company strength and weakness. What you want to find is a steady stream of progressive growth, not erratic ups and downs. The rollercoaster rides can be indicators of market trouble, poor management and leadership that you can factor into your investigation.

Assets come in many facets, property, intellectual property, human capital and in financial vehicles. Keep your mind open when searching for anything of value; you will be surprised what is considered valuable and where it can be hidden.

Six Examples of Business Asset Searching

1. Pre-assess Before Filing a Lawsuit

Looking for assets can be a costly endeavor for clients, depending on how hidden they may be. This story tells one way to find assets prior to filing a lawsuit.

The Video Store

I received a call one Friday afternoon from a longtime client for whom I had performed quite a bit of due diligence in the past. He was fuming mad about a renter of his who leased about 10,000 square feet of mini-mall space for a video business. Apparently the renter was behind three months' rent, which was unusual because he normally paid on time. When my client would call the renter, he would be continually put off by someone in the store, saying that the owner was not available.

The client was planning to hire his attorney to draft a letter threatening a lawsuit if the rent was not made up in short notice. Feeling bold I told the client not only would I be able to recover the unpaid rent, but would do so for less cost than the attorney's fees.

I began by running a D&B report. It appeared this small independent video store had been very successful with a steady stream of loyal customers for three years. His D&B showed increased revenues for the last two years, but there was a red flag in the vendor payments section, with an over 90-day payment history on several accounts. It was obvious that the landlord was not the only creditor not getting paid.

To determine if an event occurred three months prior that might have played a factor in the business problems, I searched local newspapers. I then found that a month prior to start of the payment problems a large video chain store opened a few blocks away and was attracting the community with special offers, fancy lights, more current movies always available, etc.

Figuring this explained why my client's tenant might be struggling, I visited the small video store and discovered some interesting facts per a discreet, casual chat with the clerk.

Me: "I see that new video chain moved in around the corner. Have you checked it out yet?"

Clerk: "Yea they opened a few months ago. I checked them out when they opened and they are awesome! They have video games as well as the recent videos."

Me: "No kidding. Maybe I should go there (laughs) but I like small shops, you get better customer service. But how are you guys staying alive with such a heavy competitor around the corner."

Clerk: "Just barely, this store will probably close when the boss gets back and we'll move our stuff over to his other store in [next town over]."

Me: "Oh good... you have another store [We didn't know this!]. Where is it, just in case I need to return these videos and I'm late?"

The clerk gave me the other store address, which I researched later.

Me: "When do you think you'll close, should I watch these tonight, will you be open tomorrow?" The clerk laughing told me that the boss would be back in two weeks after returning from India. He was there the entire summer; his father was dying and he was coping with his family overseas and his family in the US.

Returning to the office, I researched the second video store and found it was doing well and indeed owned by the same man. After reporting this news to my client, he took an interesting plan of attack. When the owner returned three weeks later, my client visited the store. The client showed surprise when the store owner told him about the death of his father, the long trip home, two families, two cultures, the competition moving in, and his mistake in using his nephew to manage the store while he was away. Since we had already provided this information, the client was prepared. So he smiled, told him he understood and gave him two months to make up the back payment of rent. There was no threat, no lawyers, no anger, just an understanding landlord who emphasized with family issues and competing markets. But he also did mention "Well you can always rely on your other store to carry you over during the hard times." This let the store owner know that our client did his research.

Within two months, our client collected all of his back rent. He even talked the store owner into relocating his shop to another building he also owned.

Not only did the client not have to sue, create judgments and liens on this fellow, costing him attorney fees and headaches, he maintained a valuable client relationship.

Unfortunately not all pre-searches result in happy endings. Most result in handing the claimant a list of assets and potential assets to be attached if they end up going to court.

2. Collecting on a Judgment

Once a judgment is put in place, it is up to the claimant to keep an eye on collection. There may be a judgment outstanding on an individual, but meanwhile the debtor may be acquiring extra property, cars, boats, and making investments. The claimant can sell the judgment to a judgment collector who has the legal right to attach the debtor's assets and go after them themselves. However, be careful for what you wish for. Assets do not always mean cold cash, but you could be leaving with physical assets.

Put Another Log on the Fire

Swapping stories one night with a group of judgment collectors, we were lamenting about the funniest, scariest and oddest things recovered. One judgment collector told a story regarding a visit with a fellow who owed about $5,000 on a judgment she was trying to collect. She met him on his property in northern California, an older log cabin in the back woods, and did not see anything of value. Figuring that collecting $5,000 from this fellow was as likely as getting water from a stone, she asked him his occupation. He mentioned landscaping, tree maintenance and selling wood during the winter months. She then realized his asset was wood, and the sale of wood. For her part, she lived in the same winter cold months and had a fireplace. So she told him; she would take his payment in wood split for her fireplace.

A week later a dump truck dropped 10 cords of wood on her driveway which recovered half of the payment owed.

3. Locating a Project's Funding Party or Mysterious New Investor

Sometimes an asset investigation involves trying to find the money guy or the idea guy of a new entity.

Who Are Those Guys?

A software company in a very specific transportation niche kept hearing buzz about a new competitor in the market. As the market-share leader, the software company was used to small competitors. But this new development firm seemed to have come out of nowhere and was quickly generating a lot of talk. The software company hired me to find out who was behind the mysterious new company.

I located the Web site for the new company and saw that it was partnering with other competitors, but it was not clear who was the owner. The corporate reports were all registered with the seemingly legitimate, new officers. Did the officers come from another industry and decide to create transportation software? Before I started looking deeper in the officers history, it dawned on me to check one other source.

Using the URL address of the competitor company, I visited Network Solutions at networksolutions.com, and ran the address through its WHOIS search. WHOIS gave me the registration information for the competitor's Web site. The Web site was registered to a former employee of my client's software company. My client immediately sent a cease-and-desist letter to the former employee, because the former employee was in violation of a signed non-compete clause.

The mysterious competition was a former employee re-creating my client's software. Checking the competition's asset – a Web site – led to the identity of the competitor. However, the real asset in the story was the intellectual property, and my task was to protect his software, which is his asset.

Small Companies, Big Ideas, and Borrowed Money

A common trait of new companies is trying to make themselves look bigger than they really are, to impress potential clients they are established and prepared to take on new business.

Establishing the facilities for a new business office requires space, supplies, marketing materials, staff sometimes, advertisements, and technology. In other words it requires money. A new company must rely on initial capital that usually comes from personal funds, private equity, and/or another company.

If you are asked to investigate a company, look for this situation. Sometimes these big companies are really just business fronts in rented, temporary offices and are not legitimate. If possible, visit the office to get a sense of how long the company has been at that location. The first thing to look for is the company's nameplate on the building directory.

Also, research the office address at google.com. Try searching for the address you have, 12 Main Street, New York City, to see if there are any matches to temporary offices, virtual offices, or by-the-hour offices.

Look at All Those Gold Albums!

A gentleman called me regarding a new investment he was considering with a musical production company. He had met the producers in their Manhattan office and was very impressed by the gold albums on the wall, their plush office, and the professional décor of the building. He thought they seemed legitimate, but wanted to conduct some basic due diligence on the producers before proceeding.

At the outset of my investigation, I searched online for the producers' business address and found that the suite used was a temporary office. Also, the phone and fax numbers went to an office-rental company, not the producers' office. I called their phone number and talked to a floor receptionist. When I asked about the producers, she said they were no longer renting. Then I asked how long they had rented the space, and she said it was for only one day, and they had been asked to leave because they had damaged the walls when they hung their gold albums.

The producers were part of a shell scam, set up for a day's worth of meetings to worm money out of unsuspecting investors.

Investigating this further, I contacted the furniture office-rental company and inquired about the producers' identities and their method of payment for the suite. Normally a company would be hesitant to share this information, but, in this case, was interested in legally pursuing the producers for damaging the walls. The suite was secured with a credit card, using the name of a woman who was not one of the producers. It became apparent that she was the sister of one of the likely producers and was the money behind the scam. She and the producers were reported to the police for fraudulent behavior.

In following the money trail, there was obviously a lack of real funds behind the fraudulent producers, as the real money came from the sister's credit card. If this seems like an odd example, keep in mind that many companies set up shell corporations to hide their identities and their assets. They also set up companies with liabilities in mind. They may transfer assets or liabilities to a new company and then sell it.

4. Finding Prior Ownership

It is sometimes necessary to find a prior owner of an asset, especially when the current owner is facing certain liability claims.

> **The Smelter Search**
>
> Some time ago, my company client had moved into a plant situated in an urban area. Ten years later, the EPA inspected the grounds and declared the property a superfund site. My client was producing a non-toxic product. Historical research on the building showed that the original factory was used as a smelting factory. All the burn-off of the metals leeched into the ground and poisoned the ground water. The company hired me to locate the owners of the original plant.
>
> A deed search was straightforward enough to see who owned the property. But, the deed owners were companies that changed hands year after year, and the assets and liabilities were split. The original firm was Jersey Smelting from the 1860s. It was sold to a large, publicly traded firm that merged, split, and was bought and sold more than a half dozen times because the company kept shifting and growing.
>
> Two sources really were instrumental in the search for this company's ownership. Moody's Investor Services, found at the local library usually in microfilm, listed the company's assets within its reports on publicly traded companies, and considered property an asset. The other tool was the local newspapers. I spent many hours sitting in front of the microfiche and microfilm machines, spooling through issue after issue of newspapers for any mention of the building location, or any fires, events, sales, etc.
>
> Eventually I found a piece of information that clear up a fact the attorney had presumed as a truth. The attorney found a history book about manufacturers in that city in the mid-1800s. She quoted text stating Jersey Smelting was sold to Paterson Smelting. That lead sent the attorney on a day of tracking information from state archives. Nowhere could she find that a sale had occurred. And the article I found contradicted her version.
>
> In scanning the original newspapers, I discovered the book's author was incorrect in saying the company was sold. The newspaper stated that the Jersey Smelting factory was leased to Paterson Smelting, but not sold. Hence, the assets were still with Jersey Smelting until it merged with a completely different company, which later sold its smelting practice to a foreign corporation.

5. Employment Purposes

Investigating for employment purposes is not limited FCRA purposes. The investigation outlined below dealt with an employment issue.

> **Whom Do You Trust**
>
> A friend called to complain that his accountant had misfiled his last two years of employment taxes and that he now owed almost $10,000 dollars to the IRS. He was understandably and justified in being upset. I told him I would see what I could find on the accountant.
>
> In less than twenty minutes I called back to verify the spelling of his name. Correct in my spelling, I told my cheated friend that his accountant was not licensed in his state of practice. The state consumer affairs office did not have his name listed in their database and a phone call to their customer service elaborated that his license was revoked. When I asked for the cause the friendly representative stated, "Oh... felons can't obtain their license without going through a panel review first." Felons?! While I was on the phone with my friend, I did a name search on the Bureau of Prisons Web site (bop.gov). Sure enough there was a match. His accountant had been convicted on drug possession charges and served almost 12 months. Later I following up with media and located a story about an arrest of three men charged with possession and intent to sell cocaine within a school district.
>
> Unfortunately this did not get help with the IRS bill, but my unfortunate friend learned to vet the people he does business with, for no matter how polished they seem, they could be fraudulent.

6. Investment Opportunity or New Business Venture

When an entity is considering a business relationship with another entity or investor, it is prudent to research and assess establish the financial strengths of the other party.

> **Some Got It, Some Don't**
>
> A new client asked me to I vet out a potential investor. My client had been contacted via email by an overseas investor who had offered several million dollars to buy into a partnership with the client's company.
>
> My gut reaction was to tell him this was a spam email, a fishing expedition for anyone who would reply. But he was adamant that I take the case. There was limited information about the other party. The person making the offer was from Pakistan and supposedly was part of a multi-national

firm involved in petroleum, automobiles, technology and financial industries. The firm claimed to have almost 17,000 employees and 1.7 billion in revenue.

First, checking through Bureau van Dijk, Skyminder, D&B, and other databases, I could not locate the company. This immediately raised an alarm because any company of that size and profitability would have a credit history and business reports. Further research on the company name in the news did not reveal any matches. Finally using one of my Web resources, I found the company name appearing on a listing of known spammers.

Some ventures are real though. In the same week, I was hired to research the background of a small company interested in investing in a new venture my client was spinning off. He asked that I check the credentials of the potential investor, which I did. To my surprise the little venture company was a side practice for the Berkshire Hathaway Group. My client doubled the amount of money he was going to request from the venture firm after learning the firm was a big player and could afford larger risks.

An asset and lien investigation is one of the more commonly used services provided by investigators. A good investigator performing a well-organized asset and lien search can save thousands of dollars for a client.

Ch 8:

Connecting the Dots Between Parties

*Ken Lay, the disgraced former chairman of Enron,
found a way to escape his legal problems: He died
after being convicted of fraud and conspiracy charges.*
—Robert Kiyosaki, author

Due diligence investigations is often a matter of connecting the dots between two or more parties or activities. This chapter examines the affiliations and relationships a business can develop and maintain over the years. These affiliations may include **personal** relationships with vendors, customers, investors, or employees, and **required** relationships with government vendors or contractors. Any or all of these relationships can be critical points of reference within an investigation. Often times the most important discovery in a due diligence investigation is the connection between two or more people who can be working together fraudulently.

Vendor Relationships

People judge you by those with whom you associate, and the association a business has with vendors is significant. ABC Company may make a business decision to purchase services from only a few specific vendors. Those vendors have been approved by ABC Company's procurement department and an account has been established. The fact that you might be able to buy the same product for less money from a non-preferred vendor is not as important as using the approved vendor. An investigator will ask about these types of facts. Vendor relationships often form because of necessity, bias, desire, or convenience.

Recognize Relationships Based on Necessity

Some companies select their vendors based on necessity. For example, it is necessary that a company produces a certain number of widgets on short notice. If only one vendor can supply the widget raw material in the manner that the company requires, then it becomes the vendor of choice.

Supply Chain Analysis, as discussed in Chapter 3 of this book, teaches you to recognize weaknesses within the product development lifecycle. One slowdown in development, or a weak link in the chain, will affect the entire product development. Analysis of the situation tells you that the company has vulnerability when relying on only one vendor, and if anything unforeseen should happen to that vendor, the supply chain will likely collapse.

When analyzing a competitor and identifying a relationship based on necessity, understand that the competition is going to think about opportunity. The company examined will be seeking out alternatives for its situation of having only a single source for its widget production, or will be considering bringing widget development in-house. Depending on the complexity of the product, it may be an impossible task, however, no company likes to be told its supply chain is limited, and then be forced into an arrangement not desired. Companies, like people, want choices.

Recognize Relationships Based on Bias or Desire

Many times collusion, kickbacks, and fraud can be traced to a relationship based on greed, bias, friends, or family. Laws, such as the Foreign Corrupt Practices Act (FCPA) were passed to protect stockholders, by preventing persons and companies from enjoying kickbacks after vendors were overpaid.

Investigating and analyzing biased-based vendor relationships will require analysis of the following questions:

- Does the vendor produce the product to specifications?
- Is the vendor stable, consistent, and prepared for a catastrophe?
- Do the price points match up and are they competitive?

The reason a company should pick a specific vendor is because the vendor can produce the product at the level and speed needed and for a fair price.

Check the marketplace to find who else is selling the same services. If the vendor's prices are higher than its competition, consider this a red flag. If a company is seduced by free giveaways like lunches, ballgames and other perks from a vendor, there is a possibility that the company also may be receiving kickbacks or participating in collusion. Rather than hide the collusion, some participants prefer to enjoy it.

One specific area where many companies seem to slip in their friendly vendors under the radar is customer service. A company representative might say, "Oh that vendor has terrific customer service! When I have a problem, I call the vice president and he takes care of it himself." An inquirer might retort, "No kidding, but the vice president is your spouse!"

When examining the vendor relationships using the Supply Chain Analysis, be cognizant of who is the purchaser. In large companies, there is always a procurement person. This executive authorizes invoices and purchase orders. Also, there is an executive who initially orders products or services. Both employees should be examined to determine if there is an existing relationship connecting them. Another avenue to investigate is if an outside person or company negotiated the contract. Look for ties that may produce evidence of kickbacks or collusion.

Find Ties That Spawn Fraudulent Practices

There are some typical relationship ties between a corporate individual and a vendor to examine, if there is suspicion of fraud or collusion.

1. **Past Relationship**. The procurer may have purchased products or services from the vendor prior to the relationship he has with his current company.
2. **Regional**. The seller and buyer may live in the same community, and their kids may go to the same school or attend the same college.
3. **Family**. Maybe the two parties are related through blood or marriage.
4. **Idealism**. Perhaps the two parties attend the same church, or both belong to the same organization outside of work.
5. **Infidelity**. There might be a personal or sexual relationship between the two parties that is deemed inappropriate.

When investigating parties that are suspected of any of the aforementioned relationships, be sure to scan addresses, affiliations, and family members. The tie between the two parties may be found in a shared address. Or one of the spouses may have had a different last name, a name that matches your current vendor.

Other Types of Bias

A vendor relationship may spring from a shared bias against racism, sexism, and localism. Racism and sexism seem obvious enough, but it is important to look at both sides. The president of a company may be a chauvinistic racist and not want to work with women or minorities. However, his company may be required to conduct a certain volume of business each year with females and minorities.

Localism bias is when a company wants to conduct business with only regionally specific persons. The attitude of "Buy American" is a type of localism, as is supporting local companies like contractors, store owners or farmers. Unions in the U.S. also enjoy a strong amount of support, and the mentality of "support one of us" is pervasive. Additionally, buying green or environmentally conscious products made by indigenous persons shows a bias in the purchaser.

The buying habits of a company are not too different from the buying habits of an individual. When given a choice, how does a company decide which two product manufacturers to choose? Corporate procurement rules create standards to abide by; however, there is always room for personal preference. If that is the case, then the choice between two options at the same price, supply, and value may be made on local preference.

The Role of Politics

Local, state, and federal politics often play a role in the management decisions of corporations. Gaining favor with a particular political party may assist a firm in securing contracts or jobs with government agencies. For example, if John Smith's company headquarters is located in a Democratic stronghold, John or his company might support local community projects, sponsor Democratic-agenda items, or pay for expensive campaign dinners. But, when he is not wearing his business-owner's hat, he may be a Republican at heart.

The point is, do not discount someone's personal preference for a political party when investigating business support. Righteous idealism always takes a back seat to billable work.

See Chapter 5 for a discussion of political affiliations and searching for the personal, political leanings of an executive or employee.

Discovering the Silent Partners

Silent partners can be difficult to pin down. Below are five investigative tracks that help identify these investors.

1. **Secure and read annual reports**. Depending on which state a company has its headquarters, the annual reports and available data will vary. Some states offer extensive details about the company, the partners, and the owners. Florida is a great state for gathering information on company shareholders. Whereas other states like Delaware and New Jersey, the information can be weak, often times excluding the officers.

2. **Investors can be identified through a few online services**. Check business reports from D&B and Experian. The best source for this type of search is Capital IQ from Standard & Poor's.

3. **Check legal histories**. If the company, whether large or small, has been sued in the past, all the investors, major shareholders, and partners should be listed as defendants. Also, conduct legal searches on any identified chief officers. Perhaps the company you are searching for has not been sued directly; but if one of its officers has, it may be because of his connection with a prior company. That prior company may share the same investors and shareholders as the current company. Look for connections in the UCC filings, as discussed in Chapter 7.

4. **Thoroughly examine the company's Web site**. Look for links to Partners, Management, and Investors. Some companies list their business partners as board members or advisors. Also, if the company maintains press releases, read them for leads.

5. **Check media resources**. Look for press announcements of partnerships or similar types of events. Even finding past corporate affiliations will open up leads.

The necessary diligence in reporting information should lead the investigator to writing a history for each person found. As the biographies are written, cross connections can be established.

The Obscure Connection

Years ago, I took a case that quickly went from complicated to chaotic.

My client's company was on the verge of making an announcement that would cause a dramatic increase in his company's stock price. But before the information was made public, the company owner became aware of recent investors who had developed a sudden interest in the company in a big way, each investing a minimum of $50,000. The owner suspected an internal leak and asked me to investigate connections to these investors.

At face value, the only common issue among the eight investors was that they were all male. Other than that fact, all were from different regions of the country, were of varying ages, had different religious backgrounds, and were not related.

As I investigated each man separately, outlining the highlights of each life, eight very different social and economic backgrounds emerged. None of their spouses were related and they had no common political connection.

Then, drawing out a map of their lives, one avenue made itself obvious. Each man attended the same Midwest university. With ages ranging from 28 to 67 years, the educational affiliation was not obvious at first, because the university had changed its name 30 years ago. The lead formed in two of the online biographies I located during the investigation. I noticed that the two men mentioned the same school and fraternity. Since it was a connection, I traced it back further and found out that this fraternity was affiliated with the university since the late 1920s. Given this new lead, I checked the educational background of the remaining men, and found four more with the same school and fraternity link.

Next, I searched my client's company Web site for any biographies that listed education. Listed on the site were the biographies for all the key officers and managers. I discovered one manager also was a Midwest university alumnus and fraternity member of the same university and fraternity as the investors.

An examination of the manager's email showed he was an active poster in the fraternity listserv, with his most recent posting advising his fellow fraternity brothers that his company was on the brink of a major shift and that the investment time was ripe.

There is much to be gained by drawing long biographies, with key aspects highlighted per person, per investigation. Sometimes seeing the history of a person will help pinpoint the lead that you have been looking for. For very large cases, a software program like IBM's *i2 Analyst's Notebook* or *Palantir* will help to organize information visually. As data is entered into the program, connections are cross-checked and the indicators for each person are compared to each other, with a visual map showing lines between connecting points.

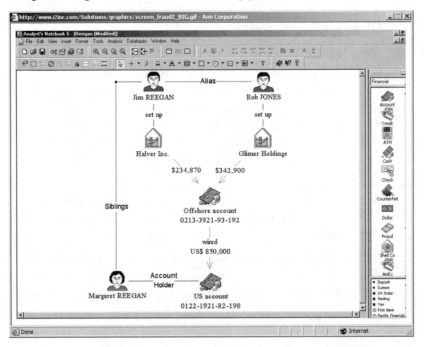

(source: <u>ibm.com/software/products/en/analysts-notebook/</u>)

Programs like *i2* and *Palantir* are expensive and take some talent to learn. However, for continuing investigations, these resources are indispensable. But for the occasional user, do not underestimate the traditional white board, as seen on TV cop shows. I am a strong believer in the white erasable board. Cases often are illustrated on the board, with the leads springing out of the center like an art project. The visual is very helpful, though, when looking at a person's life in sections. You might exclaim, "Here is education! Here is employment history! Here are family relations and bank accounts!"

Finding Their Clients

Digging into a subject company to find clients (as well as employees or vendors) will expand the association and affiliation leads for interviews, trend watching, and corporate intelligence. Also, discovery of clients is very valuable when establishing the size, scope, and capabilities of the company being evaluated.

Clients are not usually hidden. In fact, some companies like to share their client lists to show that their companies are busy and successful. However in some cases, client lists will be dissolved from company names to preserve client privacy.

There are several other areas to check that may lead to finding clients.

- Read company **press releases** to find out about potential business partnerships.

- Look for **recent events** as leads to follow up. If the company has sponsored any golf outings or charitable events, try to locate the attendees and fellow sponsors. Also, check with the vendors who worked the event. They may remember who attended and who were clients of the company.

- Key clients are often listed in a company's **annual report**.

- Review **marketing material for testimonials**. Ask for handouts that may have this information listed.

Finding Their Employees

Locating employees of a company for interview purposes is big business. Finding the right employee, either current or not, can blow an intelligence or due diligence investigation case wide open. Gaining an interview gives an investigator access to primary, firsthand experience, all of which are valuable in any case.

Several information brokers claim to sell internal corporate directories of companies. Older, but valuable, sources of corporate directory data are the published phone directories that the companies printed and passed out to their employees. All the info broker had to do was to somehow obtain a copy. Now with the advent of searchable company Intranets, these paper lists are less likely to be produced.

Once again, visit the company Web site to locate, at the very least, the company's top officers and managers. Try searching the Web, using google.com and other search engines, to find any mention of employees using expressions like "work for" or "employed by," and coupled with the company name.

Example: IBM + work for

Another method to checking on an employee is to call his company's phone number after regular business hours. Chances are the phone directory will offer a menagerie of choices, one of which will be to dial by the last name.

Two Recommended Online Resources

Zoominfo

Probably the best, free online tool to search for people listed by company is zoominfo.com.

The trick to obtaining names for free from zoominfo.com is how you go about conducting the search. Start by choosing *Find Contacts* at the top of the page. If you initially search by company and then request to see other employees, the list will be sent to you without the names. At this point, you can pay to join, or take advantage of the three-day trial period. However, if you can locate just one employee's name at that company and search that person, you will see down the Web page's left-hand side a network of individuals listed by name and company.

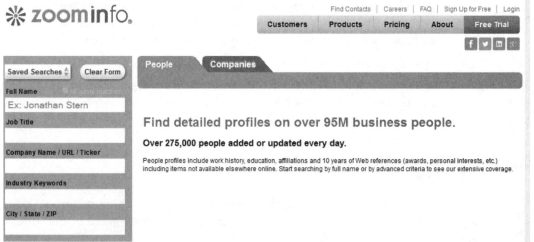

(Source: zoominfo.com)

Accurint and IRBSearch

One of the best offerings from both Accurint and IRBSearch, that sets their services apart from other public record vendors, is their respective People at Work programs. Using People at Work, you can search by name, address, phone number, Social Security number, and company name.

The results seem to be based on a variety of aggregated sources, such as secretary of state filings, business registrations, domain name registrations, and probable matches from zoominfo.com.

For example, I searched my name, Cynthia Hetherington, at both Zoominfo and Accurint. Each returned the phrase "Recurring Columnist for *PI Magazine*." True, I have had a few articles published in *PI Magazine*, but I am far from a recurring columnist and, at this writing, have not submitted an article in several years.

The point is to fact check all the results you retrieve when using fee and free online services.

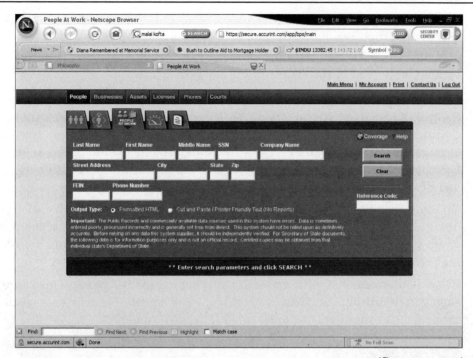

(Source: accurint.com)

Besides theses two services mentioned, there are other database services like D&B, Hoover's, and LexisNexis which offer searchable directories for individuals as well.

Remember to utilize the Web, and the company Web site, as much as possible when trying to locate connections between individuals, affiliates, and employees, or when trying to create a customer or partner list.

Finding Government Vendors and Contractors

There are no limitations to what the U.S. government will build, study, report on, or get involved with. They build bridges, study rodent populations, help small businesses grow, educate, and facilitate.

The amount of money moving between private industry and government is beyond imagination. To get a sense of how deeply the federal government is involved with the nation's economy as an employer, visit the government search engine usa.gov and browse the topic areas. The Federal Business Opportunities Web page at fbo.gov gives instructions and requirements to companies that are interested in doing business with the federal government. Business entities must be properly registered with the government before they can bid on providing services or products.

There are several essential Web pages to examine when investigating business entities and their possible connections to government contracts.

Web Resources to Find Government Vendors and Contractors

There used to be multiple systems to search for government contractors, such as the Central Contractor Registration (CCR) and the Online Representations and Certifications Application (ORCA), but in the past few years, they have all been aggregated into the System for Award Management (SAM). Sam is the Official U.S. Government system that consolidated the capabilities of CCR/FedReg, ORCA, and EPLS. (See Chapter 6.)

One stop shopping for government contractor registrations is much easier with this new system. Visit sam.gov and *Search Records*. You will be given a choice of quick or advanced search, as well as an exclusion search, which allows you to look up just the excluded party names.

Below is a screen shot with a search using my company's name. This resource will supply a multitude of facts concerning government exclusions, inclusions and conclusions as they apply to working with the government.

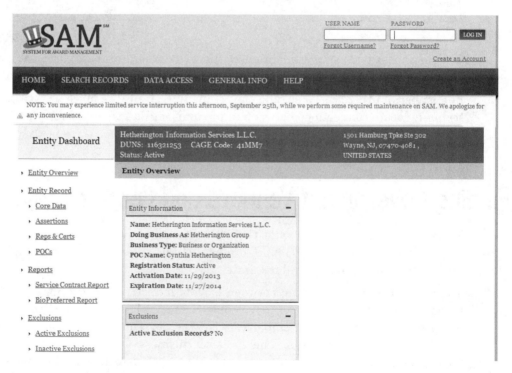

Social Media and the Connection

Online government databases of information can be one method for locating contractors who work with one another, however examining connections via the major social media networks (Facebook, Twitter, LinkedIn) may prove to be faster and easier than the databases. Recently, I worked a case where I investigated for possible connections between jurists on a trial. A Facebook search revealed there was an obvious connection between three of the jurists, and one of the jurists was connected to the defendant. Needless to say, the judge in that courtroom wasn't very pleased with the news.

Facebook, Instagram, Twitter, etc.

The likes of Facebook, Instagram, and Twitter can be more social focused than business focused in its content. I will look at these resources second in my investigation. However, don't discount these social media outlets as fluff; making a connection between two parties – no matter the source – can be invaluable to your investigation.

Many Facebook users make their profiles private, which prohibits an honest and open investigation into who they are Friends with. With that new development, the investigator simply turns to other social media sources. Twitter, Instagram, and other social media sources are increasing in popularity, rivaling that of Facebook. While Facebook users are pretty vigilant about locking down the security on their profiles, users of social media other than Facebook tend to be a bit lax in the security settings for their profiles. One Instagram photo from a user's open profile can have enough Comments and Likes on it to offer up enough affiliated names of a target to keep an investigator happily busy.

On Facebook, users tend to use their own real names for member registration. The premise is that everyone from high school will look for them by their name, not their new married name or their high school nickname, but whatever they were called on the playground or on the street. Yet, once we start exploring the social media platforms such as Instagram, we find these same people using nicknames. A good way to discover the nickname is to search for it in your favorite Internet browser, such as Google. In many cases, if the person has any social media presence, the Google search will connect his given name to his nickname.

Once you have located the nickname, attach it to any social media domain you have or that will come about. For example, if you have located hetheringtongrp as a nickname, you would then tack it onto the end of each social media URLs to search in each of the respective social media Web sites, like this:

Twitter.com/hetheringtongrp

Instagram.com/hetheringtongrp

Pinterest.com/hetheringtongrp

Another strategy for locating friends, contacts, and associates is to search in old accounts; ones that were set up when the technology was new and exciting, then abandoned once the novelty wore off. Myspace, Pinterest, Foursquare are some examples of that sort of social media Web site.

LinkedIn

LinkedIn by default blocks you from seeing connections, unless you are directly connected with the individual. There is a unique feature, however, that works in the investigator's favor. The endorsements that LinkedIn is constantly prompting for are sent only to those members within your LinkedIn community; therefore many of your target's connections are often sitting right there under your nose on the LinkedIn page under the Skills section.

 Skills

Top Skills

29	Fraud
22	Private Investigations
16	Investigation
11	Risk Assessment
11	Auditing
9	Background Checks
8	Forensic Accounting
6	Training
6	Analysis
5	Due Diligence

(source is page from linkedin.com)

When researching companies, remember it is often the associations had through vendors, clients, employees, partnerships, and sponsorships that are indicative of the direction and reputation of the company.

Ch 9:

Using Industry Sources

*If you don't want to work you have to work to earn
enough money so that you won't have to work.*

—Ogden Nash

Taking Research to a Deeper Level

Up until now this book has examined investigative research with the usual and customary resources that investigators routinely use. For example, an investigator researching a case might analyze corporate business reports from Dun & Bradstreet, obtain court records from PACER, and review articles from the online content aggregator Factiva – all good, generic investigative resources. I would encourage the researcher to use them, as well as the target company's Web site, as a starting point to ferret out the details – makeup, size, span, and function – of a company.

Hoover's (hoovers.com) is another resource for the investigator to use. A D&B product, Hoover's is comprehensive; a one-stop shop to research a wide range of generic sources and produce an overall report – for free or a nominal fee. To create its reports, Hoover's conducts its own analysis by combining basic research, press releases, data from the Hoover's proprietary database, and from the subject company's Web site. The information is helpful, and the overview section is insightful. The reports are written in an easy-to-understand, non-jargon-y style.

But, if your client can easily use the same Web sites and Hoover's reports to get the same publicly-available information that you can, then why should the client use you? What sorts of things can you do to make your investigative reports more informative, comprehensive, and worth their cost?

The answer is: Be more specific in your approach, more in-depth in your research, and more analytical in your report. Consider the following:

- Be specific about answering the questions your client has, and insure that the information you return has been verified and is accurate.

- Be in-depth about the sources you are checking and up front about where your information is coming from.

- Use a SWOT or a similar strategy in your report preparation.
- Connect the dots for your client.

As discussed throughout this book, due diligence is the examination of sources beyond a corporate report or Internet search. One of these components is the in-depth review and critical analysis within a single, or multiple industries. Given that one researcher cannot possibly know all industries, the following is a guide for the most popular industries and their sources.

Examples of Finding Industry Resources

There are plenty of industry sources and services, not necessarily known as available investigative tools, which are available to research. These sources primarily serve the industries they cater to.

For example, publishers specializing in specific markets can be as small as magazine publishers of a single, monthly monograph, or as large as *Medical Economics*, which produces volumes of journals, magazines, resource books, databases, and services specific to the healthcare industry.

Publications may be born from need or the lack of printed information for a particular group. These small, print publications may start as newsletters and eventually grow into magazines that take on a life of their own.

A good example is *Artilleryman* (civilwarnews.com). There is probably a healthy interest in Civil War cannons and other artillery, but not a great deal of literature for casually interested readers. Related article topics, found in this or similar magazines, could include recent sales, purchases, or destruction of collections, how cannons were instrumental in certain battles, or the dates of upcoming battle reenactments. Why ramble on about Civil War cannons? Because if an accident occurred involving one, perhaps during a reenactment or during a school ceremony, an authority probably would be needed to testify whether the cannon was used properly or not.

Bing Bang Theory

A unique bar in Key West, Florida is known for owning a large clipper ship, with crew, that its patrons can rent for parties, weddings, and pretend skullduggery. One of the perks of sailing on this vessel is that you can fire a flintlock and shoot the old cannon. I was involved on a case where one unfortunate fellow had a mishap – the flint from the cannon blew up in his face, burning him. He sued the restaurant, claiming medical and psychological damages as well as loss of income because he was incapacitated from his injuries.

My task was to vet the experts on behalf of the claimant's attorneys, as well as research the background of the defendant's experts. These experts were said to be well versed and respected as authorities in Civil War artillery. These experts turned out to be collectors and reenactment fans of the famous Civil War battles of the civil war. With such a small pool of experience in civil war artillery expertise, both claimant and defendant experts knew each other. The claimant's expert, whom we were bringing to court, was able to discount the defense based on former articles written, based on several inaccuracies. Odd though it may seem, he had debunked him in literature years prior, and used that to show how he was quick to judge munitions but not as clear on verifying the facts. It turned out to be a reputation blow to the defense expert.

The end result was for the claimant. With the help of our expert's testimony, the court decided the claimant should not have been given access to firearms (no matter how old they are) in his state of inebriation and that the owner of the clipper ship should have demonstrated more responsibility in passing out liquor and guns to his guests.

Sometimes the research takes you in unusual directions, as demonstrated in the story above. I would have never thought to be interested in Civil War reenactments. However, if the case takes you there, you have to learn to be interested. Sometimes it is not the expertise that is the unique aspect of the investigation, but where you find it. In the next example an historical reference led to information necessary for our case.

Which Side Are You On?

This investigation focused on evaluating the credentials of a physician who had studied diet drugs, including a combination of fenfluramine and phentermine known as fen-phen. The attorney's directions were to review any articles written by the opposing counsel's expert physician to: a) Locate the funding sponsor of the article; b) Establish if he was pro or anti in any of his theories; and c.) See if any of his articles were refuted in follow-up editorials or studies.

All of these issues were in relation to bias on the doctor's part. Was he writing articles in showing bias and support of his own funding source, such as a pharmaceutical company?

Research was located in articles written ten years earlier by the physician and funded by Wyeth Pharmaceuticals through its subsidiary, American Home Products. Wyeth was the leading producer of dexfenfluramine, used in fen-phen. The release of the physician's article and research conclusions coincided at the same time fen-phen was being re-evaluated by the FDA for causing strokes in women. After the FDA article was released, the physician was widely criticized for his findings. He then began to write new studies which were no longer funded by Wyeth, but were part of a teaching hospital study. These new articles were critical of fen-phen and its effectiveness. Thus, he completely changed his opinion from one study to the next.

Essentially, the attorney has found bias in the original study, since it was funded by the producer of fen-phen combination dexfenfluramine, and the physician changed his stand on the particular use of the drug after he left Wyeth. Neither issue is a big concern by itself; however, your research should uncover turn these events up before using a witness as an expert. Our attorneys researched the specific medical databases for articles on fen-phen and anything the physician had written or was recorded saying about fen-phen, and this resulted in huge embarrassment for the other party and their attorneys.

These two examples demonstrate how intricacies of specific information can lead a case into information sources which are unfamiliar and maybe out of your comfort zone. The important lesson here is that for each and every profession, hobby, and interest there will be magazines, Web sites, blogs, and perhaps entire publishing houses to examine and conduct research against. In these two examples, our research led us to magazines and trade journals.

Healthcare Industry Resources

In the case of the physician expert discussed earlier, how did I know where to start my search? Certainly an examination of the standard sources for any articles published on the physician would be undertaken. If results in the *New York Times* or other general press newspapers and magazines were found, I would read and analyze to decide if the information was relevant should be and included in my report. However, when targeting an expert, the goal is to find that expert's writings or things written about him, and to disclose any anomalies or opinions. To do this, you must research in the specific industry territory of the target individual. In the case of the expert physician, I needed to become familiar with the resources that physicians use, in this case medical and healthcare information.

The direction of healthcare research will depend on the type of disease or health topic the case involves, along with a common-sense approach. To start, I imagine the types of magazines and Web sites would my expert would use. What magazines or Web content does he subscribe to and how does he keep abreast with the latest news in the profession? This tactic should be used in all professions, and not just healthcare, but it certainly resounds loudest in the physical sciences. For example, with the topic regarding in the concern of fen-phen use, I focused on journals with a main theme of obesity and anorexia nervosa.

National Library of Medicine

One of the best starting point resources available in medicine and health research is the National Library of Medicine, sponsored by the U.S. National Institutes of Health (NIH). The NIH (nlm.nih.gov) offers a compendium of information cataloged under its own subject headlines, such as AIDS, influenza, and toxic chemicals.

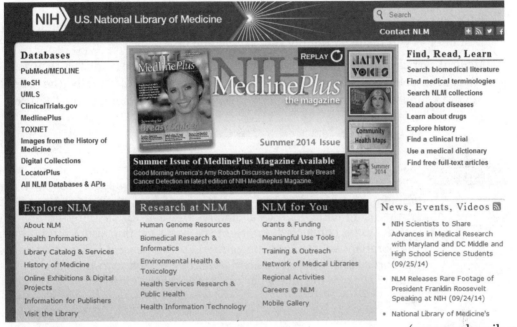

(source: nlm.nih.gov)

Since the NIH Web site is overwhelming, it helps to know specifically where to begin digging to find those searchable databases that will help educate you on a condition, or give you a source to look for concerning your expert's writings and testimonies.

In my opinion, the best starting point is MEDLINE, found at PubMed[29] by going to ncbi.nlm.nih.gov/pubmed.

MEDLINE offers searching by topic, author, or journal. I advise using the help sheets. The results of a name search will lead to abstracts, which describe each article published and where it can be located. The material and writing may seem foreign to most individuals, since the scientific nature of each article is very technical.

For example, a search of "caffeine" returned more than 21,000 hits. Using one of the top-listed results produced the following:

---

[29] PubMed is a service of the U.S. National Library of Medicine that includes over 17 million citations from MEDLINE and other life science journals for biomedical articles back to the 1950s. PubMed includes links to full text articles and other related resources.

Aguilar-Roblero R, Mercado C, Alamilla J, Laville A, Diaz-Munoz M.

Ryanodine receptor Ca(2+)-release channels are an output pathway for the circadian clock in the rat suprachiasmatic nuclei.

Eur J Neurosci. 2007 Aug;26(3):575-82.

PMID: 17686038 [PubMed - in process]

More likely, you will be searching by author, so performing an additional search of "Alamilla J" will result in finding this article and others.

Medical articles found in PubMed and similar high-end industry sources are considered refereed. In other words, a panel of experts, usually the Board of Advisors, must review them before the journal will accept the articles for publication.

AUTHOR TIP Many healthcare articles and abstractsare only referenced on the World Wide Web, but are not freely availableto download. To solve this problem, one of the fastest and least expensive ways to retrieve these articles is to visit your local library and ask for an inter-library loan request to be conducted. Print out the exact citation you are requesting. The librarian will forward the request to the nearest library that carries the particular journal. The article will be sent back to the librarian as a photocopy from the journal or perhaps in electronic form.

For extensive medical research, or searches for topical medical experts, visit the nearest teaching hospital. The library attached to the hospital most likely will contain excellent medical research sources pertinent to your subject matter.

Other Government Resources

Some free healthcare database resources can be located online for free on sites hosted by the federal government. One such service is the Food and Drug Administration (FDA), found at fda.gov. The example to follow shows how the site hosts an entire directory of cell-phone radiation and safety data.

FDA can be involved in everything from food contamination, bioterrorism, drug recalls, and livestock concerns to cell-phone effects. For example, teaming with the National Academy of Science, the FDA conducts investigations into claims that cell phones can harm individuals. In the last few years, claims have surfaced that cell phones are responsible for the honeybee population demise, the sterility of men, and brain tumors in humans.

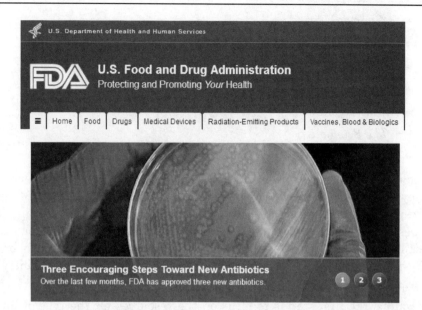

(source: <u>fda.gov</u>)

Fee-Based Resources

Perhaps the best place to find fee-based resource services for the healthcare industry is Dialog (<u>dialog.com</u>). Researchers may do a single search, subscribe monthly, or pay an in-house researcher to search within the databases for you. Dialog aggregates the majority of pharmaceutical pipeline sources, and chemical, medical, and scientific sources. Its sources range from PsychINFO® to diverse topics, such as Meteorological and Geoastrophysical Abstracts. Keep in mind that these are collected or aggregated sources on Dialog, so each service also is available independently. A researcher can access PsychINFO® through Dialog or directly at <u>psycinfo.apa.org/psycinfo</u>. The benefit to using Dialog is one-stop shopping.

Financial Industry Resources

The general media covers the finance world very well. The following is a representative list, but not all inclusive:

- Barron's
- Bloomberg
- CNBC
- CNN
- *Crain's*

- *Financial Times*
- *Forbes*
- *Fortune*
- *Investor's Business Daily*
- *Morningstar*
- *The Economist*
- *Wall Street Journal*

In addition, all large newspapers and the *USA Today* cover the financial world and many stories are archived on the Internet from their Web sites. Many large, city newspapers dedicate pull-out sections to covering world, national, and local finance issues. Much like medical and health research, finance is too broad a term to be narrowed to just a few specific topics. Finance issues can touch on economics, investments, banking, currency, regulatory issues, and a country's domestic concerns.

Of course, the first step is to focus on the resources for the type of financial issue you are investigating. This will help you focus on the sources you need. For example, if you are conducting a background investigation on a broker and you are looking for regulatory actions against the broker, begin with the Web sites for—

- Securities and Exchange Commission (SEC)
- Financial Industry Regulatory Authority (FINRA)
- National Futures Association (NFA)
- North American Securities Administrators Association (NASAA).

More information, including the web pages and how to use them for investigations, is found in Chapter 6.

But, if you are conducting a background on a new investor, or potential investment, the direction of the investigation should involve business database aggregators, like ProQuest Dialog, Thomson Reuters, and Cengage Gale are three excellent professional grade products. The only frustration I have with them is that they keep changing partners. However the core databases remain intact no matter which parent is responsible for their marketing and upkeep.

Each service is a subscription based system, and you will find them in most public libraries, certainly in academic libraries. To see the offerings of each, visit their Web sites:

- Gale: solutions.cengage.com/Gale/Database-Title-Lists
- Dialog: proquest.com/products-services/ProQuest-Dialog.html
- Thomson Reuters: thomsonreuters.com

Telecommunications and Technology Resources

If any industry has built its own directory of resources, this is the one. Telecommunications and technology are among the most readily available topics on the Internet.

ZIFF Davis

With their male genre focused glossy covers and techno-speak language, these technology magazines portray themselves as uber technical and gaming sophisticated – not to mention complicated. You would think a multitude of publishers were competing for magazine shelf space. The truth is that most of the largest and respected magazines in this market are all published by Ziff Davis (ziffdavis.com). Ziff Davis covers all geek needs from *CIO Insight* to *PC Magazine*.

Each magazine offers a search engine directly on its Web site for searching by topic, author, or business.

International Data Group

International Data Group (idg.com) is the other major player in technology news publications. Magazines like *PC World*, *Computerworld*, and *LinuxWorld* are staples in the technology market. However, these are only three of the nearly three hundred print and online sources that IDG manages and publishes.

Social Media and Technology

The best place to learn about industry changes and new markets, as well as new devices, changes, and development in the industry is through the social media sites that cater to this industry. For years Engadget (engadget.com) has been a go-to source for leaked new product releases. If you want to see what Apple is up to, no doubt Engadget members will be discussing the inner workings of the next iPhone a year before it is released. Mashable (mashable.com) is another necessary Web site for following new media and technology developments. Alongside daily media they have excellent reporting in the technospace.

Manufacturing and Construction-Related Resources

Solusource: Global Supplier Directory by Thomas Global Register

The major source for information in this category is the *Thomas Global Directory*, now part of Solusource. See worldindustrialreporter.com/solusource. The directory contains over 700,000 manufacturers and distributors from 28 countries, classified by 11,000 products and services categories. Plus the directory gives detailed product and company information in eleven languages. For example, a search of "fire doors" at this site revealed thousands of manufactures from all over the globe, which I can narrow down by country, and other easy to choose items.

Using Trade Journals and the Blue Book

Primary resources of manufacturing and industrial knowledge are trade journals and periodicals associated with the specific industries. Contractors advertise, read and keep up with their industry through trade magazines. Trade associations publish many of these sources, such as *Scrap* magazine (scrap.org), published by the Institute of Scrap Recycling Industries, Inc. (isri.org). Other trade magazines are produced by for profit entities, such as *Architectural Record* by McGraw-Hill found at:

archrecord.construction.com/Default.asp.

A great overall resource of building trade data is the **Blue Book of Building and Construction** at thebluebook.com. This site has many, many features including a links list of trade organizations, trade journals, journals, and up-coming trade shows. See Chapter 12 for a list of building trade and construction resources.

Resources of Market Research

Market Research Profound (marketresearch.com) houses over 250,000 global research reports produced by experts specific to every industry, from telecommunications to hospitality.

They collect and index each report, making them available for purchase. Using this service on an as-needed basis, you can search for free against their vast resources and then select either the total report (which is often thousands of dollars) or take advantage of purchasing only sections of the report. Sometime a paragraph with the right information is all you need. Searching Marketresearch.com is very easy, but can be hit and miss at times. Searching with a "term" will result in several possible matches. When you select a term, an abstract – which may or may not make sense – is followed by the word you searched for. It tells you the page number the word shows up on in the report, and gives you some reference to the sentence where found. This technique is called the **Key Word in Context (KWIC)** view.

While not providing a full set of data report, it does give you a sense of what may possibly be in that portion of the full report. You then must decide to purchase that section or continue searching for a better match.

The government also produces and funds a great deal of market research resources. In fact, government depository libraries are filled with free and valuable information on every industry possible, company type, whether profit, non-profit, defense oriented or horticulture, and historical or futuristic. Check out the government search engine usa.gov for a great head start on finding free reports produced by the government.

Government documents research is a difficult process and not everything is available online. My third recommendation is to visit the nearest government repository in person and ask the government documents librarian for assistance. To find the closest depository, visit gpoaccess.gov/libraries.html.

The Follow Through

Industry searching can be very uncomfortable because as an investigator you are stretching your intelligence to understand someone else's profession. Some investigators become incredibly specialized in certain types of investigations because they have investigated so many cases within the specialty area that industry is second nature to them. This is especially true for environmental investigators, financial investigators, and insurance claims investigators.

But due diligence investigations is an exercise in stretching your knowledge and critical thinking skills, so learning new materials and sources should not be intimidating. When working in unfamiliar territory, my recommendation is to consult with a professional who knows the industry. This professional may be a practitioner or even an investigator that specializes in those particular cases. The approach is to ask these experts what sources they consult, what magazines they read, the Web sites visited, and news and media preferences.

The next tip for learning about industry sources is to read everything you can. I grab and read magazines for computers, science, finance, health, home – you name it, I will read it. There may be a snippet about a new Web site specifically for some industry purpose, like a directory of manufactures of steel-related products. I will check the site to see if it provides inside information that I might need later, in this example if I have case involving steel parts and the owners behind certain products. My top three publishers are BRB Publications, Information Today and *PI Magazine*. These publishers of books, manuals, and periodicals are constantly releasing new sources of information.

The key point is to reach out to experts when applicable and not to slow down your self-learning. Collecting data resources by topic may give you an advantage when you have a case dropped on your desk a few weeks later.

A Few Final Words

Due to the variety of industries you are researching, most investigations will challenge the investigator. No one is an expert on all areas and topics. It's the investigators' challenge to get smart on any involved industry.

In order to get smart in an industry, find an industry expert, read everything they have written and been interviewed on. If possible, contact them for assistance. Below are key points to keep in mind.

- You will be researching a variety of industries, and yet no one is an expert in all areas and on all topics. It is the investigator's challenge to *get smart* on any involved industry.

- In order to *get smart* about an industry, find that industry's expert, read everything he/she has written about or reported on the industry. If possible, contact the expert for assistance.

- Use freely available online sources, such as social networks (Zoominfo, LinkedIn, etc.), for finding industry experts. Locate associations where industry experts congregate.

- The healthcare and financial industries are two industries that have many unique specialty associations and opportunities to locate experts.

- Technology and telecommunication experts are easily found online.

- Manufacturing experts can be located through unions and organized laborers.

- Market research sites (such as MarketResearch.com) offer very specific information about particular products and services, plus industry reports comparing products.

- Industry-specific resources can be readily available at the local library. Librarians can be extremely helpful in locating all sorts of information; use them.

- Intellectual property registrars, such as the U.S. Patent and Trademark office (uspto.gov), are useful to search for experts who have created and developed specific methods. These experts can be consulted on competitors' products.

- Do not get tunnel vision in your reading habits. Read everything – magazines, books, Web sites, and blogs – on topics to familiarize yourself with the industry. Extra bonus: You never know when a topic will reveal itself to be useful for a later investigation.

- Listen to the news.

Ch 10:

Internet Searches and Social Media Tactics

Little girls think it's necessary to put all their business on MySpace and Facebook, and I think it's a shame...I'm all about mystery.

—Stevie Nicks

Getting the Most Out of Google

There are several Internet search engines available to the public, Google, Bing, DuckDuckGo, Yahoo, among them. As the market-share leader of free Internet search tools, Google gets a good deal of use. In this book, we have already reviewed several search features of Google's; we've used it to search for such things as images, news, books, maps, products, and translations.

I believe Google is one of the most underappreciated search engines available, and not fully understood by investigators.

When executing a search on Google, the product has many enhancements that go far beyond entering search terms and merely clicking the Google Search or I'm Feeling Lucky buttons. An accomplished investigator should know how to use – and take advantage of – Google's advanced-search feature and operators.

Google Operators

Using Google operators will smarten a search and enable you to find the right link faster. In the table below, look in the first column for the bolded characters known as operators. They help define or narrow a search.

This Search	Operator	Finds Pages Containing ...
cooking Italian	none	With both the words cooking and Italian, but not together or in order
vegetarian **OR** vegan	**OR**	Information on vegetarian or vegan
"Can I get a witness"	""	The exact phrase "Can I get a witness"
Henry +8 Great Britain	+	Information about Henry the Eighth (8), weeding out other kings of Great Britain
automobiles ~glossary	~	Glossaries about automobiles, as well as dictionaries, lists of terms, terminology, etc.
salsa -dance	-	The word "salsa" but NOT the word "dance" (note the space before the hyphen)
salsa-dancer	-	All forms of the term, whether spelled as a single word, a phrase, or hyphenated (note the lack of a space)
define:congo	**define:**	Definitions of the word "congo" from the Web
site:virtuallibrarian.com	**site:**	Searches only one website for expression, in this case virtuallibrarian.com
filetype:doc	**filetype:**	Find documents of the specified type, in this case MS Word documents
link:virtuallibrarian.com	**link:**	Find linked pages, i.e. show pages that point to the URL

Google operators can also be combined. Follow the example below:

site:hp.com filetype:pdf 5010 LaserJet printer FAQ

This search is directed to the Hewlett Packard website, looking for an Adobe Acrobat PDF file of frequently asked questions regarding the 5010 LaserJet printer.

Also available on Google are the common mathematical operators. The following symbols between any two numbers will automatically perform a math function.

Symbol	Function
+	Addition
-	Subtraction
*	Multiplication
/	Division

To locate other advanced Google operators, use the Advanced Search Page, or you can perform the advancing searching right in the search box.

There are dozens more operators and search techniques for beginners and experts alike. A great resource for search help is googleguide.com.

Using the Preferred Results Feature

One option that can save time and help insure not to miss vital hits is to simply set the number of results from 10 (the default) to 100. To do this, go to the first screen of Google.com, click on *Search Settings*, which is a link on the upper right of the screen, and then slide down to Number of Results. You will see a pull-down menu that should be displaying 10 in the box. Change that to 100 and click the Save Preferences button at the bottom right of the page. Now every time you use Google.com on that computer, you will receive 100 results per page.

The *Preferences* option also allows you to specify the default tolerance for safe searching filtering. Google's SafeSearch blocks Web pages containing explicit sexual content from appearing in search results. The filter options are:

- Use strict filtering (filter both explicit text and explicit images)
- Use moderate filtering (filter explicit images only—default behavior)
- Do not filter my search results.

Google Proximity Searching Feature

When an asterisk * is used between words or expressions, Google offers a very rich proximity searching feature. Used between two expressions, proximity will return results that are within 15 words of each other.

For example, a search for *"cynthia hetherington" investigator* returned 755 matches in Google. Whereas, the search *"cynthia hetherington" * "investigator"* resulted in 24 matches.

Hence, the expression cynthia hetherington did appear on the same Web page as investigator 755 times, but it only occurred in close proximity to investigator 24 times out of the 755 matches.

Another example is *"Tampa Bay" * "Devil Rays"* which will return results when Tampa Bay appears within 15 words of Devil Rays.

If you are looking for a person who uses a maiden name or middle name, then put the * inside the quotes with the name. "Cynthia * Hetherington" will result in Cynthia Hetherington, Cynthia Lyn Hetherington and Cynthia L Hetherington. My name might not raise too much concern but foreign and maiden names can often be challenging. What you will notice is that this expands the number of results instead of decreases them, so now you can add another * on the outside of the quotes to narrow down your search.

As in: Cynthia * Hetherington * investigator <- this search resulted in 15 matches.

Common Phrase Searching

For English-language searches, consider using the common expressions people use in everyday language. With email, text messaging, and other basic-device communications, writing has turned into an extension of speaking. Many people no longer think about what they are writing; as far as grammar is concerned, they tend to write like they speak. Shorthand and expressions are common. Below are common expressions that can be used for creative phrase searching:

- I hate XXX (my job, my mom, my school, my employer)
- Better than XXX (<restaurant>, <product>, <any proper noun>)
- I love XXX (my job, my mom, my school, my employer)
- XXX was the nicest (<geography/location>, <company or person>)
- XXX was the worst
- XXX was off the charts
- XXX was off the hook
- XXX was off the map
- XXX was such a jerk/babe/<expletive>
- XXX was so hot/stupid/boring.

An example search using 'Better than Disney' returned hits on such pages as:

- Is Disneyland better than Disney World?
- Nick [Nickelodeon's children's network] is slightly better than Disney.

The key to using common phrase searching is to be inventive. Consider how you would describe a similar topic, and then run your searches in the same style using quotes to contain the phrases.

Google Alerts

Google Alerts is one of the handiest tools that Google offers for investigators. The Google Alerts tool sends emails automatically when new Google results match your pre-submitted list of search terms. These results are culled from Google News, Web, Blogs, Video, and Groups.

The easiest way to use the Alerts feature is to start at google.com/alerts. Here you set up your customized alert list that will email you as an event is found. Preferences may be set to alert you on an as-it-happens, or once-a-day, or even once-a-month basis. Type in your search query or key words – such as a proper name, expression, or phrase search – then use the pull-down menu to select what you want to track for your personalized alerts.

The screen shot on the next page shows a page about constructing a Google Alert.

Alerts
Monitor the web for interesting new content

🔍 "cynthia hetherington"

How often	At most once a day ⬍
Sources	Automatic ⬍
Language	English ⬍
Region	Any Region ⬍
How many	Only the best results ⬍

Enter email   **CREATE ALERT**   Hide options ▲

You will want to use a return email address specifically set up to capture heavy traffic. Use the same type of account you would when signing up to various websites and social networks.

Google Images

Image searching in Google can offer a host of interesting results. Using the same type of search queries, you can look up a personal name, company, or idea. The Advanced Image Search offers limiters by image type (such as black and white, color, and drawings) and has a search feature for finding only faces and only news content. Filtering with the "faces only" feature will narrow down large result matches. The News Content feature is terrific considering the image search happens within media and press-oriented websites.

Google Images also does facial recognition, and image recognition. If you click on the camera icon within the search box, you will see instructions to either upload a photo you want to compare, or point Google Images to a link of that photo. With their large archive of images, they will find other matches to that picture or similar looking pictures. Another source for doing this is tineye.com

Google Video

Google owns YouTube.com. YouTube is a tremendous resource for obtaining video footage of people in action, inside pictures of facilities, and location/geography snapshots. For those investigating insurance fraud, YouTube.com is a must for checking if the disabled claimant has posted any videos of himself doing heroic feats. Video.google.com also scans other video hosting sites, like https://vimeo.com, another very popular hosting service.

Google Maps

The Google Maps tool is quite useful for needs beyond the well-known driving directions and the "where is?" feature. Search an area with familiarity to see the variety and tools that go beyond directions of east to west. The My Maps tab offers a variety of features and tools where you customize your searches and zero in on certain geographic aspects.

Searches can be narrowed to show real estate listings, user-contributed photos with Picasa Web Album or Panoramio, and places of interest. Use the distance measurement tool to establish the length between two map points. Various measurement results are offered. For example, the distance between Minneapolis and St. Paul, Minnesota, is 8.73084 mi or 128.052 football fields, 13.1711 верста, 281.019 pools, and so on.

Bing.com

Just when you thought all cool single-word expressions were taken, Microsoft introduced Bing. Bing is the latest search engine to take on the formidable Google.com and Yahoo.com. Bing focuses on four key areas: shopping, local, travel, and health.

A number of features and benefits of this new search engine are reviewed below. It is worth mentioning that the interface is rather pleasant with a photo backdrop, which is fine on a computer with no bandwidth issues.

Bing Search Features and Settings

Go straight to Preferences in the right-hand corner and change the settings for Results from 10 to 50 (unfortunately the highest number). Note the obvious similarity to Google's preferences page with a few noticeable add-ons. Bing identifies your physical location based on your ISP location. My ISP is in Oakland, New Jersey, and it says so in the preferences. You can change this, but I imagine Bing is trying to use a location to determine the best marketing material to attach to my searches. You have the option to turn on (default) and off the suggestions box. It can be annoying when you start typing an expression and the Bing tries to finish your words.

The search box takes up to 150 characters, including spaces. The standard stop words (a, the, and, etc.) can be included in your search if used in quoted phrases, e.g., The Di Vinci Code.

One odd feature was the increase of results when searching with quotes against a name. A search without quotes on Cynthia Hetherington returned 60,500 results, whereas the search with the quotes returned 179,000 results.

Although, the algorithm is not clear, it is possible Bing uses a proximity command as a default when searching one or more expressions. This would make sense to limit bad results such as a document that lists Cynthia Nixon at the top of the page and Hetherington Smith LLP six pages later. A nice feature brought back to use in database searching is the Boolean terms "or" and "not." By default, search engines tend to assume the "and" (e.g., chocolate "and" cake), and the "not," which can also be represented as a "–" (minus) in the query. Although the "or" (represented as "|") gets a little lost in the advanced features, it is good to see Bing highlighting this little-used but resourceful feature.

Bing has brought back parentheses to allow you to combine expressions to be included or not. This is great for intelligence investigators who suffer due to popular names flooding their results. For example, Bill Gates returns 24 million hits. Add (Gates Foundation) to the search and you are limited to 700,000 results. If you subtract (or NOT Gates Foundation), the results jump back up, but the results will be significantly less than the original 24 million.

Bing maintains an ongoing history of your searches in the left-hand column. Avid researchers and investigators have ways of remembering what they looked up and in what order, but this list takes the questions out of doubtful searches. For example, in all my Bill Gates searches, did I ever try searching him as William Gates? A quick look to the left gives me that answer.

Also down the left-hand column are related queries and recommendations.

On the right-hand side of the results page, if you place your mouse over the returned links, you will see your search expression as it appears within the context of the website that was found. Other links offered on that page are also shown.

Bing includes many of the same resources we find in other popular engines that focus on the consumer market. There are searches specific to travel, video, pictures (images), and maps. The pictures searches are easier to manage because you see more images on the results screen as compared to only 10 per page on Google's results screen. Narrow down your search by head and shoulders shots and 'just faces' shots. Also, the type, size, and color of the picture can modify your search and are offered to the left of the screen.

The features for Bing are very well designed, even if they target a consumer market. I tried the cash back option, saved more than $5.00, and received free shipping on a new purchase through one of their vendors.

Given the popularity of Google, Bing is going to have a challenge gaining market share, but it returned surprisingly better results on traditional search queries and photo searches. The mapping queries were easier to run. Bing is a new Data2know.com top-ten choice!

Throughout this book, a number of other traditional search and social media engines have been mentioned for their products and unique features. Social media search engines come and come and go, but few have maintained themselves over time and will consistently help in online due diligence investigations. I prefer to focus strictly on using the resources mentioned.

Social Media Search Basics

Social media sites are based on XML (extended markup language). They follow certain programming protocols which makes investigating in social media much easier for the investigator.

When a user opens up an account on a social media site, he can register information about himself – for example, his name, email address, and phone number – into his profile. All content on a social media site, whether it's LinkedIn, Facebook, Vine, etc., is tagged, which means the content is indexed. Indexed content is then searchable. The most common items searched on in many social media sites are name, nickname, cell phone number, and email address. If the social media user registered any of these identifying items when creating his account, your search should turn up his profile.

Social media users tend to use their name across all their various social media sites, with a varying degree of formality. For instance, LinkedIn tends to be a social media site used almost exclusively for the professional world; it's where you'd put up your resume, where you'd look for work, and where you'd network with business colleagues. Facebook, on the other hand, tends to be a social media site used almost exclusively for, well, social activities; it's where you'd want to reconnect with high school classmates, or just share things with friends.

Given the range of function, a person's user name across the various social media sites might look like this:

- LinkedIn.com/in/RobertMcEachin
- Facebook.com/BobMcEachin
- Twitter.com/BobbyMac

The most casual of the name representations – in this case, Bobby Mac – will likely be used the most often across all the other social media sites, such as Instagram, Vine, Pandora, and others.

My preferred search resource is Google. I'm a Google girl and that's most likely not going to change. However, there are several search engines available that do just as good a job at searching as Google does. Using any one of them will pull up a social media presence for the subject on which you're searching (if that person has a social media presence), as well as plenty of information on any particular topic you may need to educate yourself on or investigate. And since search sites can sometimes cease to function, it's prudent to have more than one site ready at your fingertips.

Some search sites to use for locating information about people include:

- Google (google.com)
- Bing (bing.com)
- Pipl (pipl.com)
- Yasni (yasni.com)
- Yatedo (yatedo.com)
- Spokeo (spokeo.com)
- Peekyou (peekyou.com)
- Foupas (foupas.com)
- yoName (yoName.com)
- NameChk (namechk.com)

Some search sites to use for looking up topical information include:

- Socialmention (socialmention.com)
- BizNar (biznar.com)
- Addict-o-matic (addictomatic.com)
- Whos Talkin (whostalkin.com)
- Topsy (topsy.com)
- Clusty (clusty.com)

Hashtags and Exif Data

When searching in social media sites, it helps to know and understand the lingo used. A few key signs or key symbols might prove helpful in unlocking information for an investigation.

Hashtags and @ symbols

Sometimes referred to as a pound sign, or a number sign, the # in social media sites is referred to as a hashtag. Anything that follows the hashtag is a topic, and will always be one word or a continuous phrase with no spaces. For example:

#throwbackthursday

#tgif

The @ sign indicates a person's account and is placed in front of the account name. For example:

@hetheringtongrp

@jimmyfallon

While these signs gained popularity on Twitter, they are used across most all social media platforms. More than one can be used at a time. For example, if someone wanted to tell me that he was enjoying my new book and invite me to have coffee, the social media statement might possibly say:

@cynthiah @hetheringtongrp Enjoying your book about Online Due Diligence! #Onlineduedil #fraudfighter #letsmeetforcoffee

The @cynthiah and @hetheringtongrp indicate my addresses. The three # phrases indicate topics: Online due diligence, fraud fighter, and let's meet for coffee. If anyone else on the social media site is searching for information on the topic of fraud by using the #fraudfighter phrase, the post would show up on that person's social media stream.

Exif

Exif stands for Exchangeable Image File Format. It is the format for storing metadata in image and audio files – digital photos, digital videos, etc. Metadata can be incredibly valuable for investigators. Smart phones and modern cameras attach geographic location (geo-location) data to photographs taken with them.

When you view one of these digital photos in an Exif browser, such as Jeffrey's Exif Viewer (regex.info/exif.cgi), or via the software program Opanda (opanda.com), you can see the photo's information as clearly as you can see the photo itself.

In the example to the left, a picture of my dog was taken in my house and then uploaded to Jeffrey's Exif Viewer.

Here is the information Jeffrey's Exif Viewer returned for the photo.

Camera:	Apple iPhone 5
Lens:	iPhone 5 back camera 4.12mm f/2.4 Shot at 4.1 mm Digital Zoom: 1.710691824×
Exposure:	Auto exposure, Program AE, $^1/121$ sec, f/2.4, ISO 50
Flash:	Auto, Did not fire
Date:	**March 25, 2014** 10:29:17AM (timezone not specified) (6 months, 23 days, 17 minutes, 16 seconds ago, assuming image timezone of 5 hours behind GMT)
Location:	Latitude/longitude: **42°** 5' 29" North, **75°** 15' 28.6" West (42.091389, -75.257958) Location guessed from coordinates: *12 Lakeview Avenue, Westwood, NJ 12345, USA*

Notice the returned information includes location coordinates – the geographic location of where the photo was taken. If the user chooses to turn off his geo-location applications on his phone, then the photo's level of geographic detail will not be available. However, the date the photo was taken and the type of camera or phone that took it will still be available.

FACEBOOK

Facebook's Graph Search, a Facebook-specific search engine, allows you to search all of the things people have shared with you on Facebook. If your posts are set to Public, then by using Facebook's Graph Search, anyone can search and find the content on your Facebook account.

Your Facebook Graph Search results will differ from anyone else's results for the same search because you and they do not have the same Facebook friends. But Graph Search is not limited to only those posts on your Facebook account's Timeline; it also covers your Facebook profile information, photographs, comments, and Likes. So, for example, if you search for Photos of Boise, you'll see photos Facebook Friends took in Boise and shared with you, as well as Public photos related to Boise. As I've written in the past, this also affects searching for users, such as in an investigation, to whom you are not connected or friended. Instead of the original simple name/keyword search, such as "Cynthia Hetherington," you now have to search on the expression "People named Cynthia Hetherington'"in order to find all the Cynthia Hetheringtons out there, and from there, using Facebook's filters, usually found on the right side of the screen, you can then narrow down the results to what is likely my account.

Locking Down your Facebook Account

With Graph Search, Facebook has quite possibly made your Facebook profile visible to anyone who performs a Graph Search, whether you want that profile to be public or not. As of this book's writing, Facebook announced that it is eliminating the privacy setting that allowed a user to hide his Facebook profile from Graph Search (the option "Who can look up your timeline by name"). As always, simply be ever vigilant about your privacy settings, making sure they are set as tightly as you prefer them to be.

The explantions to follow will help you lock down your Facebook account to its most secure state.

Lock Down Posts

For future posts on Facebook, change your default audience by going to your Privacy settings and changing the setting for "Who can see my future posts?" Your best bets are to set it to Friends or a custom setting of your choosing. With this setting, any posts you create in the future will go to the limited audience of only your Friends. If you want to expand the audience for a particular post or make it publicly available, you can change the audience for that post alone. But, with your setting at Friends only, you have a safety net of sorts – your posts won't be public.

That setting covers your future posts. What about past posts; what if you were not as careful with privacy settings on them? You can make a global change to previous posts by clicking on Limit Past Posts next to Limit the Audience for posts you've shared with Friends of Friends or Public?' which will allow you to limit past posts to Friends only. However, if you have tagged someone in the post, then their Friends will also be able to view your post.

Alternatively, in Facebook's Privacy Settings, you can click on 'User Activity Log' next to "Review all your posts and things you're tagged in," or go to your own profile on Facebook and click on the "Activity Log" link. This shows you all of your activity on Facebook, including links, posts, photographs, comments, tags, etc., as well as anything that has been posted about you.

Next to each item you'll see an icon that shows the audience that the item was shared with: Friends, Only Me, Friends of Friends, Public, etc. If the item is your post – posted by you – you can change the audience to be more or less restrictive. If the post was posted by someone else on someone else's Timeline, you may remove tags, but you cannot change the audience for the post. You might want to go through the Activity Log list and remove everything you wouldn't want someone else to see.

When you've finished changing your settings, double-check the result by using the "View As" feature under the gear icon on your Timeline, or click on the lock icon in the top navigation bar and click "View As" under "What do other people see on my Timeline?" Then click on "Public" or enter a specific name to see how your Timeline is seen by that person or the public.

Lock Down Photos

Even if you restrict the audience for your Facebook posts, you still may be making some information publicly available if you don't also restrict the audience for your photos. Your purpose for using Facebook will determine whether you want to be more or less restrictive with your photos than you are with other posts. Go through all your photos with a critical eye to be sure you are not over-sharing your private life with the public.

Lock Down About Information

Take some time to review your About settings. Go to your Timeline and click on "About." For each section listed, click on the Edit button and then look for the audience icons next to each item. For example, you may be comfortable with your work and educational information being available to the public, but you may not want some other items that are more personal – such as the list of people who are your Friends on Facebook – to be visible. Don't forget that now people won't necessarily need to go to the About section of your profile on Facebook to see your Likes. If you've Liked "Breaking Bad," for example, someone doing a Graph Search on "My Friends of Friends who like Breaking Bad" will come up with a list of people whom their Facebook Friends are Friends with and who have also Liked the TV show "Breaking Bad" – and your Facebook account name will likely be on the list. Since you won't always know who your Friends' Friends are, think twice about how widely available you make this information, particularly if your Facebook use is not limited to personal friends and family. To edit who can see your various Likes, click on the pencil icon next to that section (Books, for example), and then choose "Edit Privacy" to restrict the audience for any similar Likes in the future. Or you can choose to eliminate that section entirely from your profile by clicking "Hide Section."

Where You Are Exposed

If you maintain a presence on Facebook, your name, user name, profile photo, and cover photo are all publicly available. If you post to someone's Wall, such as Liking something, and his profile is open to the public, your Like post will also be searchable. When you really do Like something the person has posted, consider conveying the Like to that person in a private message.

Facebook and Photos

For tech-savvy investigators, executing skip tracing and fugitive work on Facebook can be as easy as locating Facebook photos taken and uploaded by users at family parties and picnics. One of Facebook's really useful features was the ability to pull location information and pertinent details off of the images that Facebook users uploaded to their Facebook profiles. I did say "'was"; read the following story.

Facebook in the Netherlands

One of my best investigations was when I located a family in Amsterdam by using the fugitive husband's and wife's kids who were taking photos of themselves on the canals and uploading them to Facebook.

Since I discovered neither the husband or his wife had Facebook accounts, I began monitoring the Facebook accounts of their children. Their 16 year-old daughter, unbeknownst to her parents, was an active Facebook user. One of her posts actually read, "What my dad don't (sic) know won't hurt him." I had to chuckle at that – as I was calling in the location details to the federal agency that was looking for her dad.

Much of the young girl's Facebook status updates led me to know she wasn't in the United States. When I saw photos of her standing with her sisters in front of a scenic canal, I assumed Venice. I pulled her posted photos down from her Facebook account. I ran them through Jeffrey's Exif Viewer (regex.info/exif.cgi), which, from the Exif data on the photos, returned the latitude and longitude for the photos, placing them taken in the Netherlands.

From due diligence on the wife's outdated and abandoned LinkedIn account, I had discovered that she had worked for a Scandinavian company in prior years. I phoned the company's office that night in off hours and did a directory search of the wife's name, thus finding her extension at the company. We located them!

Soon after that successful case, Facebook started stripping out the Exif data from photos posted to Facebook.

Apparently, criminals and kids aren't the only ones posting photos of themselves to Facebook; U.S. military soldiers are updating their own Facebook accounts with photos of each other and the equipment they serviced.

Although it's been reported that military command has sent out notices to soldiers to stop adding geo-location data to their Facebook profiles, such notices are rather impossible to enforce.

As a result, with each new deployment of military helicopters, it has been reported that holiday messages and other photos were being sent to family via Facebook – and the military opposition was using the digital photos' Exif data from the digital photos to target and order missile strikes and other countermeasures.

Eventually, it was reported that the military asked Facebook to strip out the Exif data on all uploaded photographs. Facebook apparently obliged, dissolving my then rather robust skip-tracing business.

Fast-forward a few years, and now Instagram has replaced Facebook in popularity as the go-to social media service for posting photos. More and more users are flocking to Instagram, especially the kids – because their parents are on Facebook, and Instagram is much easier, faster, and cooler to use. In an ironic twist, Instagram was purchased by Facebook in April, 2012, so you can still get location data from the photos uploaded to the Facebook site.

INSTAGRAM

Instagram is a smartphone application that allows for photo-sharing over social media networks. Once the photo is taken, it can be significantly altered and any number of filters (greyscale, sepia, darker, brighter, etc.) can be applied to the photo – a mini-version of Adobe Photoshop. Additionally, the image can be placed in an online frame, cropping the photo down in size, and cutting out all the noise in the background. Apparently this is a lot of fun to do, because Instagram has 60 million photos uploaded every day to its service with more than 65 percent of the activity coming in from overseas (see instagram.com/press).

The Instagram user will index the photo by adding metadata in the form of a tag. Some photo tag examples are #silly, #tbt (abbreviation for throwback thursday), or #girlsjustwanttohavefun.

To this, the user further adds the names of friends – @SusySmith, @CarolMoore, etc. to get the attention of the people in the photo itself, or to alert an interested party of the photo now being available. The photo, with its indexed metadata content, is then uploaded to Instagram. If the user's Instagram account is connected to Facebook, Twitter, or other social media networks, the photo will land on those sites as well. Among the metadata that can be attached to the photo is the physical latitude/longitude location of the shot when it was taken. If the user has his or her smartphone's geo-location feature turned on during the taking of the photo, that data will be captured and shared for all to see.

Instagram, like Facebook, does strip the Exif data out of the photo, so the photo itself isn't relaying the location of the picture, but the phone is. I want to be particularly clear about this because while you may have access to a hard drive full of Instagram photos, you will not be able to forensically do anything with those photos. However, if you are viewing someone's Instagram account, you'll see geo-data attached to the photo. In other words, the location is simply another metadata component that you can add, or remove.

For the following examples, you will need an Instagram account. To use the sites and services I recommend here, not all the sites or services require an Instagram account, but most do.

So, let's begin by creating a blank account with a no-nonsense photo. Be sure to turn off the location tag on your smartphone. For the Apple iPhone, that is under Settings>Privacy>Location Services>Instagram. For Android, Amazon, on its site, instructs:

> "On Android devices, tap the Location option from the Settings menu. Most Android devices will allow you to turn off location services for your entire phone, such as GPS services and other companies' location services. Generally, by leaving a box unchecked, the location service is turned off."

Personally, I had to turn my location services on, just to force a map location onto a photo.

Once you have an account, the best search source for Instagram images is not Instagram. Instagram does have a web interface, but it is rather difficult to search against. Instead, I recommend, in the following order: IconoSquare (iconosquare.com), Mapgrams (http://iconosquare.com/tag/mapgram), iPhoneogram (iphoneogram.com), and Websta (websta.me).

IconoSquare

IconoSquare (iconosquare.com) is a rather straightforward application. Log into IconoSqare with your own Instagram account and then start searching by username, hashtag, or keyword in the upper right-hand corner.

If you search on the hashtag #multitaskinginvestigator (all one word), in the returned results you will see the photo I uploaded. On the page you will get my nickname, full name, and the tags I added to the photo, such as #multitaskinginvestigator and #businessowner. The photo obviously shows up and I have tagged it for Twitter with @hetheringtongrp.

Additionally, the photo was taken on 4/15/2014 of .28, which is actually Unix time (see en.wikipedia.org/wiki/Unix_time for an explanation of Unix time). After the timestamp, you may see a pencil icon with words like Hefe, or X-Pro II, or similar, which are the filters used on the photo. Finally, the word 'somewhere,' with its cute little icon next to it, when clicked on, will open a map below the photo with the location of where the photo was taken. If the user has turned off the location transfer on his phone, the space will be blank. Since Instagram is a social media tool, you will see that my friends "Heart" (Instagram parlance for Facebook's "Like") my photo – which is rather important to note because my Facebook account is locked down and you can't see my Facebook Friends list. However, since I shared my Instagram photo on Facebook and Twitter, friends who "Like" my image on Facebook will "Heart" it on Instagram. You will see most people simply connect to Instagram – and other social media sites for that matter – with their Facebook or Twitter accounts, inextricably tying all their profiles into one login. So as they "Like" my photo on Facebook, the photo automatically becomes a "Heart" on Instagram. For the investigator, the crossover function allows for developing lists of associates that the investigator previously couldn't see due to Facebook security features.

Features of the other services I recommended are very similar to IconoSquare.

Mapgrams (http://iconosquare.com/tag/mapgram) offers a great feature that allows you to search by location, in addition to hashtags and keywords. The location feature helps find much Instagram activity in a particular area, and can come in handy for post-tragic-event investigations, such as the Boston marathon bombing.

iPhoneogram (iphoneogram.com) does not require that you have an Instagram account to search.

Websta (websta.me), which is similar to IconoSquare, will actually give you a better timestamp on the photo, indicating how many seconds, minutes, or days earlier the picture was posted.

Instagram is noteworthy because it brought back geo-location data that was lost when Facebook started stripping out the Exif metadata from its photographs. Now, Instagram includes the data, and the resources I've introduced in this book will pull up a convenient map and do nearly all of the forensics work of the search for you.

With Instagram gaining in popularity over Facebook, it is very likely that your target has an Instagram account.

As with all new search strategies, first practice on something uneventful and non-work related before using for your cases, to gain a comfort level in a benign environment while learning to use these new investigative tools.

Privacy on Instagram

In short, unless you are following friends or commenting on someone's pictures, they cannot see you viewing their photos.

LinkedIn

The go-to resource for due diligence investigations in social media is LinkedIn. Mentioned often in this book, no other social media site covers the business and professional life of an individual as well as LinkedIn does. The equivalent of an online resume, LinkedIn's user profile details the person's full history, including education, degrees, certifications, and accolades.

Finding the Individual

You can look for an individual's LinkedIn account by searching for the person in an online search engine such as Google or Bing. Another method of search is to have your own LinkedIn account, set it to Private, and then search LinkedIn for the person by typing the person's name directly into the LinkedIn search box. If too many results matching your name are returned, then narrow down the search by qualifying it with country, company, or other fields LinkedIn offers up.

Set Your Profile to Anonymous

If you do not set your own LinkedIn profile to Anonymous and you then attempt to view an individual's LinkedIn profile, the individual will know that you viewed his profile. While naming you and presenting your LinkedIn account's photo, LinkedIn will send an alert to the individual that you viewed his profile. To be anonymous, you must set your LinkedIn profile to anonymous. Use the following steps to set your LinkedIn profile to anonymous:

1. Log in to your LinkedIn account, then go to the upper right-hand corner of the screen, where your settings are listed (a drop-down menu from your LinkedIn profile photo).

2. Choose Privacy and Settings, and then click Manage – don't freak out; you will be asked to Login again.

3. Go ahead and Login again.

4. Under Privacy Controls, go to the third option "Select what others see when you've viewed their profile" and click on that.

5. Choose the 'totally anonymous' option. NOTE: With this, free subscribers will lose the advantage of seeing who is viewing your LinkedIn profile.

Leave your LinkedIn setting to totally anonymous and never set it otherwise. If you are a free subscriber, yes, you will lose the advantage of seeing who is viewing your profile. However it is not worth the risk of exposing your information. Do note that Premium subscribers can both see who is viewing their profile and be anonymous.

A Few Final Comments About Social Media Sites

As new social media sites make their debut, be open minded and experiment with them. They may seem pointless in many ways – you may feel like you're working in an area that is only attractive to 15 year-old kids. However, think of the hundreds of grown-ups you daily see with their noses in their phones; they are not all reading Bloomberg headlines and texting important meeting updates. They are spilling details of their private personal lives out onto social media sites – just the information you, dear investigator, may be searching for.

The online world of open sources, along with specialized databases – resources unique to specific industries – and now with social media added to the mix, have created a wide array of tools for online due diligence investigations. Learning to effectively use these tools well will give you a head start over other non-online investigators. You will find this introduction is only the beginning. As you move about the online world, you'll find yourself discovering new resources not mentioned in these pages. The online world of information is ever-changing and ever-evolving. The more involved you get in online due diligence, the deeper into the world of online databases and open sources you will go.

Be analytical, but open minded. When new resources appear, always try them; search on a subject you are most familiar with. Only through comparison can we review and judge new services and social media sites. Keep in mind: as soon as one tool becomes a favorite bookmarked site, it can disappear overnight. The wise and effective investigator will have an arsenal of examined and vetted resources at his or her disposal to use for due diligence.

In the end, it all comes down to critical thinking and a creative approach. Sure, the online sites and services help – a lot – but truly critical thinking and a creative approach will help shape and mold your due diligence reports. With critical thinking and a creative approach, be ever vigilant in constantly improving your skills and methodology; doing so will keep your mind sharp and your investigative reports focused.

A List of Major Social Networking Sites

The list of Social Networking Sites below is taken directly from Wikipedia.org. Ths list includes sites from other countires, but it does not include dating websites. The list appears at http://en.wikipedia.org/wiki/List_of_social_networking_websites.

Name	Description/focus
43 Things	Goal setting and achievement
Academia.edu	Social networking site for academics/researchers
About.me	Social networking site
Advogato	Free and open source software developers
aNobii	Books
AsianAvenue	A social network for the Asian American community
aSmallWorld	European jet set and social elite world-wide
Athlinks	Running, swimming
Audimated.com	Independent music
Bebo	General
Biip.no	Norwegian community
BlackPlanet	Black Americans
Blauk	Anyone who wants to tell something about a stranger or acquaintance.
Blogster	Blogging community
Bolt.com	General
Busuu	Language learning community (headquartered in Madrid, Spain)
Buzznet	Music and pop-culture
CafeMom	Mothers
Care2	Green living and social activism
CaringBridge	Not for profit providing free websites that connect family and friends during a serious health event, care and recovery.
Classmates.com	School, college, work and the military
Cloob	General. Popular in Iran
ClusterFlunk	American network for students to share files with their peers
CouchSurfing	Worldwide network for making connections between travelers and the communities they visit.
CozyCot	East Asian and Southeast Asian women
Cross.tv	Faith-based social network for Christian believers from around the world
Crunchyroll	Anime and forums.
Cucumbertown	Networking for cooks
Cyworld	General. Popular in South Korea.
DailyBooth	Photo-blogging site where users upload a photo every day
DailyStrength	Medical & emotional support community - physical& mental health, support groups
delicious	Social bookmarking allows users to locate and save websites matching interests
deviantART	Art community
Diaspora*	Decentralized, privacy aware, general (open source)
didlr	Drawing service
Disaboom	People with disabilities (amputees, cerebral palsy, MS, and other disabilities)
Dol2day	Politic community, social network, Internet radio (German-speaking countries)
DontStayIn	Clubbing (primarily UK)
Draugiem.lv	General (primarily LV, LT, HU)

Name	Description/focus
douban	Chinese Web 2.0 website providing user review and recommendation services for movies, books, and music.
DXY.cn	Chinese online community for physicians, health care professionals, pharmacies and facilities
Elftown	Community and wiki around fantasy and sci-fi.
Ello	General
Elixio	Business executives jet set and global elite.
English, baby!	Students and teachers of English as a second language
Epernicus	For research scientists
Eons.com	For baby boomers and mature internet users age 40 and beyond.
eToro	Social investing, finance
Experience Project	Life experiences
Exploroo	Travel social networking.
Facebook	General: photos, videos, blogs, apps.
Faceparty	General. Popular UK.
Faces.com	Adult social network, mainly UK & USA
Fetlife	People who are into BDSM
FilmAffinity	Movies and TV series
Filmow	Movies and TV series
FledgeWing	Entrepreneural community targeted towards worldwide university students
Flixster	Movies
Flickr	Photo sharing, commenting, photography related networking, worldwide
Focus.com	Business-to-business, worldwide
Fotki	Photo sharing, video hosting, photo contests, journals, forums, flexible privacy protection, audio comments and unlimited custom design integration.
Fotolog	Photoblogging. Popular in South America and Spain
Foursquare	Location based mobile social network
Friendica	Distributed, federated, privacy aware, open source, general
Friends Reunited	UK based. School, college, work, sport and streets
Friendster	General. Popular in Southeast Asia. No longer popular in the western world
Frühstückstreff	General
Fuelmyblog	Blogging community
FullCircle	Geosocial networking and location-based services portal for mobile devices
Gaia Online	Anime and games. Most popular in USA, Canada and Europe.
GamerDNA	Computer and video games
Gapyear.com	Travel social network
Gather.com	Article, picture, and video sharing, as well as group discussions
Gays.com	For LGBT community, guide for LGBT bars, restaurants, clubs, shopping
Geni.com	Families, genealogy
GetGlue	Social network for entertainment.
Gogoyoko	Fair play in music - social networking site for musicians and music lovers.
Goodreads	Library cataloging, book lovers.
Goodwizz	Social network with matchmaking and personality games to find new contacts. Global, based in France.
Google+	General
GovLoop	For people in and around government.
Grono.net	Poland

Name	Description/focus
Habbo	General for teens. Over 31 communities worldwide. Chat room and user profiles.
hi5	General. Popular in Nepal, Mongolia, Thailand, Romania, Jamaica, Central Africa, Portugal and Latin America. Not very popular in the USA.
Hospitality Club	Hospitality
Hotlist	Geo-social aggregator rooted in the concept of knowing where users' friends are, were, and will be.
HR.com	Social networking site for human resources professionals.
Hub Culture	Global influencers focused on worth creation.
Hyves	General, mostly popular in the Netherlands.
Ibibo	Talent based social networking site that allows to promote one's self and also discover new talent. Most popular in India.
Identi.ca	Twitter-like service popular with hackers and software freedom advocates.
Indaba Music	Online collaboration for musicians, remix contests, and networking.
Influenster	Online product sampling and review platform.
Instagram	A photo and video sharing site.
IRC-Galleria	Finland
italki.com	Language learning social network. 100+ languages.
Itsmy	Mobile community worldwide, blogging, friends, personal TV-shows
iWiW	Hungary
Jaiku	General. Microblogging. Owned by Google
Jiepang	Location-based mobile social network. In Chinese language
Kaixin001	General. In Simplified Chinese; caters for mainland China users
Kiwibox	General.
Lafango	Talent-focused media sharing site
LaiBhaari	Marathi social networking
Last.fm	Music
LibraryThing	Book lovers
Lifeknot	Shared interests, hobbies
LinkedIn	Business and professional networking
LinkExpats	Social networking website for expatriates. 100+ countries.
Listography	Lists. Autobiography
LiveJournal	Blogging. Popular in Russia and among the Russian-speaking diaspora abroad.
Livemocha	Online language learning
Makeoutclub	General
MEETin	General
Meetup (website)	General. Used to plan offline meetings for people interested in various activities
Meettheboss	Business and finance community, worldwide.
MillatFacebook	General, created in response to Facebook
mixi	Japan
MocoSpace	Mobile community, worldwide
MOG	Music
MouthShut.com	Social network, social media, consumer reviews
Mubi	Auteur cinema
MyHeritage	Family-oriented social network service
MyLife	Locating friends and family, keeping in touch (formerly Reunion.com)
My Opera	Blogging, mobile blogging, photo sharing, connecting with friends, Opera Link and Opera Unite. Global

Name	Description/focus
Myspace	General
Nasza-klasa.pl	School, college and friends. Popular in Poland
Netlog	General. Popular in Europe, Turkey, the Arab world and Canada's Québec province. Formerly known as Facebox and Redbox.
Nexopia	Canada
NGO Post	Non-profit news sharing and networking, mainly in India
Ning	Users create their own social websites and social networks
Odnoklassniki	Connect with old classmates. Popular in Russia and former Soviet republics
Open Diary	First online blogging community, founded in 1998
Orkut	General. Owned by Google Inc. Popular in India and Brazil.
OUTeverywhere	Gay/LGBTQ community
PatientsLikeMe	Online community for patients with life-changing illnesses to find other patients like them, to share and learn
Partyflock	Dutch virtual community for people interested in house music and other electronic dance music.
Pingsta	Collaborative platform for the world's internetwork experts
Pinterest	Online pinboard for organizing and sharing things you love
Plaxo	Aggregator
Playfire	Computer and video games
Playlist.com	General, music
Plurk	Micro-blogging, RSS, updates. Very popular in Taiwan
Poolwo	Social networking site from India
Qapacity	A business-oriented social networking site and a business directory
Quechup	General, friendship, dating
Qzone	General. In Simplified Chinese; caters for mainland China users
Raptr	Video games
Ravelry	Knitting and crochet
Renren	Significant site in China. Was known as (Xiaonei) until August 2009.
ReverbNation.com	Social network for musician and bands
Ryze	Business
ScienceStage	Science-oriented multimedia platform and network for scientists
Sgrouples	General, with focus on privacy rights
ShareTheMusic	Music community. Sharing and listening to music for free and legally
Shelfari	Books
Sina Weibo	Social microblogging site in mainland China.
Skoob	Collaborative social network for Brazilian readers
Skyrock	Social network in French-speaking world
SocialVibe	Social network for charity
Sonico.com	General. Popular in Latin America and Spanish and Portuguese speaking regions.
SoundCloud	Repository of original music pieces and networking.
Spaces	Russian social network targeted to mobile phone users
Spot.IM	A service for webmasters to add social networking functionality to their websites
Spring.me	Social network for meeting people
Stage 32	US-based social network and educational site for creative professionals in film, television and theater
Stickam	Live video streaming and chat.
StudiVZ	University students, mostly in the German-speaking countries. School students and

Name	Description/focus
	those out of education sign up via its partner sites schülerVZ and meinVZ.
Students Circle Network	A social network connecting students, teachers and institutions to course resources, study groups and learning spaces.
StumbleUpon	Stumble through websites that match users' selected interests
Tagged	General.
Talkbiznow	Business networking
Taltopia	Online artistic community
Taringa!	General (primarily Argentina)
TeachStreet	Education / learning / teaching - more than 400 subjects
TermWiki	Learning / languages / translation - 1.2 million terms in more than 1300 subjects
The Sphere	A private online social luxury network with exclusive personalized services
TravBuddy.com	Travel
Travellerspoint	Travel
tribe.net	General
Trombi.com	French subsidiary of Classmates.com
Tuenti	Spanish-based university and high school social network.
Tumblr	Microblogging platform and social networking website.
Twitter	General. Micro-blogging, RSS, updates
Tylted	Mobile social game network[311]
Vkontakte	General, including music upload, listening and search. Popular in Russia and former Soviet republics.
Vampirefreaks.com	Gothic and industrial subculture
Viadeo	Global social networking and campus networking available in English, French, German, Spanish, Italian and Portuguese
Virb	Social network that focuses heavily on artists, musicians and photographers
Vox	Blogging
Wattpad	For readers and authors to interact and e-book sharing
WAYN	Travel and lifestyle
WeeWorld	Teenagers - 9 to 17
We Heart It	Image-based social network focused on inspiration, expression and creativity
Wellwer	Community without borders, where sharing is everything.
WeOurFamily	General with emphasis on privacy and security
Wepolls.com	Social polling network
Wer-kennt-wen	General
weRead	Books
Wiser.org	Online community space for the social justice and environmental movement[334]
Wooxie	Blogging and micro-blogging
WriteAPrisoner.com	Site networking inmates, friends, family
Xanga	Blogs and "metro" areas
XING	Business (primarily Europe (Germany, Austria, Switzerland))
Xt3	Catholic social networking, created for World Youth Day 2008
Yammer	Social networking for office colleagues
Yelp, Inc.	Local business review and talk
Yookos	General: photos, videos, blogs, games.
Zoo.gr	Greek web meeting point
Zooppa	Online community for creative talent (host of brand sponsored advertising contests)

Ch 11:

Client Interaction: Intake, Preparing the Report, and Billing

I've been rich and I've been poor; rich is much better.
—Sophie Tucker

This chapter will help make you successful not only as an investigator, but also as a business person. We will scrutinize four key functions in the relationship you establish with your clientele—

1. Taking the Order
2. Client Agreements
3. Creating the Report for the Client
4. Analyzing Your Costs and Billing Your Services

At the end of this chapter are several sample reports.

Taking the Order

I cannot emphasize enough the importance of communicating with the client to establish criteria and expectations. The expectations between the client and the investigator must be made clear at the outset of a case. This clarity starts with how you take the order or accept the case.

The rest of this subsection is adapted from a chapter in *Public Record Retrieval Industry Standards Manual*, written for members of the Public Record Retriever Network (PRRN). Carl Ernst, who was the Network's co-director at he time he wrote the original article, hits home on explaining the nuances to consider when taking a client order. I sincerely thank Mr. Ernst (who since has passed away) and of course PRRN for allowing me to modify the article and to place it in this book.

How Do You Take an Order?

Generating a great report, while protecting your firm from complaints and litigation, starts with the manner in which you take the original order.

If you receive your client's search instructions in writing – either by mail, fax, or email – your chances of making a mistake in the execution of the order is minimized, although you must still be careful that the instructions are legible and complete, as discussed below.

On the other hand if you take an order by telephone, you must be extremely diligent to follow a set of written, standard procedures. This not only insures that you took it correctly, but also protects you in the event you must convince a disgruntled client later that you did not mishear any part of the order. The reason you convert your telephone-order procedure to writing will become clear momentarily.

The Six Essential Questions

Procedure is one thing; content is another. If you do not ask all of the essential questions needed so you can complete the investigation exactly as your client wishes it to be completed, you are asking for trouble. Remember the old saying that to ASSUME makes an ASS out of U and ME. Ask all the questions. Make sure both you and the client are clear about the objectives in doing the search.

Here are six questions that are essential to include in standard, written procedures. Ask the question, record the answer.

1. What is the Purpose of the Investigation?

You must always be crystal clear about what information your client wants. Do not let your client give vague instructions. The purpose of the investigation will determine what you investigate and research. Remember the discussion in Chapter 1: If your client says, "I would like to know more about ABC Company." The investigator's follow-up questions should be, "What do you want to know about ABC Company? Is it a competitor, a potential acquisition, or a defaulted company?"

2. What is the Subject's Name?

If the subject is a **Business Entity:** Your client may ask you to find a corporate name. Would your client also like you to search LLC and limited partnership records, trademarks, or fictitious names?

Whatever the type of search, it is best to tell your client the options she has, and then let her choose from them. If the client wants less than what you would consider a full search, make this content restriction clear in your report.

If the subject is an **Individual:** The procedure followed by a national UCC search firm is to read back the subject's name letter by letter, using a version of the "Able, Baker" alphabet. A check mark is placed above each letter as it is confirmed. Then the location to be searched is repeated, and a check mark is placed over it when it is confirmed.

In the event a client later complained that you got the name wrong, you could produce the original order, point out the check marks, and show a copy of your procedures manual to affirm what the check marks meant. I can assure you that this procedure has quickly stopped a lot of complaints.

You also should use certain standards to determine if the subject name you are given is complete for your purposes. An individual's name, like "Carl Ernst," may be adequate for your purposes, or you may want to ask whether the middle initial is known, especially if the name is common. "C. Alexander Ernst" may create real search problems for you if you don't know what the C stands for.

In addition, if the subject is an individual, you must determine the purpose of the investigation or search to avoid running afoul of federal or state laws with respect to personal information privacy, such as the Fair Credit Reporting Act. If the stated purpose is, for example, employment related, you must be aware of the rules that govern the responsibilities of you and your client as a credit reporting agency or retriever.

3. What Results do You Anticipate?

A business investigation is not a test. Your job is to try to find anything that is on the records, but only within the constraints placed by your client, by the government office, and by your standard search practices. You are not Superman or Superwoman. You may be expected to find common variations of the subject name, but you cannot, nor are you responsible to, determine all the weird variations that a keypuncher might inflict on a name.

Therefore, it always helps to know whether your client is aware of any records that now exist on the subject. This is especially helpful when a filing office charges a lot for copies, and makes them for all searches automatically. If your client knows the subject has hundreds of filings, you may be able to advise her of more cost-efficient ways to search the records without incurring substantial copy charges.

Occasionally, your client may say, "That's none of your business; you do the investigating." In that case, your client may be testing you, and that is OK. But you should take the opportunity to explain that part of your investigation will involve searching public records, and these records are frequently mis-indexed by the clerks or filing officers. So you would usually extend your search procedures beyond your usual thorough methods, if you did not get a hit when one was anticipated.

If your client asks for a UCC search, does she mean to include tax liens, and if so, just federal, or federal and state tax liens? What about judgments or judgment liens? If the search is in a former dual-filing state, is only a central office search being requested, or should a local, filing office search also be conducted? Is your client aware of the different types of search methods necessary to overcome the limitations of searches, under Revised Article 9 of the UCC, in most central filing offices?

If the investigation involves real estate searches, a client needs to know if a subject owns any property in another county, and she might want to know if any properties are mortgaged.

4. What is the Time Period to Investigate?

You will need to know how far back to search many public records. When using online systems, you will need to be careful to verify that the throughput date of computerized data goes back as far as needed. Otherwise, a separate, manual search of the older records will be required. You will need to know how far back to search many public records.

5. What Documents Do You Want to Obtain?

I am not going to dwell on this aspect of the order, except to say that it can be really costly if you order or copy 500 court case filings, and then find out that your client doesn't want them and won't pay for them. If, however, you have no choice but to obtain documents as part of a search, you should inform your client of the possibility of excessive copy costs before performing the search.

6. How Do You Want the Results?

This question has two parts. First, when does your client need the results? If the client needs the information in four weeks, you say OK, but produce the results in two days. Then, you will look like a hero, which is good for your marketing. On the other hand, if your client has an unreasonable time expectation, you might as well deal with the problem up front to avoid the disgruntled phone call later.

Second, what is the form of delivery for reporting the results? Does your client want the report by email, fax, phone, express mail, or just standard mail?

––––

Creating the Client Agreements

There are several types of documents to consider when establishing an agreement with a client. Samples for each of these documents are provided at the end of this chapter.

1. A **Letter of Engagement** specifically outlines what the investigator is hired to do and how to prepare the results, and it gives an outline of the anticipated charges and fees.

2. An **Agreement to Provide Investigative Services** is similar to Letter of Engagement, but is more generalized and used for smaller cases.

3. A **Contract** is generally used for ongoing work with a client, spelling out the work and expectations.

4. A **Non-Disclosure Agreement** should be signed by both parties. This document protects you and your client from the loss of trade secrets or sensitive information. There are two add-on Exhibits than can be added to a Non-Disclosure Agreement: Confidential Information and a Form of Employee Acknowledgment.

The tradition in many client/investigator relationships is to rely primarily on verbal agreement, with a small, written component often stated on the search report and/or on the invoice for services. However, the lack of an initial written agreement or contract can prove to be a mistake for both parties. This becomes a mistake for the investigator if the responsibilities are never clearly stated, and perhaps, not well understood. The lack of a written agreement will become a mistake for the client if she or he is never required to thoroughly think about to expect, and what not to expect, from the investigator.

About the Letter of Engagement and Letter of Agreement

A written agreement using a standard form document allows you to enter the specifics about the case and about the client in an easy to use format. This can also be on company stationery. The following information should be included:

- Your company's name, address, and contact information
- Your client's name, address, and contact information
- Date and time order was placed
- Client instructions
- Any agreed upon specifics, like turnaround time or pricing
- Anticipated results, if applicable.

About Contracts

If your written contract needs to be negotiated, then use the contract as an opportunity to educate your client about the real world where disclaimers are necessary, because of the vagaries of resources, public records, and the artfulness of the search process.

There are multiple styles and formats for writing a contract. They should include financial terms, timeline expectations, expected deliverables, and legal jurisdiction.

AUTHOR TIP **Where to Find a Good Master Contract**
Nolo Press offers many contracts for sale via its Web site at nolo.com. You also can inquire with a state or national investigator association for any samples or templates from other investigators.

Hiring an attorney to advise you on the creation of basic paperwork templates is a good idea and will also give you some peace of mind.

About the Non-Disclosure Agreement

A Non-Disclosure Agreement (NDA) should be a standard item, signed by both parties when an investigator takes on a new client. In fact, every new client should ask you to sign his own NDA. If the client does not suggest this, then offer one of your own. The NDA can be part of a package for the new client, with the Letter of Agreement or the Contract.

An NDA is especially important for compliance with federal regulations mentioned previously, such as SOX and HIPPA, but should be an expected requirement from all clients due to the sensitive nature of investigative work.

There are two recommended Exhibits (add-ons) also:

- Exhibit A: Confidential Information
- Exhibit B: Form of Employee Acknowledgement

As mentioned above, samples of all of these documents are provided at the end of this chapter.

Establishing the Cost of the Report

Many investigators often find two of the more difficult tasks is recognizing costs and mastering the procedure of billing the client. With experience you can gauge and anticipate your costs; however, even seasoned investigators have been surprised by greater than anticipated expenses. For example, if a court document needs to be pulled, copied and sent to a client, what if it contains dozens of pages more than anticipated. If the copy fee is $1.00 page, and you quoted $6.00 instead of $48.00, you are in trouble. Just the management of subcontractors, database search cost, as well as any other reports purchased, can escalate the cost of conducting an investigation very quickly.

Use a Tracking System

The best way to monitor these is to create a tracking system and checklist. There are Case Management Software Programs that provide this type of service. They can be quite helpful if you have large caseloads and even if you have many investigators working for you. However, a simple system where you write down each report that you pull and each database you use also works well. Create a checklist or file for each case, and list all the costs you encounter. Even generic check-book programs like QuickBooks or Quicken can be used for cost accounting purposes.

Another key point is to take advantage of cost tracking features that database and online vendors offer. For example, when you log into systems for TransUnion TLO, Accurint, LexisNexis, and D&B, etc., use the place or field they provide to record a specific project name or number. When invoices arrive at the end of the month, simply separate the costs by the respective client names or numbers so you can then record the figures as you would any other project cost. Be prepared for some slow-coming invoices, such as PACER which send bills quarterly.

Other costs in a case may involve hiring outside record retrievers, ordering unusual reports specific to the case, office expenses such as printing, binding and mailing the report, and the traditional expenses such as mileage, film (surveillance), meals, etc.

AUTHOR TIP   If you you hire a public record retriever or sub-contractor in a foreign country, make sure you clarify all the costs up front. In instances when costs are uncertain (i.e. record retriever doesn't know how many pages until file is found), ask to be contacted to verify the final cost or set a limit of a dollar amount not to exceed without approval from you.

Tracking Database Costs

Database costs should be somewhat predictable if you pay by the report. The following is an example of an investigator's hard or true costs on a basic due diligence of one small U.S. company with three executives:

- 3 comprehensive reports $60.00 @ $20 per report.
- 1 D&B Business Report $75.00
- 1 Experian Business Report $30.00
- 20 News Media Articles $60 @ $3.00 per story.

The investigator's hard cost for this case's particular set of searches is $225.00.

However, if you pay a vendor by subscription or on an 'all you can eat' program, then you have two choices:

1. If you know how many persons or companies you are investigating for the subscription's billing period, you can devise a simple matrix that will calculate the cost. And for goodness sake round up to make it easier.

2. Standardize your costs. Say you figure you average X cases a month that use a particular service, simply divide the subscription cost by X. If you have a busy month, then the better for you.

Tracking Your Time

There is one cost you do not want to forget. **Yourself!** Investigators often discount their own hours in order to keep the price down. Remember your client is hiring you for your skill set, not the fancy databases and marketing expertise you have. Do not ever discount your own fee; otherwise your client will expect a reduced fee every time and will not understand your value and your worth. If you want to impress a client, then slice a percentage off the bill, but explain that this is a special situation.

Preparing the Report

As discussed earlier, while there are many styles used to write reports, using a format that is simple, clean, and professional is a definite must. An excellent reference for report writing is what I have called my go-to guide since college, *The Publication Manual of the American Psychological Association* also known as the *APA Style Manual*. Although using this reference may seem like overkill for some reports, keep in mind that your report could be read by attorneys and judges. By using a format commonly used in graduate schools, your client will understand the style and appreciate your attention to detail. That said, not everything I do is applicable to this style guide.

Depending on the type of investigation you are conducting, SWOT and CARA are interchangeable in many ways. SWOT (probably the most widely used analytical tool), CARA, and Supply Chain Analysis are used in the sample reports to follow.

The Investigative Report on a Principal

The following example provides a report style for a standard due diligence check on an individual with an emphasis on using the CARA method of analysis. This example has instructional text mixed in with sample, reporting language, which is in italics. Although presented on a bullet-list basis, a numeric-list presentation is also very acceptable. Sample report text is shown in *italics*.

Sample Report Format on a Principle

1. Cover Page

The cover sheet should include your company's name, the client's name, the date, and the name of the report.

Also on the cover page, place the words *Privileged* and *Confidential*. If you are working with an attorney, place the words *Attorney Work Product*.

2. Summary Analysis

If the report exceeds 30 pages, create a table of contents. If not, then just continue to the next point.

- **The Objective**

Stating the basics of who hired you and why is sufficient, but you can expand on this as well.

ABC Company has engaged XYZ Investigative Services, Inc. to conduct a personal due diligence/background check on Joseph Smith. This investigation was conducted utilizing public records, legal filings, media sources, and discreet interviews.

- **Executive Summary**

Summarize the individual's background and highlight any key issues. Draw out key findings from documents you have analyzed so that the client reads these first. You do not want to force the client to find out about the subject's criminal history ten pages into your report. Very clearly itemize what is important in your summary, and what needs to be done. Also you can make recommendations and follow-ups in this section.

- CARA Analysis

Here, state any very notable CARA indicators that developed during the course of your investigation. This text also may be incorporated into the summary statement.

Characteristics give a sense of the subject's personality. Look at his rank or position and the type of car he drives. Is he litigious? Has he been convicted of any crimes or rewarded for any heroic acts?

Military records indicate John Smith spent 20 years in the United States Army and retired honorably with Purple Heart and Meritorious Service Medals.

Associations with other people, either professional or personal, help in understanding the socio-economic position of the subject, whether he is wealthy, an average worker, or a criminal.

A marriage announcement, located from ten years ago, [put the actual date in] states that John Smith married Antoinette Vanderbilt of the Vanderbilt Estates, a wealthy and well- established family.

Reputation searches present the best opportunities to hear what people say about the person and his affiliates.

According to interviews with former subordinates, Smith was considered a fair commander, a brave soldier, and lived very much by the book. However, an interview with a female former staff sergeant who served under his command, revealed that Smith held a bias against women in the military, and was opposed to females in combat. And although he never publicly stated as such, he "showed a bias against known homosexual military personnel."

Affiliations with certain companies, organizations, associations, and educational facilities are very telling.

Currently, Smith is connected to the Republican Party and it is rumored that he is considering running for public office. Local media have asked him if he is considering entering the race for the U.S. Senate, but he will neither confirm nor deny this speculation.

3. Body of Report

- Vital Information

Public records reveal the subject's full name and his date of birth, as well as his spouse's full name (need maiden name) and her date of birth.

> *The couple have resided at 170 Dryer Road, Swisstown, in Morris County, New Jersey 07524, since June 1993. The telephone number listed to both is (908) 555-4567. He has five children, with their names and ages also listed.*

- Professional History

Discuss the type of professional business career your subject has had and note if there are any discrepancies in his employment dates. If the subject does not have any companies listed for two years and you cannot fill that gap, make sure you mention that fact. It might be an indicator that the subject was out of the country or in prison.

If any questionable information turns up, you should write it directly at the beginning of this section. Otherwise, list the following in descending order:

> Years of service
>
> Company that employed the subject
>
> Subject's job title
>
> Short definition of the company's practice

For example:

> *Here is information that was located on the subject, listed in descending order:*
>
> ○ *1994 to 1996*
>
> ○ *DEF Group L.P.*
>
> ○ *Limited Partner*
>
> ○ *Capital investment group with major investments in emerging markets, petroleum, and generic pharmaceuticals.*

- Board Positions

Chapter 4 goes into depth on why board positions are so important. This section of the report should be presented in the same itemized style as the professional history. Again, highlight any incongruence or possible collusion issues directly at the beginning of this section.

> *Subject has sat on several boards, but one of note is Reliance Hospital. This might seem inappropriate, as the subject is also the lead developing contractor for the new wing of Reliance Hospital. Recommend further research into this matter to insure no collusion or favoritism was bestowed on the subject, considering his role as a board member.*

1996 to present

    ○ IBM

    ○ Board Member

    ○ Chair of Compliance

- Political Affiliations

Political affiliations will enlighten you on where the subject spends his money, and how he feels about hot-button issues, like stem cell research and the environment. However, do not judge too quickly because many corporate executives play both sides of the political race to get the best advantage for their company.

If the subject is active in politics, explain that here. Mention any donations to campaigns. If you locate his voter registration information, mention it.

- Charitable Works

If your subject sits on the board of a charitable organization, take note of who else is a board member. Many corporate people sign up for feel-good projects because it is great networking. They like to attend swanky annual fundraisers and mix with the rich and famous. Keep in mind though, if they are dedicating a good deal of their time to charities, or if you are reading a lot about their activities, then they may have real reasons to be involved. People often join children's health charities because of personal interests regarding their own children or a friend's children.

Mention any notes regarding the subject's personal interest versus professional interest; mention any donations to charities; describe charitable works, projects and activities; and list any charity board seats.

> *Subject is a board member for the United Way of Greater New York. Also on this board are several corporate CEOs [name a few]. Subject also is active in the Children's Diabetes Foundation. A New York City metro newspaper article, published on January 5, 1999, talked about the subject's involvement with the Children's Diabetes Foundation because of his "son's severe diabetic condition."*

- Academic Credentials and Special Licenses

If your subject attended college or trade school and has received special certifications in his profession, highlight the achievements here. But, you should verify these claims. Education is one of the most frequently exaggerated sections of a report.

Once the information is collected and vetted, report it in a manner that is consistent with section on board positions. Note: The following academic records information can be verified by contacting the records departments for each school:

Level of education

Year graduated

University, college, or trade school

Certifications, if any

Elaborate on certifications if they are pertinent to the case.

- Identified Assets

Physical assets such as properties, automobiles, luxury boats, vacation or investments homes, business licenses, and significant shareholder wealth should be identified in this section. This works as a great pull-out section for the reader to get to the bottom dollar. Many times these background checks are performed to see if the subject is worth going after in court. A prejudgment search to identify any assets, prior to litigating, might help the client collect on his debts.

Types of assets are indicated below:

Real Property

Subject is the registered owner of 170 Dryer Road, Swisstown, in Morris County, New Jersey 07062. The property was purchased on January 15, 1999 for $8,000,000.

Previous and unverified addresses include:

123 5th Avenue, Floor 15, New York, New York 10017

101 Knights Palace, Bronx, New York 10468

Physical Assets (Note: motor vehicles, vessels, airplanes, etc.)

Subject is the registered driver of a 2007 Mercedes-Benz Coupe. Mercedes-Benz Credit Leasing, Inc. is listed as the registered owner. There is also luxury watercraft listed for the subject, a 2004 Sea Ray 390 Motor Yacht.

Financial Assets

Financial assets are certainly an indicator of wealth. If your subject has a trust account named for him, he may come from a wealthy lineage. If not, he may be protecting his assets. Indicate the investigation results for the following items:

Trusts

Significant shareholders

Recipients of any judgments

UCCs

Intellectual Properties

One of the most valuable items that could be in your subject's coffer is any patent that he may hold. Make sure you report these items correctly. A corporate scientist may be the patent creator, but his company is the patent holder. In terms of intellectual property, I always grab a PDF copy of the stated asset and append it to my report. And, in this particular case, I would mention that the subject was shown to have 12 registered patents under his name, in what appeared to be a fuel-processing methodology.

Copyrights and trademarks are much more straightforward. For instance, in the example above, I would report that the subject has had several copyrighted works published on fuel processing and that he owned the trademark to the mark fuel methods.

Following the APA Style Manual in citing works for papers, I use the same style guide for professional reports. See the following examples.

Sample text using fonts from APA Style Manual:

- Copyrights

  - Smith, J. (1999). *Fuel: Processing Methods*. Chicago, IL: CCR Publishing.

- Patents

  - Smith, J. (1995). U.S. Patent No. 123,434. Washington, D.C.: U.S. Patent and Trademark Office.

- Trademarks

  - Smith, J. (1995). *Fuel Methods*. Washington, D.C.: U.S. Patent and Trademark Office.

- **Legal Findings**

Civil and criminal matters should be cited clearly and separately in this portion of the report. Report criminal matters first. Make sure you know the search variables of the sources you used so that you can accurately report what was and was not searched. For example, many states only offer convictions history and do not indicate arrests without dispositions.

Example:

For the last seven years in [State], there were no convictions, misdemeanors, or felonies located.

A domestic dispute charge was filed in [County] on 12/24/1999.

Then list the details.

There are two format methods to use to report civil cases. The first example is reported as follows:

Case name

Date filed

Date terminated

Office

Nature of suit

Cause

Plaintiff

Defendant

If you notice names or further content in the dockets or summary, continue your listing with a short narrative.

The second example is:

> *On January 15, 1999, ABC Company filed a breach-of-contract claim against the Smith Group in New York County Supreme Court. Defendants named, in addition to the Smith Group, were Kathy and John Smith. The case was voluntarily dismissed on June 9, 1999.*

- **Regulatory, Sanction, and Disciplinary Issues**

Chapter 6 discusses how to investigate regulatory and disciplinary issues. Below shows how to report the findings. Use the headings as shown in the sample text below:

Reporting Regulatory Issues

Online searches, through various U.S. regulatory agencies like the Office of Foreign Asset Control, the Central Contractors Registry, and the Excluded Parties Database, did not reveal any matches to the subject.

Reporting Disciplinary Issues

A search in the Health and Human Services Office of Inspector General did not reveal any matches to the subject. Nor were any matches located in the State of Florida Disciplinary Actions database for physicians.

- **Financial Troubles**

Liens and debts, caused by lawsuits and bankruptcies, are straightforward for reporting purposes. Below is sample text:

Tax Liens – Judgments

Subject is seen to have an unsatisfied federal tax lien of $10,000 from 1998, registered in the state of Montana.

Subject has an unsatisfied judgment/lien for $5,000, resulting from a lawsuit filed in 1999 by the ABC Company.

Bankruptcies

Subject filed for Chapter 7 bankruptcy protection on August 2, 1998. Bankruptcy was granted and a list of his debts and creditors can be provided, if requested.

You can list the creditors and the money owed, but appending or offering for further information later is better, unless you see something significant in the creditor's report.

- **Media**

The media findings should be reported in descending order. There are two schools of thought on how to report media issues, and both are certainly acceptable.

You can summarize the story for brevity sake, which is a more professional approach to report writing. Sample:

> *Date – Source – Title*
>
> *Truncated article, italicized, justified, and indented .5 on each side.*

Or you can include key portions of the article, quoting it entirely or paraphrasing the report. In some cases, this is necessary because the subject material may be beyond your comprehension of the topic, and the paraphrasing could turn out to be inaccurate. Sample:

> *Summary of article as follows:*
>
> *On June 2, 1996, the New York Times reported that Bob Smith was found guilty of racketeering.*

The Investigative Report on a Company

Much of the company reporting style is the same as the principal's style just outlined. In this sample breakdown report on a company, the supply chain method of analysis will be demonstrated. A bullet-list method is used below for presentation. Again, sample text is shown in *italics*.

Sample Report Format on a Principle

1. Cover Page

The cover sheet should include your company's name, the client's name, the date, and the name of the report.

Also on the cover page, place the words *Privileged* and *Confidential*. If you are working with an attorney, place the words *Attorney Work Product*.

2. Summary Analysis

If the report exceeds 30 pages, create a table of contents. If not, then just continue to the next point.

- **The Objective**

Stating the basics of who hired you and why is sufficient, but you can expand on this as well.

> *ABC Company has engaged XYZ Investigative Services, Inc. to conduct a personal due diligence/background check on Joseph Smith. This investigation*

was conducted utilizing public records, legal filings, media sources, and discreet interviews.

- **Executive Summary**

Summarize the corporate location, key managers, and history. Bring to light any current and important issues that may have been revealed in recent media reports or through your research and analysis. Make recommendations based on the supply chain analysis. Draw out key findings from documents you have analyzed so that the client reads these first. Again, you do not want to force the client to find out about a company's criminal history ten pages into your report. Very clearly itemize what is important in your summary, and what needs to be done.

- **Supply Chain Analysis**

Logistics - Inbound – Warehousing and Internal Handling of Products

What sorts of warehouse conditions apply? Be ready to define how the product is handled and stored. If refrigeration is necessary, is that addressed? Which vendors are being used to service and repair those air conditioners? If the company produces a controlled substance, a foodstuff or a potentially hazardous product, consider which oversight agency (EPA, OSHA, FDA, local labor commission, or labor union) would be on-site and writing reports about the internal logistics.

EPA and OSHA reported multiple violations over the course of five years. OSHA deemed the equipment "hazardous" in light of an employee accident that was caused by a faulty processing belt in shipping. Additionally, the EPA has cited the company two years in a row for health-code violations related to mouse feces.

Logistics – Outbound – Distribution

How are the products shipped? Find out if the company itself ships the products or if it uses an outside contractor to haul the products to stores or the final location.

From all accounts, it appears that the company is using a third-party vendor, Johnson Trucking Co., to deliver its product to market. No violations or disparaging information was located in a brief search on Johnson.

Operations – Product Development and Manufacturing

Who is making the product? Is there special machinery involved in the creation of the manufactured goods?

According to interviews with local union members, the products are made completely on-site; however, twice a year, when the plant shuts down for maintenance, the company subcontracts its product development to Temporary Product Developers located in (Location).

Support Teams – Research & Development, Manufacturing Groups, and Unions

The workforce for the product could be spread out among disparate groups throughout the country and the world.

The subject company appears to be a local small mom-and-pop operation, based on the size of office space they lease and the number of employees in the United States mentioned in their business report. This was verified as well through an interview with the chairman of another company, when he mentioned he thought too that they were a "local company." He referred to a conversation he had with the subject company's CEO. During that conversation the CEO revealed the U.S. location was only for marketing team, and their research and development lab was located in Tel Aviv, Israel.

Human Resources – Support for Support Teams and Management

This is management analysis.

No mention of union problems was located in the media. When interviewing several members of the union, they expressed overall satisfaction with the employers. However, they did mention a formal complaint about the aging equipment, as cited in an OSHA report. They said the equipment was a concern and that they were lobbying management to make the necessary upgrades.

No legal filings were located against the company management.

Infrastructure – Location, Security, and Risk Management

What contingency plans are in place to get the business back into manufacturing?

The company did not have a disaster-recovery plan in place. To date, it has not suffered any unscheduled closings, but it does close twice a year for maintenance. In a discrete interview with the COO, he stated that the company was developing a disaster-recovery plan to meet the risk-assessment requirements of its insurance policy.

Technology – Tracking of Products, Customer Intelligence, and Market Basket Analysis

Customer relationship management (CRM) tools are standard for companies selling products.

The company does not have a standard CRM program in place. Orders are currently generated through phone and on-site sales.

3. Body of Report

- **Corporate Information**

The company headquarters and manufacturing plant are located at 170 Dryer Road, Swisstown, in Morris County, New Jersey 07524. The phone number is

(908) 555-4567 and its Web site is www.company.com. The company's research and development division is based in Tel Aviv, Israel, the original location of the company before it established its headquarters in the U.S. The company also has a small sales division based in New York, New York.

- **Company History and Current Standing**

Written in paragraph form, discuss the history of the company, which is usually found on its Web site or in the annual report. In this section, detail the financial health of the company and add any other details that seem appropriate.

- **Management**

List the management-team members, their positions, if they sit on any boards, and any biographies that can be located. Write any affiliations they may have outside of their particular company. If necessary, a principal report for each of the top managers should be conducted.

- **Board Positions**

List the board members, their positions on the board, if they sit on any other boards and any short biographies that can be located about them.

Political Affiliations and Charitable Works

Companies also can have political affiliations. Be sure to mention if a company is sponsoring any fundraisers for one political party or the other. Note that companies will often play both sides and will not automatically discount any future powers.

Companies often sponsor charitable events as well. Find out what is the cause or mission of the event. It might be connected to a personal matter for one of the company's chief officers. For example, if the chairman of the board's son has autism, there is a good chance that his company will be sponsoring a fundraiser to help raise autism awareness.

- **Certifications, Credentials, and Special Licenses**

If your company holds a business license or has received special certifications in ISO[30] or other regulatory organizations, list each independently.

    Certification

    Expiration

    Issuing Agency

    Disciplinary actions, if any

    Identified Assets

If you were conducting an asset investigation, this section would become voluminous, as you outlined the company's physical assets, such as property, automobiles, vessels, and possibly airplanes. However, standard reports should

---

[30] International Organization for Standardization, see iso.com.

include subsidiaries, UCC filings, intellectual properties, and any low-hung assets worth mentioning.

- **Financial Assets**

Financial assets to investigate and include are:

Subsidiaries

Stock ownership

UCCs

Vessels, Airplanes, and Automobiles

- **Intellectual Property**

Following the APA Style Manual in citing works for papers, I use the same style guide for professional reports. See the following examples. Sample text using fonts from APA Style Manual:

- Copyrights

- Smith, J. (1999). *Fuel: Processing Methods*. Chicago, IL: CCR Publishing.

- Patents

- Smith, J. (1995). U.S. Patent No. 123,434. Washington, D.C.: U.S. Patent and Trademark Office.

- Trademarks

- Smith, J. (1995). *Fuel Methods.* Washington, D.C.: U.S. Patent and Trademark Office.

- **Legal Findings**

Civil and criminal matters should be cited clearly and separately in this portion, just as in the principal report. Report all criminal matters first. Make sure you know the search variables of the sources you used so that you can accurately report what was and was not searched. For example, many states only offer convictions history and do not indicate arrests without dispositions. Example:

For the last seven years in (STATE), there were no convictions, misdemeanors, or felonies located.

A domestic dispute charge was filed in (COUNTY) on 12/24/1999.

[Then list the details.]

There are two format methods to use to report civil cases. The first example is reported as follows:

Case name

Date filed

Date terminated

Office

Nature of suit

Cause

Plaintiff

Defendant

If you notice names or further content in the dockets or summary, continue your listing with a short narrative. The second example is:

On January 15, 1999, ABC Company filed a breach-of-contract claim against the Smith Group in New York County Supreme Court. Defendants named, in addition to the Smith Group, were Kathy and John Smith. The case was voluntarily dismissed on June 9, 1999.

- **Regulatory, Sanction, and Disciplinary Issues**

Reporting Regulatory Issues

Online searches, through various U.S. regulatory agencies like the Office of Foreign Asset Control, the Central Contractors Registry, and the Excluded Parties Database, did not reveal any matches to the subject.

Reporting Disciplinary Issues

A search in the Health and Human Services Office of Inspector General did not reveal any matches to the subject. Nor were there any matches located in the State of Florida Disciplinary Actions database for physicians.

- **Financial Troubles**

Liens and debts, caused by lawsuits or bankruptcies, are reported straightforward.

Tax Liens – Judgments

Company is seen to have an unsatisfied federal tax lien of $10,000 from 1998, registered in the state of Montana.

Company has an unsatisfied judgment/lien for $5,000, resulting from a lawsuit filed in 1999 by the ABC Company.

Bankruptcies

Company filed for Chapter 11 bankruptcy protection on August 2, 1998. Bankruptcy was granted and a list of the debts and creditors can be provided, if requested.

You can list the creditors and the money owed, but appending or offering for further information later is better, unless you see something significant in the creditor's report.

- **Media**

The media findings should be reported in descending order. There are two schools of thought on how to report media issues and both are certainly acceptable.

You can summarize the story for brevity sake, which is a more professional approach to report writing. Sample:

Date – Source – Title

Truncated article, italicized, justified, and indented .5 on each side.

Or you can include key portions of the article, quoting it entirely, or paraphrasing the report. In some cases, this is necessary because the subject material may be beyond your comprehension of the topic, and the paraphrasing could turn out to be inaccurate. Sample:

Summary of article as follows.

On June 2, 1996, the New York Times reported that Bob Smith was found guilty of racketeering.

Disclaimer for Database Errors

Sometimes databases and online sources make mistakes, or the details cannot be verified. In the footer, on the last page of all my reports, I add the following statement to protect myself against errors and omissions that occur from badly obtained data:

> "Information is obtained from a multitude of databases, records-keeping systems, and other sources, of which [Company Name] and/or its suppliers have no control. These are fallible, electronic and human sources. There can be absolutely no warranty expressed or implied as to the accuracy, completeness, timeliness, or availability of the records listed, nor to the fitness for the purpose of the recipient of such records or reports.

> Information provided may be limited or not totally current. There is absolutely no guarantee that the information exclusively pertains to the search criteria information, which was submitted by the requesting party"

Your reports have serious implications in the business world and the personal lives of people you investigate. Yet, as investigators we rely heavily on the database services we use, and albeit we try to discern and verify every last detail, no system, database or analysis is ever 100% perfect. Take the time to consult with a business attorney or a veteran investigator to understand the implications of the information you are selling as a report. Also, consider talking with a business insurance specialist who sells Errors and Omissions Liability insurance, and make sure you understand what the policy will cover and what it will not. A smart investigator will must research any and all possible inherent liability exposures and risks.

Billing the Client

After a few years of conducting the same types of investigations over and over again, you develop a sense of how much a case will cost. Nonetheless, if your normal procedure is to create invoices on the fly and by the seat of your pants, you are inviting trouble and establishing poor precedent. Using an established pricing method goes a long way to insure that you will not be losing money or overcharging when sending an invoice. It also sends a message to your clients that you are a professional service firm and have checks and balances in place for your own financial affairs. However, the invoice to the client should come out to them within 30 days of closing the case and sending the final report.

Marking Up Your Hard Costs

A rule of thumb is to mark up or write up your hard costs for research work and database expenses for U.S. company searches by 15%. Increase the mark up for foreign searches, depending on the time it takes you to find and hire someone overseas to pull documents, research legal and business filings by hand.

Billing Models

The four most popular and efficient billing models are:

1. **By the Investigation**
2. **By the Hour**
3. **Time and Expense**
4. **Hybrid**

Charge by the Investigation

This is a good method for repeat clients who regularly order the same types of investigations. They can anticipate cost and budget for it. However, you have to be careful when taking in the new project. A standard U.S. company due diligence may run a few thousand dollars, which is enough to do your job and make a profit. However, if a client orders a due diligence report on a much larger company, perhaps even foreign, with dozens of subsidiaries, you must realize that the case will need a larger budget. The trick is to always do a little pre-search on the company or person you are investigating first to get a sense of how large they are and how involved your investigation may be.

Charge by the Hour

Analyze your database costs in relation to the type of investigation and compare that hourly rate to your own hourly rate. For example, if you know your database costs always come in at about 20 percent of your hourly rate, then you can bump your hourly costs up by 20 to 25 percent. This enables you to give your client a flat hourly rate. Clients like to know they can anticipate costs by the hours you work and are not surprised with extra database costs on the invoice.

However, you have to be able to pre-assess which databases you will need to conduct your work and quote your client in hourly increments. If you believe you are going to need $1,000 dollars' worth of reports and database costs before you even start, then use the next method by all means.

Time and Expense

This method combines a flat hourly rate for your time, plus the databases fees and reports that you provide. This is the fairest of billing methods, because it is the most detailed. However, the downside is that you will have to wait to bill the client until you to get all of your monthly invoices from all the vendors used. The client also might ask for a breakdown by database vendor on the invoice.

Hybrid

Hybrid is a combination of the above three billing styles. During the course of a 'By the Investigation' billable case, you may come across information the client never anticipated and wants you to pursue. This is out of the scope of your original flat rate billable time, so now you have to charge additional fees. For example, four subsidiaries appear when the client thought it was only one. Now that you have to investigate the other three, calculate what it will cost including time involved and project a new budget to the client.

If your hourly rate is stated in the agreed upon Letter of Agreement, you must first clear the extra charges before proceeding. If you do not know how costly the additional direction of the investigation will be and if that doubt concerns your client, offer a few stopping points. Give yourself enough room in the budget to obtain what is needed initially and tell the client you will check in when you hit that budget amount.

Overall

Any one of these billable methods is acceptable, so long as you can remain consistent with your clients and they are fine with your billing methods.

If you have a fully staffed office, the third option might be best because an administrator can calculate the invoices by project numbers and database costs per the firms work. The first and second invoicing methods are easiest, but you should be able to produce your vendor invoices for specific database usage if necessary.

No matter which billing method you utilize **clear it with the customer before you start.** Have them agree to the price per job or price per hour in an email, fax or signed contract. A verbal agreement is not enough.

Occasionally a client may be unhappy about the amount of the invoice. If you met your obligations, did a terrific job, but the answer you returned was not what the client wanted to hear, stick by your guns. I have handed over pretty empty reports on occasion because there was nothing to be found. The report essentially highlighted all the places I looked and all the basic information discovered, but there was no fraud, as client claimed, and the company examined was on the up and up. I did my investigation, reported in as stated and invoiced the client. The client was upset because 'you did not find anything.' I clearly pointed out all the details of the investigation and that there was nothing to find and firmly told the client that the invoice would stay put.[31]

However, if you missed something in the report of if your work was sub par and there you are handing over a big invoice at the end, you will not see that client again.

Customer Satisfaction Pointers

When a client calls you to conduct an investigation, your purpose is to conduct the best investigation possible without compromising your ethics or your client's reputation when gathering information. You must pool that information, present a reasonably intelligent and smart looking report to the client and follow up after the client has had a chance to review the findings. The client's opinion of you and your work is based on bringing the client information that is accurate, timely and helpful to the decision making process.

The Follow-up Process

A week later, be sure to pick up the phone or send an email to the client, asking if there are any questions about the report. Surely there may be something in the document that might be very clear to you as the author; however, the client may not fully understand. This interaction will also give the client a chance to say what a great job you did or give the client a chance to comment on an aspect of the case you might have missed.

On the follow-up, there are **four questions** to remember to always ask–

1. Do you have any questions or concerns on the report I sent to you last week?

2. Was the report style to your liking? Or do you have a preference to layout or analysis methodology?

---

[31] A year later the other company sued my client for fraud. My client tried to establish a smear campaign using investigators to insinuate fraudulent activity, when the client was actually the suspicious party. I am SO GLAD I stuck to my findings!

3. Is there anything you would like me to follow up on? (Refer the client to any recommendations you made.)

4. Is there any other investigation I may be of assistance with at this time? Or is there someone else in your practice or office that also may require an investigator.

Never be afraid to ask for additional work! The client knows you are in business. Just be professional about it and not annoying. If the client has nothing for you at the time and seems satisfied with what you sent, then ask a final fifth question—

5. Would you mind if I followed up in a few weeks to make sure there are no remaining issues on this case or solicit you for more work?

One Last Comment

Not long ago I disappointed a serious and prestigious client. Failures happened on both sides, I was too busy to talk to her often and when I did she wouldn't listen and. Despite these circumstances we made much progress and the case was coming to a close. She then sent me a sendoff email that stung like no other. Not because of her abrasive and rude (she's famously rude) language, but because she was correct. Her statement to me was that I was too busy doing other things, and not focused on helping her. Although this woman was quite taxing and demanding, she is still the client. While I know we may not agree on all issues, I did want her to be satisfied with the work and effort we put into her case. She wanted more handholding and I was not there to hold her hand.

I tell this story to everyone who works for me. The key point is when someone calls an investigator for a due diligence assignment, it is because they need to remove all doubt. Doubt is not a good feeling. Our task is to make sure we cover all the bases, including the customer service, handholding if need be, to make the customer feels sure about their decisions. And if you keep the client rated as first in all things though, they will always keep them coming back, despite the fancy databases.

The rest of this chapter contains a series of sample agreements. The last two chapters of this book include many great lists of useful sources and Web pages.

In closing, I hope I have given you insight and education on how to perform quality online due diligence investigations. And I wish you the very best in your investigative endeavors.

❖❖❖

Sample Letter of Engagement

This letter will confirm the terms of the engagement between the firm Investigative Group ('IG' or 'us') and _____ ('client' or 'you').

It is our understanding that the scope of our engagements will include, under your direction, investigative consulting services. Our work may include online and investigative research, public record searches, interviews and other legally permissible investigative tactics. If you so request, we will be in a position to provide a written report of our findings. Because our engagements are limited in nature and scope, it cannot be relied upon to discover all documents and other information or provide all analyses which may have importance. Attached hereto is a specific list of services to be performed and exclusions, which may be modified upon written authorization by the Client and agreement by us.

Communications and Use of Materials

We consider all communications between us and the Client either written or oral, as well as any materials or information developed or received by us during this engagement, as confidential and protected by the attorney work-product privilege doctrine or other applicable legal privileges. Accordingly, it is agreed that all materials prepared or received by us pursuant to this engagement will be maintained as confidential material. We agree not to disclose any of our work, work product, communications, or any of the information we receive or develop during the course of this engagement to third parties without the Client's consent, except as may be required by law, regulation or judicial or administrative process. You agree that we may be required to abide by any court orders provided to us in writing and signed by us regarding confidentiality.

We will, at your request, transmit information to you by facsimile, e-mail, or over the Internet. If you wish to limit such transmission to information that is not highly confidential, or seek more secure means of communication for highly confidential information, you will inform us. The Client shall select the specific communication media to use when transmitting information to you or other parties working with you. If any confidentiality breaches occur because of data transmission you agree that this will not constitute a violation of our obligations of confidentiality.

We agree to notify the Client promptly of any request by a third party to access any of the materials regarding this engagement which are in our possession and will cooperate with you concerning our response thereto. In the event that we are subpoenaed or are required by government regulation or other legal process to produce our documents or our personnel as a result of the work performed with respect to this engagement, the Client agrees to compensate Investigative Group for time and expenses, attorneys' fees and costs incurred in responding to the subpoenas.

Compensation

Our fees are based on an hourly rate and the actual hours incurred and are not contingent upon the outcome of the engagement. Our current rates range from $XXX - $XXX per hour depending upon the professional. Where appropriate, we may utilize the services of vetted subcontractors to assist our employees and control costs to the Client. Those costs will be billed to the Client.

Prior to undertaking a particular engagement, we will confirm the assignment in writing. When possible, we will provide an estimate of anticipated professional fees. Please note that estimates may not reflect the actual amount of work necessary to complete a project.

We may revise our rates from time to time to reflect market conditions and professionals' experience and will inform you of such changes. You agree to reimburse Investigative Group for reasonable and documented expenses incurred in connection with the performance of our services with respect to the engagement, including database costs, travel, and lodging, outside research, mailing, telephone, messengers and other direct costs; as long as we receive prior approval from the Client with respect to nature and amount of such expenses.

An itemized invoice outlining professional fees and expenses will be delivered monthly, during the term of the project. An estimate of expenses tends to be 10% to 25% of the quoted professionals' time. Payment is to be made within ten (10) days of receipt of such invoice. In the event Client fails to make payments as required, we reserve the right to suspend the work until payments are made.   In the event IG is required to initiate litigation to enforce its rights under this Agreement, it is entitled to attorney's fees and court costs related to such litigation, should it be successful.

Retainer

We request a retainer of _____ to begin this investigation. The initial retainer will be billed against work performed, with an itemized invoice monthly explaining charges and fees. Twenty percent of the retainer is non-refundable in the event the case closes early, in order to compensate our pre contract expenses.

Deliverables:

A report will be drafted at the conclusion of the project.   For extended projects preliminary-draft reports will be provided and we will be available for telephone updates and meetings.

Miscellaneous

Either party may terminate this Agreement on ten (10) days' notice to the other. In such case, IG shall be entitled to payment for work performed through the termination.

All services provided by IG are provided on an 'AS IS' basis and without any warranty. The parties agree that IG shall not be liable for any damage to systems, equipment or software as a result of its actions, except where IG is grossly negligent. Client shall indemnify IG against any and all damages, including attorneys' fees and court costs suffered by IG as a result of claims made against IG by third parties relating to Client, the work or this contract.

IG warrants that it carries liability insurance and workers compensation insurance in statutory amounts.

IG shall be considered a Subcontractor to Client. Nothing in this Agreement shall be constructed to create an employer/employee relationship between the parties.

If these terms are in accordance with your understanding and meets with your approval, please sign and date one copy of this letter and return it to the address shown on the first page and retain a copy for your files.

Very truly yours,

President

_____

Acknowledged by:

_____

_____

Date

AGREEMENT TO PROVIDE INVESTIGATIVE SERVICES

THIS AGREEMENT, dated _____, is made **BETWEEN** the Client,

> **<CLIENT NAME>**

whose address is _____

AND   **<YOUR INVESTIGATIVE AGENCY>**

whose address is _____

1. **Investigative Services to be Provided**

   Research of given parties such as companies and individuals to include public record, open source information and databases. Discreet inquires may also include interviews and site visits with client pre-approval.

2. **Legal Fees**

   A. Initial Payment. You agree to pay the INVESTIGATIVE AGENCY $x,xxx for fees and expenses in connection with services under this Agreement.

   B. Hourly Rate. You agree to pay the INVESTIGATIVE AGENCY for investigative services at the hourly rate of $xxx.xx per hour.

   C. Expenses. In addition to hourly rate, any expenses incurred such as database costs, report fees, any travel related costs, will be the responsibility of the Company.

   The INVESTIGATIVE AGENCY reserves the right to increase the above hourly rates after one year from the date hereof.

3. **Your Responsibility**

   You must fully cooperate with the INVESTIGATIVE AGENCY and provide all information relevant to the issues involved in this matter.

4. **Bills**

   The INVESTIGATIVE AGENCY will send you itemized bills from time to time.

5. **Signatures**

You and the INVESTIGATIVE AGENCY have read and agreed to this Agreement. The INVESTIGATIVE AGENCY has answered all of your questions and fully explained this Agreement to your complete satisfaction. You have been given a copy of this Agreement.

BY: INVESTIGATIVE AGENCY

_____

NAME

_____

POSITION

_____

DATE

BY: CLIENT

_____

CLIENT NAME

_____

POSITION

_____

DATE

MUTUAL NON-DISCLOSURE AGREEMENT

This Mutual Non-disclosure Agreement (this 'Agreement') is entered into by CLIENT COMPANY ('CLIENT COMPANY'), and _____, a YOUR COMPANY ('Company'), effective as of _____, 200_.

BACKGROUND

CLIENT COMPANY and Company (each, a 'Party', and collectively, the 'Parties') intend to enter into discussions concerning a possible business transaction (the 'Transaction').   In connection with those discussions, each Party will need to disclose certain of its confidential and proprietary information and materials to the other Party. The Parties wish to enter into this Agreement to provide for the disclosure of that confidential and proprietary information and to restrict the use and disclosure of that information and materials by the receiving Party.

The Parties agree as follows:

1. Definition of Confidential Information. 'Confidential Information' means (a) information and materials that are identified in writing as CONFIDENTIAL at the time of disclosure, (b) information disclosed orally and subsequently identified in writing as CONFIDENTIAL within thirty days following the initial disclosure of such information, (c) information or materials that the disclosing Party treats as confidential and does not disclose publicly, or (d) the information and materials identified on Exhibit A to this Agreement. The Party disclosing Confidential Information is referred to in this Agreement as the 'Disclosing Party,' and the Party receiving such Confidential Information is referred to as the 'Receiving Party.' The term 'Confidential Information' includes any modifications or derivatives prepared by the Receiving Party that contain or are based upon Confidential Information disclosed by the Disclosing Party, including analysis, reports or summaries of that information. Notwithstanding anything to the contrary set forth herein, no provision in this Agreement is, or is intended to be construed as, a condition of confidentiality within the meaning of Sections 6011, 6111 or 6112 of the Internal Revenue Code of 1986, as amended, or the regulations thereunder, or any similar state legislation. The CLIENT COMPANY, Inc., and its subsidiaries and affiliates ('CLIENT COMPANY'), and each employee representative, or other agent of CLIENT COMPANY, may disclose to any and all persons, without limitation of any kind, the tax treatment and tax structure of any transaction within the scope of this Agreement that reduces or defers federal tax or state income or franchise taxes and all materials of any kind (including opinions or other tax analyses) that are provided to CLIENT COMPANY relating to such tax treatment or tax structure.

2. Limitations on Use. Confidential Information must be used by the Receiving Party only in connection with analysis of, and discussions concerning a proposed Transaction with the Disclosing Party as contemplated in the Background or as directed in writing by the Disclosing Party. Receiving Party must not use Confidential Information at any time, in any fashion, form or manner, for any other purpose.

3. Limitations on Disclosure. Receiving Party will use the same measures to protect the confidentiality of the Confidential Information that it uses to protect the confidentiality of its own proprietary and confidential information and materials of like kind, but in no event less than a reasonable standard of care. Receiving Party will take (and will cause its employees and agents to take) any steps required to avoid inadvertent disclosure of materials in Receiving Party's possession.

4. Access to the Confidential Information. Access to the Confidential Information must be restricted to personnel of Receiving Party engaged in the analysis and discussions concerning a possible Transaction with the Disclosing Party as contemplated in the Background Statement. Receiving Party will furnish access to the Confidential Information to its employees and third party contractors solely on a need-to-know basis. Each Party will furnish the other with a complete list of its employees and agents who have been furnished access to the Confidential Information of the other Party.

5. Ownership of Confidential Information. No Licenses. Confidential Information disclosed by the Disclosing Party to the Receiving Party will at all times remain the property of the Disclosing Party. No license under any trade secrets, copyrights, or other rights is granted under this Agreement or by any disclosure of Confidential Information under this Agreement.

6. Copies of Confidential Information. Confidential Information must not be copied or reproduced by Receiving Party without the Disclosing Party's prior written approval.

7. Return of Confidential Information. All Confidential Information made available under this Agreement, including copies of Confidential Information, must be returned to the Disclosing Party upon the termination of discussions concerning a possible Transaction between the Parties, or, if earlier, upon the request by the Disclosing Party. Any materials prepared by the Receiving Party which include any Confidential Information of the Disclosing Party, including summaries or extracts thereof, must be destroyed, and written certification of such destruction provided to the Disclosing Party.

8. Exceptions. Nothing in this Agreement will prohibit or limit Receiving Party's use of information (a) known to Receiving Party prior to disclosure by the Disclosing Party, (b) that is independently developed by the Receiving Party, without reference to the Confidential Information, or (c) that is or becomes publicly available through no breach of this Agreement by the Receiving Party.

9. Binding Agreement. This Agreement is and will be binding upon the Parties and each of their respective affiliates, and upon their respective heirs, successors, representatives and assigns.

10. Governing Law. The validity, performance, construction and effect of this Agreement will be governed by the laws of the State of <CLIENT COMPANY'S STATE>, without regard to that state's conflict of laws provisions.

11. Equitable Remedies. The Parties recognize that serious injury could result to the Disclosing Party and its business if the Receiving Party breaches its obligations under this Agreement. Therefore, Receiving Party agrees that the Disclosing Party will be entitled to a restraining order, injunction or other equitable relief if Receiving Party breaches its obligations under this Agreement, in addition to any other remedies and damages that would be available at law or equity.

12. Compelled Disclosures. If Receiving Party receives a subpoena or other validly issued administrative or judicial process demanding Confidential Information, Receiving Party must promptly notify Disclosing Party and tender to it the defense of that demand. Unless the demand has been timely limited, quashed or extended, Receiving Party will thereafter be entitled to comply with such demand to the extent permitted by law. If requested by the Disclosing Party, Receiving Party will cooperate (at the expense of the Disclosing Party) in the defense of a demand.

13. No Use of Names. Receiving Party may not use the name or logo of CLIENT COMPANY or any of its affiliates, or any abbreviation or adaptation thereof, in any advertising, trade display, or published statement or press release, or for any other commercial purpose, without the prior written consent of CLIENT COMPANY(in its sole discretion). The fact that the Parties are engaged in discussions concerning a Possible Business Arrangement, and the terms of those discussions, is Confidential Information and may not be disclosed for any purpose.

14. Non-Solicitation of Employees. During the tendency of discussions concerning a possible Transaction between the Parties, and for a period of one year following termination of such discussions, (a) neither Party will solicit the employment of any employee of the other Party, and (b) if a Party is approached by an employee of the other Party concerning employment, that Party will notify (or cause the employee to notify) the other Party before making an offer of employment.

15. Term; Survival of Obligations. This Agreement will terminate upon the first to occur of (1) termination of discussions between the Parties concerning the Transaction (or if a Transaction is entered into, upon termination of the Transaction), or (2) delivery of written notice of termination by either Party to the other Party. Following termination, the obligations of Receiving Party under this Agreement with respect to the Confidential Information of Disclosing Party will continue in full force and effect as follows: (a) in the case of any information or materials that constitute a trade secret within the meaning of applicable law, for as long as such information and materials remain as a trade secret, or (b) in the case of any other information or materials, for a term of two (2) years from the date of disclosures.

16. Interpretation. The following rules of interpretation must be applied in interpreting this Agreement: (1) the headings used in this Agreement are for reference and convenience only and will not enter into the interpretation of this Agreement, (2) the provisions of the Exhibits to this Agreement are incorporated into this Agreement, (3) as used in this Agreement, the term 'including' will always be deemed to mean 'including, without limitation,' and (4) this Agreement shall not be construed against either Party as the drafter of this Agreement.

17. No Commitment. Nothing in this Agreement will constitute a commitment by either Party to develop or disclose any information or materials, including any Confidential Information, or to acquire or recommend any product, service or asset of the other Party. The provision of Confidential Information to Receiving Party as contemplated under this Agreement and discussions held in connection with the proposed business arrangement between the Parties will not prevent either Party from pursuing similar discussions with third parties or obligate either Party to continue discussions with the other Party, nor will either Party otherwise be obligated to take, continue or forego any action with respect to the proposed business arrangement.

Disclosing Party makes no warranty as to the accuracy or completeness of any information or materials provided in connection with this Agreement.

18. Entire Agreement. This Agreement constitutes the entire agreement and understanding of the Parties with respect to the subject matter of this Agreement and supersedes all prior discussions and agreements, either oral or written, relating to the subject matter of this Agreement.

Agreed and Accepted: Agreed and Accepted:

CLIENT COMPANY   *[COMPANY]*

By:_____   By:_____
            [Signature]   *[Signature]*

_____   _____
            [Title]   *[Title]*

_____   _____
            [Date]   *[Date]*

EXHIBIT A

CONFIDENTIAL INFORMATION

Confidential Information will include:

1. All application, operating system, database, communications and other computer software, whether now or hereafter existing, and all modifications, enhancements, and versions thereof and all options with respect thereto, and all future products developed or derived there from;

2. All source and object codes, flowcharts, algorithms, coding sheets, routines, sub-routines, compilers, assemblers, design concepts and related documentation and manuals, and methodologies used in the design, development and implementation of software products;

3. Marketing and product plans, customer lists, prospect lists, and pricing information (other than published price lists);

4. Financial information and reports;

5. Employee and contractor data; and

6. Research and development plans and results.

EXHIBIT B

FORM OF EMPLOYEE ACKNOWLEDGMENT

The undersigned is an employee of _____ ('Receiving Party'), and, in connection with such employment, is being furnished access to confidential and proprietary materials of _____. ('Disclosing Party'). The undersigned has been advised and acknowledges that such materials are the confidential and proprietary materials of Disclosing Party, the use and disclosure of which is subject to the terms and conditions of a Non-Disclosure Agreement between Disclosing Party and Receiving Party effective as of _____, 200_, and the undersigned agrees to comply with the terms and conditions of such nondisclosure agreement.

_____

[Name]

_____

[Date]

Ch12:

Lists of Investigative Resources — U.S. Based

Rule #3: Don't believe what you're told. Double check.

—TV's NCIS Agent Leroy Jethro Gibbs

This section of the Guide to Online Due Diligence Investigations provides four useful resource lists to investigators—

- State Agency Links with Free Web Access (subscription sites not listed) to These Records:
    - Business Entities; UCC Filings, Trademarks
    - Incarceration (Inmate Locator)
    - Sex Offender Registry
    - Election Campaign Finance, Lobbyists, and PACs (Political Action Committees)
    - Selected Motor Vehicle-Related Records
    - Selected Election-Related Records
- National Trade Associations with Investigation Interests
- Contributors to the Excluded Parties List System (EPLS)
- Building and Construction Trade: Industry Journals and Magazines

Although all URLs were verified at press time, please keep in mind URLs will and do change over time.

Links to Free Searches of State Agency Records

The links below are selected sites where one can search for free for business entities, UCC filings, incarceration or Inmate records, sex offender registries, certain motor vehicle-related data, and certain election-related data such as PACs and campaign finance.

Editor's Notes:
- All 'www.http' omitted from URLs.
- These are the direct search sites
- Content is supplied by BRB Publications (BRBPublications.com)

Alabama
Business Entities	sos.alabama.gov/vb/inquiry/inquiry.aspx
Fugitive Search	dps.alabama.gov/Community/wfSearch.aspx?Type=25
Incarceration Records	doc.alabama.gov
Securities Administrative Actions	asc.state.al.us/admin_action.aspx
Sex Offender Registry	dps.alabama.gov/Community/wfSexOffenderSearch.aspx#1
Trademarks	sos.state.al.us/vb/inquiry/inquiry.aspx?area=Trademarks
UCC	sos.state.al.us/vb/inquiry/inquiry.aspx?area=UCC

Alaska
Business Entities	commerce.state.ak.us/CBP/Main/SearchInfo.aspx
Business Licenses	commerce.state.ak.us/CBP/Main/CBPLSearch.aspx?mode=BL
Election Campaign Disclosure Records	https://webapp.state.ak.us/apoc/searchcampaigndisclosure.jsp
Recorded Documents	dnr.alaska.gov/ssd/recoff/searchRO.cfm
Sex Offender Registry	dps.state.ak.us/sorweb/Search.aspx
UCC	dnr.alaska.gov/ssd/recoff/searchUCC.cfm

Arizona
Candidate Campaign Finances	azsos.gov/cfs/CandidateSummarySearch.aspx
Corporation Commission Dockets and eFilings	edocket.azcc.gov/Search
Incarceration Records	https://corrections.az.gov/public-resources/inmate-datasearch
Business Entities, Trade Name, Trademark)	starpas.azcc.gov/scripts/cgiip.exe/WService=wsbroker1/main.p
Registered Names	azsos.gov/scripts/TNT_Search_engine.dll
Sales Tax Registration Verification	https://www.aztaxes.gov/LicenseVerification
Securities Actions, Orders, Admin. Decisions	azcc.gov/divisions/securities/enforcement/
Sex Offender Registry	https://az.gov/app/sows/home.xhtml
UCC	azsos.gov/apps/ucc/search/
Vehicle Lien Status Check	https://servicearizona.com/webapp/lienmvr/search?execution=e1s1

Arkansas
Business Entities, Trademarks	sos.arkansas.gov/BCS/Pages/default.aspx
Incarceration Records	adc.arkansas.gov/inmate_info/index.php
Securities Company State Registration	securities.arkansas.gov/star/portal/arasd/portal.aspx
Sex Offender Registry	acic.org/offender-search/index.php
Trademark	sos.arkansas.gov/corps/trademk/index.php

California

Business Entities (Corporation, LLC, LLP, LP) ... kepler.sos.ca.gov/
Campaign Finances .... cal-access.sos.ca.gov/campaign/
Delinquent Taxpayers .... https://www.ftb.ca.gov/aboutFTB/Delinquent_Taxpayers.shtml
Incarcerations - Inmate Locator............................ inmatelocator.cdcr.ca.gov
Publicly Traded Disclosure Search .... ptsearch.sos.ca.gov/app/basic_search.html
Securities Company/Franchise .... dbo.ca.gov/CalEASI/CalEASI.asp
Sex Offender Registry .... meganslaw.ca.gov/index.htm
UCC Filings .... https://uccconnect.sos.ca.gov/acct/acct-login.asp
Vehicle Smog Test History Search...................... smogcheck.ca.gov/pubwebquery/Vehicle/PubTstQry.aspx
Workers Comp - Active Disputed Cases .... dir.ca.gov/dwc/eams/EAMS_PublicInformationSearch.htm

Colorado

Business Entities .... sos.state.co.us/biz/BusinessEntityCriteriaExt.do
Charitable Non-Profit Association Members .... coloradononprofits.org/help-desk-resources/find-a/
Election & Finance Information .... tracer.sos.colorado.gov/PublicSite/Search.aspx
Incarceration Records .... doc.state.co.us/oss/
Registered Charities and Fundraisers................ sos.state.co.us/ccsa/CcsaInquiryMain.do
Securities Dept Enforcement Actions..........cdn.colorado.gov/cs/Satellite/DORA-SD/CBON/DORA/1251627123688
Sex Offender Registry .... https://www.colorado.gov/apps/cdps/sor/?SOR=home.caveat
Stolen Vehicles... https://www.colorado.gov/apps/dps/mvvs/public/entry.jsf
Trade Names and Trademarks .... sos.state.co.us/biz/BusinessEntityCriteriaExt.do
UCC Filings .... https://www.sos.state.co.us/ucc/pages/home.jspx

Connecticut

Business Entities, Business Filings .... concord-sots.ct.gov/CONCORD/index.jsp
Delinquent Taxpayers .... ct.gov/drs/cwp/view.asp?a=1453&q=328618
Incarceration Records .... ctinmateinfo.state.ct.us/searchop.asp
Securities Division Enforcement Actions............. ct.gov/dob/cwp/view.asp?a=2246&q=401762
Sex Offender Registry .... icrimewatch.net/index.php?AgencyID=54567&disc=54567
UCC... concord-sots.ct.gov/CONCORD/

Delaware

Business Entities .... https://delecorp.delaware.gov/tin/GINameSearch.jsp
Business License .... https://dorweb.revenue.delaware.gov/bussrch/
Delinquent Taxpayers .... revenue.delaware.gov/ddt.shtml
Incarceration Records .... doc.delaware.gov/offenderLocate.shtml
Political Financial Disclosures...............elections.delaware.gov/information/campaignfinance/pdfs/PAC%20List.pdf
Sex Offender Registry .... https://sexoffender.dsp.delaware.gov/
Trade, Business, Fictitious Names..................... courts.delaware.gov/tradenames/

District of Columbia

Business License Search .... pivs.dcra.dc.gov//BBLV/Default.aspx
DL/ID Card Verification...... https://public.dmv.washingtondc.gov/BusinessPages/DL/DriverLicenseVerification.aspx
Elections - Contributions and Expenditures .... ocf.dc.gov/dsearch/dsearch.asp
Expanded Business Entity Search............https://corp.dcra.dc.gov/Account.aspx/LogOn?ReturnUrl=%2fHome.aspx
Inmate Locator .... https://www.vinelink.com/vinelink/siteInfoAction.do?siteId=9900
Political Financial Reports .... ocf.dc.gov/IMAGING/SEARCHIMAGES.ASP

Recorded Documents...https://gov.propertyinfo.com/DC-Washington/

Sex Offender Registry..mpdc.dc.gov/service/search-sex-offender-registry

Veh. Registration..... https://public.dmv.washingtondc.gov/BusinessPages/VR/VehicleRegistrationVerification.aspx

Florida

Attorney General Active Investigations List.........myfloridalegal.com/lit_ec.nsf/investigations

Business Entities, Trademark, Judgment Liens .. sunbiz.org/

Campaign Financial & Disclosure Reports..........election.dos.state.fl.us/campaign-finance/cam-finance-index.shtml

Drivers License Status ....https://services.flhsmv.gov/DLCheck/?Aspx

Federal Liens Search ....sunbiz.org/lienlis.html

Incarceration Records ....dc.state.fl.us/inmateinfo/inmateinfomenu.asp

Parental Check of Minor's Driving Record ....https://services.flhsmv.gov/DLCheck/?Aspx

Sex Offender Registry...offender.fdle.state.fl.us/offender/homepage.do

Stolen Vehicles, Boats, Plates, etc.....................pas.fdle.state.fl.us/pas/pashome.a

UCC...floridaucc.com/UCCWEB/SearchDisclaimer.aspx?

Georgia

Campaign Contribution & Disclosure Reports.....sos.ga.gov/elections/disclosure/disclosure.htm

Delinquent Taxpayers ....https://etax.dor.ga.gov/DeT/DebtInterior.aspx

DL Status Check ....https://online.dds.ga.gov/DLStatus/default.aspx

Find Business Entities ....https://cgov.sos.state.ga.us/Account.aspx/SearchRequest

Incarceration Records ....dcor.state.ga.us

Lobbyist List, Political Action Committee (PAC).. media.ethics.ga.gov/Search/Lobbyist/Lobbyist_ByName.aspx

Recorded Documents, Notaries ....https://www.gsccca.org/search/

Sex Offender Registry...gbi.georgia.gov/georgia-sex-offender-registry

Trademarks....................sos.ga.gov/index.php/corporations/search_the_trademarks_and_service_mark_database

UCC Transactions - All Counties.........................search.gsccca.org/UCC_Search/default.asp

Hawaii

Bureau of Conveyances.......................................https://boc.ehawaii.gov/docsearch/nameSearch.html

Campaign Disclosure & Enforcement Reports.... ags.hawaii.gov/campaign/

Legislative Ethics: Gift Disclosures ....ethics.hawaii.gov/alldisc/

Legislative Ethics: Spending ethics.hawaii.gov/2014-legislator-financial/

Recorded Documents..dlnr.hawaii.gov/boc/online-services/

Registered Businesses..https://hbe.ehawaii.gov/documents/search.html

Sex Offender Registry...sexoffenders.ehawaii.gov/sexoffender/search.html

Idaho

Business Entities...accessidaho.org/public/sos/corp/search.html?SearchFormstep=crit

Campaign Spending Disclosure, PACs...............sos.idaho.gov/elect/finance.htm

DL Status Check ....https://www.accessidaho.org/secure/itd/reinstatement/signin.html

Incarceration Records ....idoc.idaho.gov/content/prisons/offender_search

Sexual Offender Registry ....isp.idaho.gov/sor_id/search.html

Trademarks ....accessidaho.org/public/sos/trademark/search.html

UCC...https://www.accessidaho.org/secure/sos/liens/search.html

Illinois
Business Entities .... apps.ilsos.gov/corporatellc/
Campaign Disclosure.............elections.state.il.us/campaigndisclosure/ContributionsSearchByAllContributions.aspx
Incarceration Records www2.illinois.gov/idoc/Offender/Pages/default.aspx
LP, LLP, LLLP, RLLP .... apps.ilsos.gov/lprpsearch/
Parental Look up Child's Driving Record............. https://apps.ilsos.gov/parentalaccess/
Political Committees and PACs......................... elections.state.il.us/CampaignDisclosure/CommitteeSearch.aspx
Sex Offender Registry .... isp.state.il.us/sor/
Title and Registration Status Inquiry .... apps.ilsos.gov/regstatus/
UCC... ilsos.gov/UCC/

Indiana
Business Entities .... https://secure.in.gov/sos/online_corps/name_search.aspx
Campaign Finance, PACs in.gov/sos/elections/2394.htm
Election Contributions, Expenditures .... campaignfinance.in.gov/PublicSite/Search.aspx
Incarceration Records .... in.gov/apps/indcorrection/ofs/ofs
Securities Company State Registration............... in.gov/apps/sos/securities/sos_securities
Sex Offender Registry .... icrimewatch.net/indiana.php
Trademarks in.gov/sos/business/2374.htm
UCC...https://secure.in.gov/sos/bus_service/online_ucc/browse/default.asp

Iowa
Business Entities .... sos.iowa.gov/
Campaign Spending Disclosure, PACs..............https://webapp.iecdb.iowa.gov/publicview/ContributionSearch.aspx
Incarceration Records .... doc.state.ia.us/
Sex Offender Registry .... iowasexoffender.com/
Treasurer's Office - Search Names by County.... https://www.iowatreasurers.org/mapsearch.php
UCC & Federal Liens .... sos.iowa.gov/search/ucc/search.aspx?ucc
UCC Alternative (broader scope) .... sos.iowa.gov/search/uccAlternative/search.aspx

Kansas
Business Entities, Trademark/Service-Mark .... https://www.kansas.gov/bess/flow/main?execution=e1s1
DL Status Check .... https://www.kdor.org/DLStatus/login.aspxElections - Campaign
Finance, PACs .... sos.ks.gov/elections/cfr_viewer/cfr_examiner_entry.aspx
Incarceration Records .... dc.state.ks.us/kasper
Sex Offender Registry .... kbi.ks.gov/registeredoffender/
Trademarks/Servicemarks .... kssos.org/business/trademark/trademark_search.aspx
Voter Registration Look-up................................ https://myvoteinfo.voteks.org/VoterView/RegistrantSearch.do

Kentucky
Business Entities .... https://app.sos.ky.gov/ftsearch/
Campaign Finance, PACs .... kref.state.ky.us/krefsearch/
Incarceration Records .... corrections.ky.gov/communityinfo/Pages/KOOL.aspx
Sex Offender Registry .... kspsor.state.ky.us/
Trademarks .... apps.sos.ky.gov/business/trademarks/
UCC... https://app.sos.ky.gov/ftucc/

Louisiana

Business Entities...................sos.la.gov/BusinessServices/SearchForLouisianaBusinessFilings/Pages/default.aspx

Certified Louisiana Capital Companies ....ofi.state.la.us/

Campaign Finance, PACs, Lobbyists..................ethics.la.gov/default.aspx

Fugitives, Escapees, Absconders ....doc.la.gov/fugitives/

Sex Offender Registry.......................................lsp.org/socpr/default.html

Maine

Business Entities...https://icrs.informe.org/nei-sos-icrs/ICRS

Current, Adult Inmates ....https://www.maine.gov/online/mdoc/search-and-deposit/index.htm

Election Finance, PACs, Lobbyists ....mainecampaignfinance.com/PublicSite/homepage.aspx

Securities Enforcement Actions/ Agreements .....maine.gov/pfr/securities/enforcement.shtml

Sexual Offender Registry ....sor.informe.org/cgi-bin/sor/index.pl

UCC...maine.gov/sos/cec/ucconline/index.htm

Maryland

Business Entities...sdat.resiusa.org/ucc-charter/Pages/CharterSearch/default.aspx

Charities ....sos.state.md.us/Charity/SearchCharity.aspx

Campaign Finance ....elections.state.md.us/campaign_finance/index.html

PACs ....https://campaignfinancemd.us/Public/ViewCommittees

Incarceration Records www1.dpscs.state.md.us/inmate/

Recorded Land Instruments...............................mdlandrec.net/main/

Sex Offender Registry..socem.info/

State Inmate Locator..dpscs.state.md.us/inmate/

Trademarks & Service Marks..............................sos.state.md.us/Registrations/Trademarks/TMSearch.aspx

UCCs..sdatcert3.resiusa.org/ucc-charter/Pages/UCCSearch/default.aspx

Massachusetts

Business Entities...corp.sec.state.ma.us/corpweb/corpsearch/CorpSearch.aspx

Driver License/ID/Permit Inquiry........................https://secure.rmv.state.ma.us/LicInquiry/intro.aspx

Hazardous Waste Sites......................................mass.gov/eea/agencies/massdep/toxics/

Sex Offender Registry..sorb.chs.state.ma.us/

UCC...corp.sec.state.ma.us/uccfiling/uccSearch/Default.aspx

Vehicle Title/Lien Inquiry ....https://secure.rmv.state.ma.us/TitleLookup/intro.aspx

Michigan

Business Entities...dleg.state.mi.us/bcs_corp/sr_corp.asp

Incarceration Records mdocweb.state.mi.us/otis2/otis2.html

Sex Offender Registry..communitynotification.com/cap_main.php?office=55242/

Trademarks,Service Marks........dleg.state.mi.us/dms/results.asp?docowner=BCSC&doccat=Mark&Search=Search

UCC...https://services.sos.state.mi.us/UCC/QuickSearch.aspx

Minnesota

Business Entities...mblsportal.sos.state.mn.us/

Department of Corrections - Level 3 Search https://coms.doc.state.mn.us/Level3/

Department of Corrections - Offender Search.....https://coms.doc.state.mn.us/PublicViewer/main.asp

Driver License Status Report ....https://dutchelm.dps.state.mn.us/dvsinfo/mainframepublic.asp

Methamphetamine Offender Search ....https://mor.state.mn.us/MorOffenderSearch.aspx

Predatory Offender Program ....https://por.state.mn.us/OffenderSearch.aspx

UCC...da.sos.state.mn.us/minnesota/ucc_order/ucc_filing_search.asp

Mississippi

Business Entities................................https://corp.sos.ms.gov/corp/portal/c/page/corpBusinessIdSearch/portal.aspx
Incarceration Records .... mdoc.state.ms.us/InmateTest.asp
Parole Board Records .... mpb.state.ms.us/inmatesearch.asp
Securities.. sos.ms.gov/Applications/Pages/Securities-Filings-Search.aspx
Sex Offender Registry .... state.sor.dps.ms.gov/
Statewide Property Rolls .... dor.ms.gov/inquiry.html?dept=PropertyTax
UCC Debtor.. sos.ms.gov/BusinessServices/Pages/UCC-Search.aspx
Unclaimed Property .... missingmoney.com/main/index.cfm

Missouri

Business Entities .... https://bsd.sos.mo.gov/loginwelcome.aspx?lobID=1
Inmates, Offenders.. https://web.mo.gov/doc/offSearchWeb/
Sex Offender Registry mshp.dps.mo.gov/CJ38/search.jsp
UCC.. https://bsd.sos.mo.gov/

Montana

Business Entities .... https://app.mt.gov/bes/
Campaign Finance, Disclosures.......................... https://camptrackext.mt.gov/CampaignTracker/dashboard
Incarceration Records .... https://app.mt.gov/conweb/
Lobbyists and Lobbyist Principals .... https://app.mt.gov/cgi-bin/camptrack/lobbysearch/lobbySearch.cgi
PACs .... campaignreport.mt.gov/forms/committeesearch.jsp
Sex Offender & Violent Offender Registry........... https://app.doj.mt.gov/apps/svow/search.aspx

Nebraska

Business Entities .... https://www.nebraska.gov/sos/corp/corpsearch.cgi?nav=search
Campaign Finance .... nadc.nebraska.gov/ccdb/search.cgi
Driver License Status Check............................... https://www.nebraska.gov/dmv/reinstatements/client.cgi
Incarceration Records .... dcs-inmatesearch.ne.gov/Corrections/COR_input.html
Lobbyist Look-up .... nebraskalegislature.gov/reports/lobby.php
Registered PACs.. nadc.nebraska.gov/cf/active_pacs.html
Securities Company State Registration............... ndbf.ne.gov/searches/securities.shtml
Sex Offender Registry .... https://sor.nebraska.gov/
Title Status - Lien Inquiry.................................... nebraska.gov/dmv/els/index.cgi

Nevada

Business Entities .... nvsos.gov/sosentitysearch/
Campaign Finance Reports.................................. https://nvsos.gov/index.aspx?page=3
Incarceration Records .... doc.nv.gov/
PACs .... nvsos.gov/index.aspx?page=111
Trademark, Service mark .... nvsos.gov/sosentitysearch/
UCC (Must Register) .... https://nvsos.gov/NVUCC/user/login.asp
Vehicle Registration Inquiry...............................https://dmvapp.nv.gov/dmv/vr/vr_dev/VR_reg/VR_Reg_Default.aspx

New Hampshire

Business Entities .... https://www.sos.nh.gov/corporate/soskb/csearch.asp
Incarceration Records .... business.nh.gov/Inmate_locator/
Sex Offender Registry .... business.nh.gov/NSOR/search.aspx

New Jersey

Business Entity, Trade Name, Service Mark	https://www.njportal.com/DOR/businessrecords/
Inmate Search	https://www6.state.nj.us/DOC_Inmate/inmatefinder?i=I
Sex Offender Registry	njsp.org/info/reg_sexoffend.html
Trade Name, Trademarks, and Status	https://www.njportal.com/DOR/businessrecords/
UCC	https://www.njportal.com/ucc/
Validate Business Registration	https://www1.state.nj.us/TYTR_BRC/jsp/BRCLoginJsp.jsp

New Mexico

Business Entities	https://portal.sos.state.nm.us/Corps/
Campaign Finance - PACs	https://www.cfis.state.nm.us/media/PACMain.aspx
DUI Offender History	nmcourts.gov/dwi.php
Inmate Locator	corrections.state.nm.us:8080/OffenderSearch/
Sex Offender Registry	sheriffalerts.com/counties.php?state=nm
UCC	https://portal.sos.state.nm.us/corps/Corplookup/Lookdn.aspx

New York

Business Entities	dos.ny.gov/corps/bus_entity_search.html
Campaign Ethics Reports	nycourts.gov/ip/jcec/
Campaign Finance Reports	elections.ny.gov/CFViewReports.html
Incarceration Records	nysdoccslookup.doccs.ny.gov/kinqw00
Sex Offender Registry	criminaljustice.ny.gov/SomsSUBDirectory/search_index.jsp
Child Support Enforcement Warrant	dos.ny.gov/corps/child_support_search.html
Tax Warrant Notice	dos.ny.gov/corps/tax_warrant_search.html
Title/Lien Status Check	https://transact.dmv.ny.gov/TitleStatus/
UCC	appext20.dos.ny.gov/pls/ucc_public/web_search.main_frame

North Carolina

Business Entities	secretary.state.nc.us/Corporations/
Campaign Finance, PACs	ncsbe.gov/ncsbe/Campaign-Finance/report-search
Delinquent Taxpayers	dor.state.nc.us/collect/delinquent.html
Federal Tax Liens	secretary.state.nc.us/taxliens/filingsearch.aspx
Incarceration Records	webapps6.doc.state.nc.us/opi/offendersearch.do?method=view
Lobbyists	ncsbe.gov/ncsbe/Campaign-Finance/report-search
Sex Offender Registry	sexoffender.ncdoj.gov/disclaimer.aspx
Tax Debtors List	dor.state.nc.us/collect/delinquent.html
Trademarks	secretary.state.nc.us/trademrk/search.aspx
UCC	secretary.state.nc.us/UCC/FilingSearch.aspx

North Dakota

Business Entity Name Search	https://apps.nd.gov/sc/busnsrch/busnSearch.htm
Campaign Finance, PACs	https://vip.sos.nd.gov/PortalListDetails.aspxChild Support Lien
Search	https://apps.nd.gov/dhs/application/lienRegistry/
Driver License Status Check	https://apps.nd.gov/dot/dlts/dlos/requeststatus.htm
Inmate Locator	nd.gov/docr/search/
Lobbyists	sos.nd.gov/lobbyists/registered-lobbyists
Securities Industry Professionals	nd.gov/securities/industry-registration
Sex Offender Registry	sexoffender.nd.gov/

Ohio

Business Name Search	www2.sos.state.oh.us/pls/bsqry/f?p=100:1:0:::::
Campaign Finance Reports	sos.state.oh.us/SOS/CampaignFinance/Search.aspx
Debarred Contractors	sos.state.oh.us/SOS/recordsIndexes/debarredcontractors.aspx
DOC Inmate, Offender (for most counties)	https://www.vinelink.com/vinelink/siteInfoAction.do?siteId=36001
Elections - PACs	www2.sos.state.oh.us/pls/cfonline/f?p=119:1:0:::::
Campaign Finance Disclosures	sos.state.oh.us/SOS/CampaignFinance/pfdisclosure.aspx
Incarceration Records	drc.ohio.gov/OffenderSearch/Search.aspx
Registered Lobbyists	www2.jlec-olig.state.oh.us/olac/Reports/FormsFiledHome.aspx
Securities Enforcement Orders	https://www.comapps.ohio.gov/secu/secu_apps/FinalOrders/
Sex Offender Registry	icrimewatch.net/index.php?AgencyID=55149

Oklahoma

Business Entities	https://www.sos.ok.gov/corp/corpInquiryFind.aspx
Campaign Finance and Disclosure	ok.gov/ethics/public/index.php
Incarceration Records	ok.gov/doc/Offenders/index.html
Parole Status	gov.ok.gov/parole/parole_lookup.php
Securities Enforcement Actions	securities.ok.gov/Enforcement/Orders/OrdersDisplay.asp
Securities Firms, Advisors	securities.ok.gov/Firms-profs/DBSearch/DatabaseSearch.asp
Sex Offender & Violent Offender Registry	sors.doc.state.ok.us/
Trademarks	https://www.sos.ok.gov/trademarks/default.aspx
UCC and Recorded Land Documents	countyclerk.oklahomacounty.org/registrar-of-deeds/rod-ucc-search

Oregon

Active Trademarks	sos.oregon.gov/business/Pages/trademarks.aspx
Business Entities	egov.sos.state.or.us/br/pkg_web_name_srch_inq.login
Campaign Finance, PACs	sos.oregon.gov/elections/Pages/orestar.aspx
Complaints on Businesses	sos.oregon.gov/business/Pages/business-consumer-complaints.aspx
Inmates, Offenders	https://www.vinelink.com/vinelink/siteInfoAction.do?siteId=38000
UCC Recent Filing Lists	sos.oregon.gov/business/Pages/ucc-data-lists.aspx
Sexual Offender Records	sexoffenders.oregon.gov/SorPublic/Web.dll/main
UCC	https://secure.sos.state.or.us/ucc/searchHome.action
UCC Farm Products Registration List	sos.oregon.gov/business/Pages/farm-products-master-list.aspx
UCC Recent Filing Lists	sos.oregon.gov/business/Pages/ucc-data-lists.aspx

Pennsylvania

Business Entities	https://www.corporations.state.pa.us/corp/soskb/csearch.asp
Incarceration Records	inmatelocator.cor.state.pa.us/inmatelocatorweb/
Sexual Offender Records	pameganslaw.state.pa.us
UCC	https://www.corporations.state.pa.us/ucc/soskb/SearchStandardRA9.asp

Rhode Island

Business Entities	ucc.state.ri.us/CorpSearch/CorpSearchInput.asp
Campaign Finance, PACs	elections.ri.gov/finance/publicinfo/
Inmates, Offenders	doc.ri.gov/inmate_search/index.php
Sex Offender Registry	paroleboard.ri.gov/sexoffender/agree.php
Trademark/Servicemark	ucc.state.ri.us/trademarks/trademarksearch.asp
UCC	sos.ri.gov/business/ucc/database/

South Carolina

Business Entity Filings scsos.com/Search%20Business%20Filings

Campaign, Political Ethics Violations .... ethics.sc.gov/Debtors/Pages/index.aspx

Campaign Finance Reports................................ apps.sc.gov/PublicReporting/Index.aspx

Delinquent Taxpayers .... sctax.org/delinquent/delinquent.shtml

Driver License Status and Points .... https://www.scdmvonline.com/DMVpublic/trans/DRecPoints.aspx

Incarceration Records .... doc.sc.gov/pubweb/InmateSearchDisclaimer.jsp

Lobbyists Lists and Reports .... apps.sc.gov/LobbyingActivity/LAIndex.aspx

Sex Offender Registry.. icrimewatch.net/index.php?AgencyID=54575&disc=54575

South Dakota

Business Entities .... https://sos.sd.gov/business/search.aspx

Campaign Finance Reports, PACs .... sdsos.gov/elections-voting/campaign-finance/default.aspx

Fictitious Name Registration .... https://apps.sd.gov/st08bnrs/secure/ASPX/BNRS_Search.aspx

Sex Offender Registry.. sor.sd.gov/

Tennessee

Business Entities .... https://tnbear.tn.gov/ECommerce/FilingSearch.aspx

Campaign Finance Reports, PACs, Lobbyists .... tn.gov/tref/cand/cand.htm

Felony Offender Lookup..................................... https://apps.tn.gov/foil-app/search.jsp

Securities Enforcement Actions .... tn.gov/securities/enfaction.shtml

Sex Offender Registry.. tbi.tn.gov/sorint/SOMainpg.aspx

Trademarks .... tn.gov/sos/bus_svc/TrademarkSearch.htm

UCCs... https://tnbear.tn.gov/UCC/Ecommerce/UCCSearch.aspx

Texas

Business Entities .... sos.state.tx.us/corp/sosda/index.shtml

Campaign Finance and Lobbyist Reports .... ethics.state.tx.us/main/search.htm

Cemetery Inscription Search .... obitcentral.com/cemsearch/tx-cem.htm

Delinquent Campaign Finance/Lobbyist Reports ethics.state.tx.us/dfs/delinquent_filers.htm

Inmates, Offenders... offender.tdcj.state.tx.us/OffenderSearch/index.jsp

Insurance Agency Enforcement Actions .... tdi.texas.gov/commish/actions.html

Motor Carrier Complaint History......................... https://apps.txdmv.gov/apps/mccs/cms/CMS.asp?reload_id=3

Securities Enforcement Actions .... ssb.state.tx.us/Enforcement/Recent_Enforcement_Actions.php

Sex Offender Registry..https://records.txdps.state.tx.us/SexOffender/PublicSite/Index.aspx

Taxable Entity (From Comptroller's Office) .... https://mycpa.cpa.state.tx.us/coa/Index.html

Utah

Business Entities, Registered Principles .... utah.gov/services/business.html?type=citizen

Campaign Finance Reports, PACs .... elections.utah.gov/campaign-finance

Financial Disclosure - Election Related............... disclosures.utah.gov/

Inmates, Offenders... corrections.utah.gov/index.php/services/offender-search.html

Lobbyist Reports .... https://secure.utah.gov/lobbyist/lobb

Sex Offender Registry.. communitynotification.com/index.php

State Cemetery and Burial Database.................. heritage.utah.gov/history/cemeteries

UCC... https://secure.utah.gov/uccsearch/uccs

Vermont

Business Entities	https://www.vtsosonline.com/online
Inmate Locator	doc.vermont.gov/offender-locator/
Securities/Investment Professionals	dfr.vermont.gov/securities/investor/find-registered-professional
Sex Offender Registry	communitynotification.com/index.php
UCC	https://www.sec.state.vt.us/corporations/ucc-service-center.aspx
Verify Good Standing of Business	https://www.vtsosonline.com/online/Certificate

Virginia

Business Entities & UCC Filings	https://sccefile.scc.virginia.gov/
Campaign Finance Reports	cfreports.sbe.virginia.gov
Incarceration Records	vadoc.virginia.gov/offenders/locator/
Sex Offender Registry	sex-offender.vsp.virginia.gov/sor/
Trademarks and Service Marks	scc.virginia.gov/srf/index.aspx

Washington

Business Entities	sos.wa.gov/corps/corps_search.aspx
Delinquent Taxpayers	dor.wa.gov/content/fileandpaytaxes/latefiling/delinquenttaxpayerlist.aspx
Driver Status Display	https://fortress.wa.gov/dol/dolprod/dsdDriverStatusDisplay/
Election Disclosures, PACs, Lobbyists	pdc.wa.gov/MvcQuerySystem
Incarceration Search - Inmates	doc.wa.gov/offenderinfo/default.aspx
Sex Offender Registry	icrimewatch.net/index.php?AgencyID=54528
UCC	https://fortress.wa.gov/dol/ucc/

West Virginia

Business Entities	apps.sos.wv.gov/business/corporations/
Campaign Finance Reports, PACs	sos.wv.gov/elections/campaignfinance/Pages/default.aspx
Driver Status Display	transportation.wv.gov/dmv/Pages/DLVerify.aspx
Inmate Search	wvdoc.com/wvdoc/OffenderSearch/tabid/117/Default.aspx
Sex Offender Registry	https://apps.wv.gov/StatePolice/SexOffender/Disclaimer
UCC	https://ucc.state.wy.us/ExLogin.asp

Wisconsin

Business Entities	https://www.wdfi.org/apps/CorpSearch/Search.aspx?
Campaign Finance Reports	https://cfis.wi.gov/
Child Support - Lien Docket	dwd.state.wi.us/liendocketweb/
Delinquent Taxpayers	revenue.wi.gov/html/delqlist.html
Driver License Status	https://trust.dot.state.wi.us/occsin/occsinservlet?whoami=statusp1
Inmates, Offenders	https://www.vinelink.com/vinelink/siteInfoAction.do?siteId=50001
License Plate Status	https://trust.dot.state.wi.us/pinq/PinqServlet?whoami=pinqp1
Securities Investment Advisor	wdfi.org/fi/securities/
Securities Registration and Exemption	https://www.wdfi.org/apps/SecuritiesSearch/search.aspx
Sex Offender Registry	offender.doc.state.wi.us/public/
Trademarks, Trade Names	https://www.wdfi.org/apps/TrademarkSearch/Search.aspx
UCC	https://www.wdfi.org/ucc/search/
Vehicle Lien Inquiry	on.dot.wi.gov/applicationdoc/lien/index.htm

Wyoming

Business Entities	https://wyobiz.wy.gov/Business/Default.aspx
Campaign Finance, PACs	https://www.wycampaignfinance.gov
Sex Offender Registry	wysors.dci.wyo.gov/sor/
Trademark Search	will.state.wy.us/trademarks/
Validate Certificate of Good Standing	https://wyobiz.wy.gov/Business/ViewCertificate.aspx

National Trade Associations With Investigation Interests

Editor's Notes:
- 'www.http' omitted from URLs.
- Content supplied by BRB Publications (BRBPublications.com)

Name	Acronym	URL
American Assn of Motor Vehicle Administrators	AAMVA	aamva.org
American Assn of Professional Landmen	AAPL	landman.org
American Association for Justice	AAJ	justice.org/
American Banking Assn	ABA (2)	aba.com/default.htm
American Bankruptcy Institute	ABI	abiworld.org
American Bar Assn	ABA	americanbar.org/aba.html
American Board of Forensic Examiners	ABFE	acfei.com
American Intellectual Property Law Assn	AIPLA	aipla.org/Pages/default.aspx
American Land Title Assn	ALTA	alta.org
American Society for Industrial Security	ASIS	https://www.asisonline.org
American Society of Law Enforcement Trainers	ASLET	aslet.org
America's Mortgage Banking Attorneys	USFN	http://imis.usfn.org
Assn of Certified Fraud Examiners	ACFE	acfe.com
Assn of Collectors and Collection Professionals	ACA	acainternational.org
Assn of Former Intelligence Officers	AFIO	afio.com
Assn of Independent Information Professionals	AIIP	aiip.org
Assn of Professional Genealogists	APG	https://www.apgen.org/
Council of Intl Investigators	CII	cii2.org
Direct Marketing Assn	DMA	http://thedma.org/
Electronic Security Association	ESA	alarm.org/
Environmental Assessment Assn	EAA	eaa-assoc.org/
Evidence Photographers Intl Council	EPIC	epic-photo.org
Intl Assn of Arson Investigators	IAAI	fire-investigators.org
Intl Assn of Healthcare Security & Safety	IAHSS	iahss.org
Intl Assn of Law Enforcement Intelligence Analysts	IALEIA	ialeia.org
Intl Assn of Security & Investigative Regulators	NASIR	iasir.org
Intl Narcotics Officers Assn	INOA	ineoa.org
Intl Trademark Assn	INTA	inta.org/Pages/Home.aspx
Investigative Open Network	ION	ioninc.com
Investigative Reporters and Editors	IRE	ire.org
NALS...the Assn of Legal Professionals	NALS	nals.org
National Assn of County Recorders, Elec. Officials ad Clerks	NACRC	nacrc.org/
National Assn of Credit Managers	NACM	nacm.org
National Assn of Fire Investigators	NAFI	nafi.org
National Assn of Law Firm Marketers	NALFM	legalmarketing.org
National Assn of Legal Assistants	NALA	nala.org

National Assn of Legal Investigators	NALI	nalionline.org
National Assn of Legal Search Consultants	NALSC	nalsc.org
National Assn of Professional Background Screeners	NAPBS	napbs.com
National Assn of Professional Process Servers	NAPPS	napps.org
National Assn of Public Insurance Adjustors	NAPIA	napia.com
National Assn of Unclaimed Property Administrators	NAUPA	unclaimed.org
National Consumer Reporting Assn	NCRA	ncrainc.org
National Council of Investigation & Security Services	NCISS	nciss.org
National Court Reporters Assn	NCRA	ncra.org/
National Defender Investigator Assn	NDIA	ndia.net
National Federation of Independent Businesses	NFIB	nfib.com
National Federation of Paralegal Assns	NFPA	paralegals.org/
National Genealogical Society	NGS	ngsgenealogy.org
National Human Resources Assn	NHRA	humanresources.org/website/c/
National Insurance Crime Bureau	NICB	https://www.nicb.org/
National Lawyers Guild	NLG	nlg.org
National Public Record Research Assn	NPRRA	nprra.org
National Sheriffs' Assn	NSA	sheriffs.org
Professional Bail Agents of the United States	PBUS	pbus.com
Professionals in Human Resources Assn	PIHRA	pihra.org
Property Records Information Professionals Assn	PRIA	pria.us
Public Record Retriever Network	PRRN	prrn.us
Society of Competitive Intelligence Professionals	SCIP	https://www.scip.org/
Society of Former Special Agents of the FBI	SFSA	socxfbi.org
Society of Human Resources Management	SHRM	shrm.org
Software & Information Industry Assn	SIIA	siia.net
World Assn of Detectives	W.A.D.	wad.net

The Excluded Parties List System Contributors

The Excluded Parties List System (EPLS) housed at SAM.gov contains information on individuals and firms which have been excluded by the federal government agencies listed below from receiving federal contracts or federally approved subcontracts, and certain types of federal financial and non-financial assistance and benefits.

Agency for International Development
Agriculture, Department of
Air Force, Department of
Appalachian Regional Commission
Army, Department of
Broadcasting Board of Governors
Central Intelligence Agency
Commerce, Department of
Commerce, Department of
Commission on Civil Rights
Consumer Product Safety Commission
Corporation for National and Community Service
Customs and Border Protection, Bureau of
Defense Advanced Research Projects Agency
Defense Information Systems Agency (DISA)
Defense Logistics Agency
Defense Threat Reduction Agency (DTRA)
Defense, Department of
Education Department of
Energy, Department of
Environmental Protection Agency
Export-Import Bank of the U.S.
Farm Credit Administration
Federal Communications Commission
Federal Deposit Insurance Corporation
Federal Election Commission
Federal Labor Relations Authority
Federal Mediation and Conciliation Service
Federal Trade Commission Inc
General Services Administration
Government Accountability Office
Government Printing Office
Health and Human Services, Department of
Homeland Security, Department of

Housing and Urban Development, Department of
Immigration & Customs Enforcement, Bureau of
Interior, Department of
International Trade Commission
Justice, Department of
Labor, Department of
Missile Defense Agency (MDA)
National Aeronautics and Space Administration
National Archives and Records Administration
National Endowment for the Arts
National Endowment for the Humanities
National Gallery of Art
National Geospatial-Intelligence Agency (NGA)
National Labor Relations Board
National Science Foundation
National Security Agency/Central Security Service
Navy, Department of
Nuclear Regulatory Commission, United States
Office of Foreign Assets Control
Office of Personnel Management
Overseas Private Investment Corporation
Peace Corps
Pension Benefit Guaranty Corporation
Postal Service
Railroad Retirement Board
Small Business Administration United States
Social Security Administration
State, Department of
Transportation Security Administration
Transportation, Department of
Treasury, United States Department of the
United States Coast Guard
United States Trade and Development Agency
Veterans Affairs, Department of

Building and Construction Trades: Industry Journals and Magazines

Editor's Notes:
- 'www.http' omitted from URLs.
- This list is a select group maintained by the author

Name of Journal or Magazine	URL
Access International	access-industry.com
Air Conditioning, Heating & Refrigeration News	achrnews.com
Automated Builder Magazine	automatedbuilder.com
BNPMedia	bnpmedia.com
Building Design and Construction	bdcmag.com
Buildings.com	buildings.com
Cement Americas	cementamericas.com
CMDaec	cmdg.com/products/cmdaec.html
CoatingsPro magazine	coatingspromag.com
Construction Claims Online	constructionclaims.com
Construction Equipment Guide	constructionequipmentguide.com
Construction Equipment Magazine	constructionequipment.com/about
Construction Europe Magazine	construction-europe.com
Construction Exec	constructionexec.com
Crane Hot Line	cranehotline.com
Demolition & Recycling International	khl.com
Elevator World	elevator-world.com
Engineering News Record	enr.com
Equipment Connection	equipmentconnection.com
Equipment Journal	equipmentjournal.com
Equipment World	equipmentworld.com
European Rental News	khl.com
Expressways Publishing Project	expresswaysonline.com
Federal Publications/West Group	fedpub.com
Floor Covering Installer	fcimag.com
FW Dodge's Northwest Construction	nwc.fwdodge.com
Green Building Insider	greenbuildinginsider.com
Hard Hat News	hardhat.com
HousingZone.com	housingzone.com
International Cranes	craneworld.com
International Dredging Review	dredgemag.com
KHL International Publishing Group	KHL.com
Manufacturing Management	khl.com
Masonry Edge	masonryedge.com

Modern Steel	modernsteel.com
National Driller	drilleronline.com
National Floor Trends	ntlfloortrends.com
On-Site	econstruction.ca
Pit & Quarry	pitandquarry.com
Plant & Works Engineering	khl.com
Plumbing & Mechanical	pmmag.com
PM Engineer	pmengineer.com
Point of Beginning	pobonline.com
Project Controls	projectcontrols.com
Public Works Journal	pwmag.com
Reed Business Information	reedbusiness.com
Reed Construction Data	reedconstructiondata.com
Rental Product News	equipmentconnection.com
Retail Construction magazine	retailconstructionmag.com
Roads & Bridges Magazine	roadsbridges.com
Rock Products	rockproducts.com
Roofing Contractor	roofingcontractor.com
Site Prep	SitePrepMag.com
Southern California Contractors Association Magazine	sccaweb.com
The Construction Zone	nvczone.com
The Electrical Distributor (TED) magazine	tedmag.com
Underground Construction	oildompublishing.com
Underground Focus	underspace.com
Walls & Ceilings	wconline.com

Ch13:

Lists of Investigative Resources — Foreign Based

The reason for having diplomatic relations is not to confer a compliment, but to secure a convenience.
—Winston Churchill

Chapter 13 contains three very useful lists.

- Foreign Security Identifiers
- Company Extensions by Country
- Foreign Regulatory and Enforcement Agencies

The first two lists are provided by the **Winthrop Corporation**. The author and the publisher wish to thank the Winthrop Corporation for allowing us to include this excellent material herein. Please visit www.CorporateInformation.com for details on the competitive analysis and research that the Winthrop Corporation provides to clients.

Foreign Security Identifiers

Bonds and Stocks usually have one or more identifier codes, issued by various clearing houses or other agencies. The purpose of these identifiers is to prevent confusion when discussing a particular security, particularly a bond. While a company will usually only have one class of stock, it can have many different bond issues. The following is a list of various security identifiers along with information about their structure and issuers.

ID	Description
Cedel	No longer used; replaced by the Common Code on January 1, 1991.
CIN	*CUSIP International Number.* Used for non-U.S. and non-Canadian securities. Nine

ID	Description
	characters. The first character is always a letter, which represents the country of issue. The country codes are as follows: A=Austria, B=Belgium, C=China, D=Germany, E=Spain, F=France, G=Great Britain, H=Switzerland, J=Japan, K=Denmark, L=Luxembourg, M= MiddleEast, N=Netherlands P= South America, Q=Australia, R=Norway, S=South Africa, T= Italy, U= United States, V =Africa(Other), W= Sweden, X=Europe (Other), Y=Asia. The next five characters are numbers which represent the issuer, followed by two digits representing the security. The final digit is the check digit.
Common Code	Issued in Luxembourg, replaces CEDEL and Euroclear codes. Nine digits. Final digit is a check digit, computed on a multiplicative system.
CUSIP	*Committee on Uniform Securities Identification Procedures.* Standard & Poor's assigns a nine character code to stocks and bonds. The first six characters identify the issuer. The next two characters represent the security that was issued, and the ninth character is a check digit, which is computed using a modulus 10 double add double calculation. For Canadian and U.S. securities, the first character is always a digit. Other countries use an alphabetic first character. See CIN number, above.
Euroclear	Not used anymore; replaced by the Common Code on January 1, 1991.
ISIN	*International Securities Identification Number.* This is a twelve character code developed by the International Standards Organization (ISO) that represents a security. The first two letters always represent the country code, and the ISO standards are used. Basically, these are the same two letters as used in Internet addresses (however GB, not UK, is used for the United Kingdom of Great Britain and Northern Ireland). The next nine characters usually use some other code, such as CUSIP in the United States, SEDOL in Great Britain, etc. Leading spaces are padded with 0. The final digit is the check digit, also computed with modulus 10 double add double, but it is different from the method used in CUSIP's.
RIC	*Reuter Identification Code.* Used on the Reuters Terminal to pull up a particular security. When an equal sign is the last character, that symbol is a master RIC. An RIC that has an equal sign followed by some additional letters means that this string contains the price quoted by some entity. That entity is denoted by those letters following the equal sign.
SEDOL	*Stock Exchange Daily Official List.* Securities identification code issued by the London Stock Exchange. Has a built in check digit system.
SIC	*Standard Industrial Code.* Denotes the company's line of business. Does not symbolize a security.
SICC	*Security Identification Code Conference.* Used in Japan instead of ticker symbols, usually four digits.
Sicovam	*Société Interprofessional Pour La Compensation des Valeurs Mobiliers.* Used in France.
SVM	Used in Belgium.
Valoren	Identifier for Swiss securities. No check digit system.
Wertpapier Kenn-nummer	Issued in Germany by the Wertpapier Mitteilungen. Six digits, no check digit. Different ranges of numbers represent different classes of securities. Sometimes called WPK. Note that this number has widespread use in Germany: much more so than the CUSIP in the United States, for instance.
WKN	See Wertpapier Kenn-Nummer.
WPK	See Wertpapier Kenn-Nummer.

Company Extensions by Country

This section provides definitions of company "extensions" and security identifiers. While U.S. companies are usually followed by "Inc.", many foreign companies have different endings. This section tells what these terms mean, and where they are used. If you don't know what country a company is based in, this list of identifiers might help narrow your search.

Ext.	Country	Description
A. en P.	Mexico	*Asociación en Participación.* Joint venture
AB	Sweden	*Aktiebolag.* Aktiebolag. Stock company -- can be publicly-traded or privately-held. In Sweden, privately-held AB's must have capital of at least SEK 100,000 upon incorporation. AB's are also required to allocate at least 10% of the profits for reserves per year until reserves are at least 20% of the start-up capital. Publicly-traded AB's in Sweden must have capital of at least SEK 500,000. There must be at least three board members for Swedish AB's. An Annual General Meeting is required. AB's are registered with the Swedish Patent and Registration Office (*Patent- och Registreringsverket* or PRV). The Swedish automobile and aircraft manufacturer SAAB is actually an acronym -- Svenska Aeroplan Aktiebolaget. Aktiebolaget is sometimes used instead of Aktiebolag, since the definite article is appended to the end of the word in Swedish (Aktiebolaget means THE stock company whereas Aktiebolag means just Stock Company).
AB	Finland	*Aktiebolag.* In Finland, many companies use both this Swedish abbreviation and the Finnish language Oy designation, since Finland is a bilingual country. In Finland, an AB is only private (Apb is the public equivalent).
A.C.	Mexico	*Asociación Civil* Civil Association of a non-commercial nature.
ACE	Portugal	*Agrupamento Complementar de Empresas.* Association of businesses
AD	Bulgaria	*Aktzionerno Druzhestvo.* Limited Liability company, can be publicly-traded.
AE	Greece	*Anonymos Etairia.* Limited company. Must have a board of three to nine members.
AG	Austria	*Aktiengesellschaft.* Translates to "stock corporation". Minimum share capital is ATS 1 million. Par value of each share must be ATS 100, ATS 500, or a multiple of ATS 1,000. As in Germany, an Austrian AG must have both a *Vorstand* and an *Aufsichtsrat.*

Ext.	Country	Description
AG	Germany	*Aktiengesellschaft*. Translates to "stock corporation." In Germany, all publicly traded companies are AG's, but not all AG's are publicly traded. AG's have two sets of boards -- the *Vorstand*, which usually consists of the CEO, CFO and other top management, and an *Aufsichtsrat*, which translates to "supervisory board," which has the function of overseeing management and representing the shareholders. German law prohibits individuals from being members of both boards at the same time. AG's in Germany require a minimum of DM 100,000 share capital and at least five shareholders at incorporation. Minimum par value for shares is DM 50.
AG	Switzerland	*Aktiengesellschaft*. Translates to "stock corporation." In Switzerland, AG's must have at least CHF 100,000 share capital, and each share must be at least CHF 0.01 par value. When a Swiss entity registers as an AG, 3% of the capital must be paid to the authorities as a Tax if the share capital is equal to or more than CHF 250,000. There must be three shareholders (although they can be nominees). An annual audit is required, and an annual directors meeting and shareholders meetings must be held in Switzerland.
AL	Norway	*Andelslag*. Co-operative society. Note: this was formerly written as A.L. and A/L, but financial law reform has dictated that periods and slashes should no longer be used.
AmbA	Denmark	*Andelsselskab*.
ANS	Norway	*Ansvarlig selskap*. Trading partnership.
Apb	Finland	*Publikt Aktiebolag*. Public limited company. This is the Swedish language equivalent to the more commonly used Oyj in Finland. Finland is technically bilingual, so this could be used, but is not likely.
ApS	Denmark	*Anpartsselskab*. Limited liability corporation, required minimum share capital of DKK 200,000.
ApS & Co. K/S	Denmark	Similar to a K/S, but the entity with unlimited liability is a company (ApS) instead of an individual.
AS	Norway	*Aksjeselskap*, translates to "stock company," and gives owners limited liability. In Norway, publicly traded companies now use the ASA notation, and no longer use this notation. Private companies still use this AS notation. An AS requires minimum share capital of NOK 100,000, of which at least 50% must be paid up at incorporation. Note: this was formerly written as A.S. and A/S, but financial law reform has dictated that periods and slashes should no longer be used.
A/S	Denmark	*Aktieselskap*, translates to "stock company", and gives the owners limited liability. Danish companies require minimum share capital of DKK 500,000.

Ext.	Country	Description
A.S.	Czech Republic	*Akciova spolecnost*. Joint stock company. Owners have limited liability. Share capital must be at least CZK 1 million. The company must put at least 20% of the capital into a reserve fund, which is funded by after-tax profits. The accounts must be audited annually. There must be at least three members on the board of directors, and each member must be a Czech citizen or resident.
A.S.	Estonia	*Aktsiaselts*, Joint stock company.
A.S.	Slovakia	*Akciova Spolocnost*, Joint stock company
A.S.	Turkey	*Anonim Sirket*, a limited liability company
ASA	Norway	*Allmennaksjeselskap*. Stock company. This acronym was chosen because Aas is a very common surname in Norway, which might have created some confusion. Since 1996, all publicly traded Norwegian companies are now incorporated in this legal structure, but not all ASA's are publicly traded. Note: this was formerly written as A.S.A. and A/S/A, but financial law reform has dictated that periods and slashes should no longer be used.
AVV	Aruba	*Aruba Vrijgestelde Vennootschap*. Aruba Exempt Company. This type of company is intended for non-residents of Aruba: and such a company pays no taxes (but must instead pay an annual registration fee of AFl 500, or about US$280). Registered or bearer shares may be issued, and preference shares are also allowed. Minimum share capital is AFl 10,000. There are no financial statements that are required to be filed, but there must be representation by a local Aruban company (usually a Trust Agent).
Bpk	South Africa	*Beperk*
Bt	Hungary	*Beteti társaság*. Limited liability partnership.
B.V.	Belgium	*Besloten Vennootschap*. Limited liability company.
B.V.	Netherlands	*Besloten Vennootschap*. Limited liability company. Capital of at least 40,000 NLG is required to start at BV.
B.V.	Netherlands Antilles	*Besloten Vennootschap*. Limited liability company. Many companies incorporated in the Netherlands Antilles are merely shells created for tax purposes.
BVBA	Belgium	*Besloten Vennootschap met Beperkte Aansprakelijkheid* Flemish language equivalent of the SPRL. It means that the company is a private limited company. Capital must be at least BEF 750,000, with at least BEF 250,000 paid up.
CA	Ecuador	*Compania anonima*.
Corp.	USA	*Corporation*. Same meaning as Incorporated.
C.V.	Netherlands	*Commanditaire Vennootschap*. Limited Partnership. One partner must have unlimited liability, and the others can have limited liability.
CVA	Belgium	*Commanditaire Vennootschap op Aandelen. Limited partnership with shares. Flemish language equivalent to the French language SCA*

Ext.	Country	Description
CVoA	Netherlands	*Commanditaire Vennootschap op Andelen*. Limited Partnership, with shares
DA	Norway	*Selskap med delt ansar*. Limited Partnership Note: this was formerly written as D.A. and D/A, but financial law reform has dictated that periods and slashes should no longer be used.
d/b/a	USA	*Doing Business As*. Used often by individuals who want to have a business name, but don't want to incorporate. Companies also use this designation when they operate under a name other than the owner's personal name or the name of a filed corporation/LLC.
d.d.	Croatia	*dionicko drustvo*. Joint stock company.
d.d.	Slovenia	*Delniska druzba*. Stock company -- all publicly traded companies must have this structure. Must have capital of SIT 3 million, and each share must have par value of SIT 1,000. Minimum of five shareholders.
d.n.o.	Slovenia	*Druzba z neomejeno odgovornostjo. Partnership -- all partners have unlimited liability.*
d.o.o.	Croatia	*drustvo s ogranicenom odgovornoscu*. Limited Liability company.
d.o.o.	Slovenia	*Druzba z omejeno odgovornostjo*. Limited Liability company. Must have a share capital of at least SIT 1.5 million, and each partner must invest at least SIT 10,000.
EE	Greece	*Eterrorrythmos*. Limited liability partnership.
EEG	Austria	*Eingetragene Erwerbsgesellschaft*. Professional Partnership.
EIRL	Peru	*Empresa Individual de Responsabilidad Limitada*. Personal business with limited liability.
ELP	Bahamas	*Exempted Limited Partnership*. Has one or more limited partners, and one general partner, which must be a resident of the Bahamas or a company incorporated in the Bahamas. Cannot conduct business in the Bahamas, but may conduct business elsewhere. Usually set up for tax purposes.
EOOD	Bulgaria	*Ednolichno Druzhestvo s Ogranichena Otgovornost*. Limited liability company. Requires only one shareholder.
EPE	Greece	*Etairia periorismenis evthinis*. Limited liability company.
EURL	France	*Enterprise Unipersonnelle à Responsabilité Limitée*. Sole proprietorship with limited liability.
e.V.	Germany	*Eingetragener Verein*. Non profit society/association.
GbR	Germany	*Gesellschaft burgerlichen Rechts*. Partnership without a legal name. Mainly used for non-commercial purposes. Partners have full liability.

Ext.	Country	Description
GCV	Belgium	*Gewone Commanditaire Vennootschap*. Limited Partnership. The Flemish language equivalent to the French language SCS.
GesmbH	Austria	See GmbH. This abbreviation is only used in Austria (not Germany or Switzerland).
GIE	France	*Groupement d'intéret économique*. Economic Grouping of Interest. Two or more persons or entities form an alliance with the goal of facilitating or developing economic activity of the members.
GmbH & Co. KG	Germany	Like a KG, but the entity with unlimited liability is a GmbH instead of a person. (See the KG entry for more information).
GmbH	Austria	*Gesellschaft mit beschränkter Haftung*. Translates to "Company with limited liability." In Austria, this is often GesmbH, although this abbreviation is not used in Germany or Switzerland. In Austria, there must be at least two founding shareholders of a GmbH. Insurance companies and mortgage banking companies are not permitted to exist in this form. Minimum share capital is ATS 500,000, and at least half of this must be raised in cash. Minimum par value is ATS 1,000 per share. No citizenship or residence requirement for shareholders exists, and shareholders can be other companies. A general meeting must be held at least annually. If an Austrian GmbH controls companies with 300 or more employees, or if the company has more than 300 employees itself, there must be a supervisory board, which must have at least three members, one of whom represents the workers. The supervisory board must meet at least three times annually.
GmbH	Germany	*Gesellschaft mit beschränkter Haftung*. Translates to "Company with limited liability." In Germany, a GmbH means that the company is incorporated, but it is not publicly traded (as public companies must be AG's). GmbH's are essentially partnerships without a legal name, and there must be at least two partners. There must be nominal capital of at least DM 50,000. Subsidiaries of AG's can be GmbH's.
GmbH	Switzerland	*Gesellschaft mit beschränkter Haftung*. Translates to "Company with limited liability." In Switzerland, a GmbH cannot have shares, and the owners of the company are entered into the commercial registry. Nominees can be used for anonymity.
HB	Sweden	*Handelsbolag*. Trading Partnership
hf	Iceland	*Hlutafelag*. Limited liability company.
IBC	Various	*International Business Company*. Used for offshore companies, in places such as Bahamas, Turks & Caicos Islands, etc.
Inc.	USA	Means a company is Incorporated, and the owners have limited liability. In the United States, companies can be registered in any of the 50 states -- many of the bigger corporations are registered in Delaware due to various regulations. Incorporation in the United States is very easy, and can be done for minimal fees.
Inc	Canada	Incorporated. Limited liability

Ext.	Country	Description
I/S	Denmark	*Interessentskab*. Used in Denmark. General partnership; all partners have unlimited liability.
j.t.d.	Croatia	*Javno trgovacko drustvo*. Unlimited liability company.
KA/S	Denmark	*Kommanditaktieselskab*. Limited partnership with share capital
Kb	Sweden	*Kommanditbolag*. Limited partnership. There must be at least one partner with unlimited liability, although some partners can have limited liability. In Sweden, all Kommanditbolags must be registered with the Patent and Registration Office. Annual reports must be filed annually. If there are more than 10 employees, then the annual accounts must be audited. If there are more than 200 employees, the annual reports must be filed with the Patent and Registration Office.
Kb	Finland	*Kommanditbolag*. Limited partnership. This is a Swedish term, and since Finland is technically bilingual, this abbreviation can be used there, although the Ky designation is more common.
KD	Bulgaria	*Komanditno drushestwo*. Partnership
k.d.	Croatia	*komanditno drustvo*. Limited Partnership.
k.d.	Slovenia	*Komanditna druzba*. Limited Partnership -- there must be at least one limited partner and one unlimited partner.
KDA	Bulgaria	*Komanditno drushestwo s akzii*. Partnership with shares.
k.d.d.	Slovenia	*Komanditna delniska druzba*. Limited Partnership with shares.
Kft	Hungary	*korlátolt felelösségû társaság*. Limited liability company. Similar to the German GmbH, this type of company offers limited liability, although the shares cannot trade publicly. Requires only one shareholder. Minimum share capital is HUF 1 million.
KG	Austria	*Kommanditgesellschaft*. A partnership under a legal name. There must be two partners, at least one limited and at least one unlimited partner. The limited partner's liability is listed in the commercial register.
KG	Germany	*Kommanditgesellschaft*. A partnership under a legal name. There must be a minimum of two partners, at least one limited and at least one unlimited.
KGaA	Germany	*Kommanditgesellschaft auf Aktien*. A Limited Partnership that has shares.
KK	Japan	*Kabushiki Kaishi*. Joint Stock Company
Kkt	Hungary	*közkereseti társaság*, General Partnership. All partners have unlimited liability.
Kol. SrK	Turkey	*Kollektiv Sirket*. Unlimited liability partnership.
Kom. SrK	Turkey	*Komandit Sirket*. Limited liability partnership.
k.s.	Czech Republic	*komanditni spolecnost*. Limited partnership. One partner must have unlimited liability, although other partners can carry limited liability.

Ext.	Country	Description
K/S	Denmark	*Kommanditselskab.* Limited partnership: at least one partner has unlimited liability and at least one partner has limited liability.
KS	Norway	*Kommandittselskap.* Limited partnership: at least one partner has unlimited liability and at least one partner has limited liability. Note: this was formerly written as K.S. and K/S, but financial law reform has dictated that periods and slashes should no longer be used.
Kv	Hungary	*Közös vállalat.* Joint Venture
Ky	Finland	*Kommandiittiyhtiö.* Limited Partnership.
Lda	Portugal	*Sociedade por Quotas Limitada.* Must have at least two shareholders, and paid in capital of at least 400,000 Escudos (800 Euros)
LDC	Bahamas	*Limited Duration Company.* A company, but it has a life of 30 years or less. Sometimes, these companies can be classified as partnerships in the United States.
LLC	USA	*Limited Liability Company.* Not really a corporation, and not really a partnership; it's something different altogether. Most states require at least two people to form an LLC, but some states require only one. An LLC has limited liability (hence the name), and unlimited life (i.e., the charter does not expire). In the United States, Corporations typically pay taxes, then distribute the profits via dividends, and the recipients must pay taxes on the dividends. An LLC allows for *pass through taxation*, which means that the income a company makes goes directly to the owners on their tax forms (even if the profits were not distributed). LLC's may have several different classes of stock.
LLP	USA	*Limited Liability Partnership.*
Ltd.	Various	*Limited.* Used in the UK and many former British colonies, as well as in other countries such as Japan. Indicates that a company is incorporated and that the owners have limited liability. This can also be used in the United States, and has the same meaning as Inc.
Ltda	Brazil	*Sociedade por Quotas de Responsabiliadade Limitada.* Means the owners have limited liability.
Ltée.	Canada	*Limitée.* French language equivalant of Ltd. (Limited). Indicates that a company is incorporated and that the owners have limited liability.
N.A.	USA	*National Association.* Used by Banks in the United States as a way of getting the word national into their name, which is a legal requirement under certain banking regulations.
NT	Canada	*iNTermediary.* Indicates that a company is a financial intermediary. However, companies are not required to use this abbreviation in their name if they are a financial intermediary -- it's merely a description.

Ext.	Country	Description
NV	Netherlands	*Naamloze Vennootschap*. All publicly traded Dutch companies are NV's, but not all NV's are publicly traded. Dutch NV's require 100,000 NLG share capital or more.
NV	Belgium	*Naamloze Vennootschap*. This is Flemish (Dutch): In Belgium, many companies use both NV and SA (the French language equivalent).
NV	Netherlands Antilles	*Naamloze Vennootschap*. In the Netherlands Antilles, many foreign companies establish subsidiaries to shelter taxes.
NV	Suriname	*Naamloze Vennootschap*. All publicly traded companies are NV's, but not all NV's are publicly traded. NV's require SRD 5000 (USD 1850) share capital or more.
OE	Greece	*Omorrythmos*. Partnership. All partners have unlimited liability.
OHG	Austria	*Offene Handelsgesellschaft*. Partnership, with at least two partners. Partners have unlimited liability.
OHG	Germany	*Offene Handelsgesellschaft*. Partnership with a legal name, and must have at least two partners. Partners have unlimited liability.
OOD	Bulgaria	*Druzhestvo s Ogranichena Otgovornost*. Limited liability company. Requires at least two shareholders. Minimum share capital is 5000 leva (2550 Euro).
OÜ	Estonia	*Osaühing*. Private limited liability company. Minimum capital of EEK 40,000. This type of company doesn't trade on the stock exchange (as those are of the AS variety).
Oy	Finland	*Osakeyhtiö*. All corporations in Finland used to have this legal structure, although now, publicly traded companies will be OYJ (julkinen osakeyhtiö).
OYJ	Finland	*Julkinen osakeyhtiö*. Used by publicly-traded companies in Finland.
P/L	Australia	*Pty. Ltd.* Proprietary Limited Company.
PC Ltd	Australia	*Public Company Limited by Shares*
PLC	Various	*Public Limited Company* A publicly traded company and the owners have limited liability. Used in the UK, Ireland, and elsewhere. In the UK, a PLC must have at least UKP 50,000 in authorized capital, with UKP 12,500 paid up.
PMA	Indonesia	*Penenaman Modal Asing*. Foreign joint venture company.
PMDN	Indonesia	*Penanaman Modal Dalam Negeri*. Domestic Capital investment company
PrC	Ireland	*Private Company limited by shares*.
Prp. Ltd.	Botswana	Private company limited by shares.
PT	Indonesia	*Perseroan Terbuka*. Limited liability company.

Ext.	Country	Description
Pty.	Various	Stands for Proprietary. Used in South Africa, Australia and elsewhere.
RAS	Estonia	*Riiklik Aktsiaselts.* State (owned) Joint Stock company.
Rt	Hungary	*Részvénytársaság.* Stock Company. All Hungarian publicly-traded companies are incorporated via this structure. However, an Rt doesn't necessarily mean that a company is publicly traded, and Rt companies may have as few as one shareholder. However, there are three board members required. Minimum share capital is HUF 10 million.
S. de R.L.	Mexico	*Sociedad de Responsabilidad Limitada.* Limited Partnership
S. en C.	Colombia & Peru	*Sociedad en Comandita.* Limited Partnership
S. en N.C.	Mexico	*Sociedad en Nombre Colectivo.* General Partnership
S/A	Brazil	*Sociedades Anônimas.* In Brazil, there must be at least two shareholders of an S/A, and they must have paid in cash at least 10% of the subscribed capital. The Capital must be deposited with the Bank of Brazil or other approved entity of the Brazilian Securities and Exchange Commission. Annual accounts must be published.
SA	Belgium	*Société Anonyme*, the Dutch language equivalent is NV. Initial capital must be BEF 2.5 million, and must be fully paid up upon incorporation.
SA	France	*Société Anonyme.*
SA	Greece	*Société Anonyme.* A Greek SA must have share capital of GRD 10 million.
sa	Italy	*Societá in accomandita per azioni.* Limited partnership with shares.
SA	Ivory Coast	*Société Anonyme.* Requires a minimum of seven shareholders. Each share must have a par value of at least 5000 CFA Francs.
SA	Luxembourg	*Société Anonyme.* There is a minimum of two shareholders, and a minimum share capital of LUF 1.25 million.
SA	Mexico	*Sociedad anónima.* Mexican SA's require a minimum capital of N$50,000. At least 20% of this must be paid-in at the time of incorporation. There is a minimum of two shareholders, but no maximum. Ordinary shareholder meetings can be called with 1/2 of the shares voting, and extraordinary meetings require a 3/4 vote. Shareholder meetings must take place in the city where the company is located, but board meetings can be abroad. 5% of annual profits must be allocated to a reserve until the reserve totals 20% of the capital.
SA	Morocco	*Société Anonyme.* SA's must have at least seven shareholders and a share capital of at least 10,000 dirhams, with each share having a minimum par value of 1000 dirhams.
SA	Poland	*Spolka Akcyjna.* Stock company

Ext.	Country	Description
SA	Portugal	*Sociedad Anónima.* Share capital minimum of PTE 5 million, and a minimum par value of PTE 1000 per share. There is a minimum of 5 shareholders. Companies are registered in the Commercial Registry.
SA	Romania	*Societate pe actiuni.* Limited liability company, can be publicly-traded. Can be set up by one or more shareholders (but not more than 50) and must have a minimum capital of RL 2 million (about $100.00). At present, capital contributed by a foreign investor is converted to lei at the prevailing market exchange rate in effect at the time the capital is contributed for accounting purposes only. Companies may maintain bank accounts in foreign currency. The registered capital is divided into equal shares whose value cannot be less than RL 100,000 (about $5.00 USD) each.
S.A.	Brazil	*Sociedade por Ações.* Privately-held company
SA de CV	Mexico	*Sociedad Anónima de Capital Variable* In Mexico, SA's can have either fixed or variable capital; this abbreviation is used for those with variable capital.
SAFI	Uruguay	*Sociedad Anonima Financiera de Inversion.* Offshore company.
S.A.I.C.A.	Venezuela	*Sociedad Anónima Inscrita de Capital Abierto.* Open Capital Company
SApA	Italy	*Societa in Accomandita per Azioni.*
Sarl	France & Other	*Société à responsabilité limitée.* Used in France and other French speaking countries. Private company.
Sarl	Luxembourg	*Société à responsabilité limitée.* Private company -- must have share capital of at least LUF 500,000, and 100% must be paid up on formation. Requires a minimum of one director and two shareholders.
SAS	Italy	*Societá in Accomandita Semplice. Limited Partnership.*
SC	France	*Société civile.* Partnership with full liability.
SC	Poland	*Spólka prawa cywilnego.* Partnership with all partners having unlimited liability.
S.C.	Spain	*Sociedad en commandita.* General Partnership.
SCA	Belgium	*Societe en commandite par actions.* Limited partnership with share capital.
SCA	Romania	*Societate in còmandita pe actiuni.* Limited liability partnership with shares.
SCP	Brazil	*Sociedade em Conta de Participacão.* This is a partnership where there is one partner assumed responsible for running the business. The other partners carry liability, but they do not have to be revealed.
SCS	Belgium & France	*Societe en Commandite Simple.*

Ext.	Country	Description
S.C.S.	Brazil	*Sociedade em Comandita Simples*. Limited Partnership
SCS	Romania	*Societate in comandita simpla*. Limited liability partnership.
Sdn Bhd	Malaysia	*Sendirian Berhad*. Limited Liability Company.
SENC	Luxembourg	*Société en Nom Collectif*. General Partnership
SGPS	Portugal	*Sociedade gestora de participações socialis*. Holding Enterprise.
SK	Poland	*Spólka komandytowa*. Limited liability partnership.
SNC	France	*Société en nom collectif*. General Partnership
SNC	Italy	*Società in Nome Collettivo*. General Partnership.
SNC	Romania	*Societate in nume colectiv*. General Partnership.
SNC	Spain	General Partnership
SOPARFI	Luxembourg	*Société de Participation Financiére*. Holding company.
sp	France	*Societe en participation*.
SpA	Italy	*Società per Azioni*. Limited share company.
spol s.r.o.	Czech Republic	*Spolecnost s rucenim omezenym*. Limited liability company. This type of company cannot trade on the stock exchange, but owners have limited liability up to their unpaid deposits. This type of company must have share capital of at least CZK 100,000, and each shareholder must contribute at least CZK 20,000. A reserve fund of at least 10% of the share capital must be created from the profits. There is a maximum of 50 shareholders. Directors must be Czech citizens or residents. An annual audit is usually not required.
SPRL	Belgium	*Société Privée à Responsabilité Limitée*. French language equivalent to BVBA -- see that definition for more information.
Sp. z.o.o.	Poland	*Spólka z ograniczona odpowiedzialnoscia*. Limited liability company, privately-held.
Srl	Chile	*Sociedad de responsabilidad limitada*, Limited Liability company
Srl	Italy	*Società a Responsabilità Limitata*. Limited liability company.
Srl	Mexico	*Sociedad de responsabilidad limitada*. This type of limited liability company is really not that common in Mexico. A minimum of N$3,000 is required.

Ext.	Country	Description
Srl	Romania	*societate cu raspondere limitata*. Limited-liability company, privately-held. Can be set up by one or more shareholders (but not more than 50) and must have a minimum capital of RL 2 million (about $100.00). At present, capital contributed by a foreign investor is converted to lei at the prevailing market exchange rate in effect at the time the capital is contributed for accounting purposes only. Companies may maintain bank accounts in foreign currency. The registered capital is divided into equal shares whose value cannot be less than RL 100,000 (about $5.00) each.
Srl	Spain	*Sociedad Regular Colectiva*
td	Slovenia	*Tiha druzba*. Sole proprietorship.
TLS	Turkey	*Türk Limited Sirket*. Private Limited Liability Company
VEB	East Germany	*Volkseigner Betrieb*. Term for East German companies before Reunification. They were all either shut down, or converted into AGs or GmbHs by the Privitization Agency (Treuhandanstalt).
VOF	Netherlands	*Vennootschap onder firma*. General partnership.
v.o.s.	Czech Rep	*Verejna obchodni spolecnost*. General partnership. Partners are fully liable.

Enforcement and Regulatory Agencies

These 472 agencies are listed by country.

Africa	African Development Bank Group
Albania	Albanian State Police
Albania	Balkan Insight
Albania	District Court of Tirana
Albania	General Prosecutor's Office
Albania	High Appellate Court
Antigua & Barbuda	Antigua and Barbuda Directorate of Offshore Gaming
Antigua & Barbuda	Antigua and Barbuda International Financial Sector Authority
Antigua & Barbuda	Office of National Drug Control Policy
Argentina	Central Bank of Argentina (PEPs)
Argentina	Comision Nacional de Valores
Argentina	Judiciary Branch
Argentina	Ministerio de Justicia y Derechos Humanos
Argentina	Unidad de Informacion Financiera
Armenia	Central Bank of Armenia
Armenia	National Security Council
Armenia	Police of the Republic of Armenia
Armenia	Prosecutor General's Office of Armenia
Australia	Australian Competition and Consumer Commission
Australia	Australian Crime Commission
Australia	Australian Customs and Border Protection Service
Australia	Australian Federal Police
Australia	Australian Prudential Regulatory Authority
Australia	Australian Securities & Investments Commission
Australia	Australian Stock Exchange
Australia	Transactions Reports and Analysis Centre
Austria	Austrian Financial Markets Authority
Austria	Bundeskriminalamt .BK (Austrian Federal Investigation Bureau)
Austria	POLIZEI (Austrian Federal Police)
Azerbaijan	Head Police Department of Baku City
Azerbaijan	Ministry of Internal Affairs of the Republic of Azerbaijan
Azerbaijan	Ministry of National Security
Azerbaijan	Office of the Prosecutor General
Bahamas	Central Bank of the Bahamas
Bahamas	Royal Bahamas Police Force
Bahamas	Securities Commission of the Bahamas
Bangladesh	Bangladesh Securities and Exchange Commission
Barbados	Royal Barbados Police Force
Belarus	General Prosecutor's Office
Belarus	Ministry of Internal Affairs
Belarus	Ministry of Internal Affairs of Brest region
Belarus	Ministry of Internal Affairs of Gomel region
Belarus	Ministry of Internal Affairs of Grodno region
Belarus	Ministry of Internal Affairs of Minsk region
Belarus	Ministry of Internal Affairs of Mogilev region
Belarus	Ministry of Internal Affairs of Vitebsk region

Belarus	State Security Agency of Belarus
Belgium	Banking Finance and Insurance Commission
Belgium	Belgium Federal Police
Belgium	Financial Services and Markets Authority
Belize	Belize International Financial Services Commission
Belize	Central Bank of Belize
Bermuda	Bermuda Monetary Authority (BMA)
Bosnia & Herzegovina	Council of Competition Bosnia and Herzegovina
Bosnia & Herzegovina	Federal Police Directorate of Bosnia and Herzegovina
Bosnia & Herzegovina	The Court of Bosnia and Herzegovina
Bosnia & Herzegovina	The Prosecutor's Office of B&H
Botswana	Directorate on Corruption and Economic Crime
Brazil	DENARC (Departamento de Investigations sobre Narcoticos
Brazil	Ministrie do Trabalho e Emprego (M.T.E.) do Brasil
Brazil	Policia Civil de Santa Catarina (Brazil)
Brazil	Portal DA Transparencia
Brazil	Procuradoria Geral da Republica do Brasil
Brazil	Supremo Tribunal Federal do Brasil
Brunei	Anti Corruption Bureau
Bulgaria	Bulgarian State Agency for National Security
Bulgaria	Prosecutor of the Republic of Bulgaria
Bulgaria	Commission for Protection of Competition
Cambodia	Extraordinary Chambers Courts of Cambodia
Canada	Canada Revenue Agency
Canada	Department of Justice Canada
Canada	Financial Services Commission of Ontario
Canada	Investment Industry Regulatory Organization of Canada (IIROC)
Canada	Office of the Superintendent of Financial Institutions Canada
Canada	OSFI Enforcements
Canada	Public Safety Canada
Canada	Royal Canadian Mounted Police
Canada	Tax Court of Canada
Cayman Islands	Cayman Islands Monetary Authority
Chile	Chile Superintendencia de Valores y Seguros
Chile	Fiscalia de Chile
Chile	Ministerio de Hacienda
China	Banking Regulatory Commission
China	Central Commission for Discipline Inspection
China	Central Commission for Discipline Inspection Anti Corruption Network
China	China Securities Regulatory Commission
China	Hangzhou Police Wanted List
China	Insurance Regulatory Commission
China	Ministry of Public Security
China	Ministry of Supervision
China	National Bureau of Corruption Prevention of China
China	Supreme People's Procuratorate of China
Colombia	Armada Nacional de Colombia
Colombia	Contraloría General de la República de Colombia
Colombia	Ministerio de Ambiente y Desarrollo Sostenible
Colombia	Registraduria Nacional del Estado Civil

Colombia	Superintendencia de Sociedades
Costa Rica	Superintendencia General de Valores de Costa Rica (SUGEVAL)
Cote d'Ivoire	Platform Fighting Cybercrime
Croatia	Croatia's State Prosecutor's Office
Cyprus	Commission for the Protection of Competition
Cyprus	Cyprus Securities and Exchange Commission
Cyprus	Federal Police Most Wanted
Cyprus	Supreme Court
Czech Republic	Czech National Bank
Czech Republic	Czech Office for the Protection of Competition
Czech Republic	Czech Police Most Wanted
Denmark	Finanstilsynet (Financial Supervisory Authority of Denmark)
Dominica	Financial Services Unit, Ministry of Finance & Planning
Dominican Republic	Dirección Central de Investigaciones Criminales
Dominican Republic	Poder Judicial
Dominican Republic	Policía Nacional Dominicana
Dubai	Dubai Financial Services Authority
Dubai	Dubai Police
Ecuador	Fiscalia General del Estado de Ecuador
Ecuador	Policia Judicial Ecuador
Ecuador	Policia Nacional del Ecuador
Egypt	Egyptian Financial Supervisory Authority
Egypt	Ministry of Interior
Egypt	Stock Exchange
El Salvador	Fiscalía General de la República, El Salvador
El Salvador	Ministerio de Gobernación, República de El Salvador
El Salvador	Policía Nacional Civil de El Salvador
El Salvador	Superintendencia de Valores, El Salvador
Estonia	Estonian Internal Security Service
Estonia	Estonian Police
Estonia	Financial Supervision Authority of Estonia
Estonia	Prosecutor's Office
Ethiopia	Ethiopia Revenues and Customs Authority
Ethiopia	Federal Ethics and Anti-Corruption Commission of Ethiopia
Fiji	Fiji Independent Commission Against Corruption
Finland	Finanssivalvonta (Financial Supervisory Authority of Finland)
Finland	Prosecutor's Office
Finland	Supreme Court
France	Banque De France
France	French Autorité des marchés financiers
France	Legifrance
France	Ministre de l'Intérieur, Police nationale (France)
Georgia	Ministry of Internal Affairs of Georgia
Georgia	Office of the Prosecutor General of Georgia
Germany	Bundesanzeiger Appointments (Germany)
Germany	Bundesanzeiger courts' decisions (Germany)
Germany	Bundeskartellamt (Federal Cartel Office)
Germany	Federal Office for Protection of the Constitution
Germany	German Federal Criminal Police Office
Germany	Ministry of Justice Federal Gazette

Ghana	Bank of Ghana
Ghana	Securities and Exchange Commission of Ghana
Gibraltar	Gibraltar Financial Services Commission
Greece	Hellenic Competition Commission
Greece	Hellenic Police
Greece	Hellenic Republic Capital Market Commission
Guatemala	Ministerio de Gobernación de Guatemala
Guatemala	Ministerio Público de Guatemala
Guatemala	Policia Nacional Civil de Guatemala
Guernsey	Guernsey Financial Investigation Unit
Guernsey	Guernsey Financial Services Commission
Honduras	Secretaria de Defensa Nacional de Honduras (Ministry of Defense)
Hong Kong	Financial Services and the Treasury Bureau of Hong Kong
Hong Kong	Hong Kong Customs and Excise Department
Hong Kong	Hong Kong Monetary Authority
Hong Kong	Hong Kong Police
Hong Kong	Independent Commission Against Corruption (Hong Kong)
Hong Kong	Judiciary
Hong Kong	Market Misconduct Tribunal
Hong Kong	Securities and Futures Commission of Hong Kong
Hungary	Competition Commission
Hungary	Hungarian Courts
Hungary	Hungarian Financial Supervisory Authority
Hungary	Hungarian National Police
Iceland	Fjármálaeftirlitið, Financial Supervisory Authority, Iceland (FME)
India	India Courts
India	Indian Central Bureau of Investigation
India	Ministry of Defense
India	Ministry of Finance of India, Department of Revenue
India	Ministry of Home Affairs of India
India	National Investigation Agency
India	Reserve Bank of India
India	Securities and Exchange Board of India
Indonesia	Attorney General of Indonesia
Indonesia	Bank Indonesia
Indonesia	Capital Market Supervisory Agency of Indonesia
Indonesia	Corruption Eradication Commission
Indonesia	Indonesian Financial Services Authority
Indonesia	Indonesian Financial Transaction Reports & Analysis Centre
Indonesia	National Police
Indonesia	Supreme Court
Ireland	Central Bank of Ireland
Ireland	Irish Financial Services Regulatory Authority
Ireland	Revenue Commissioners-Irish Tax & Customs
Isle of Man	Isle of Man Financial Supervision Commission
Israel	Bank of Israel Sanctions Committee
Israel	Israel Securities Authority (ISA)
Israel	Israel Security Agency
Israel	Israeli Intelligence and Terrorism Information Center
Israel	Israeli Ministry of Justice

Israel	Ministry of Finance
Israel	Ministry of Foreign Affairs
Italy	Autorita Garante Concorrenze Mercato
Italy	Guardia di Finanza
Italy	Ministero dell'Interno (Italy)
Italy	Polizia di Stato
Jamaica	Jamaica Financial Services Commission
Japan	Fukuoka Prefecture
Japan	Japanese Financial Services Agency
Japan	Japanese National Police Agency
Japan	Ministry of Defense
Japan	Ministry of Economy, Trade and Industry
Japan	Ministry of Finance Japan
Japan	Ministry of Foreign Affairs
Japan	Securities and Exchange Surveillance Commission of Japan
Japan	Tokyo Stock Exchange
Jersey	Courts
Jersey	Jersey Financial Services Commission
Jersey	Police
Kazakhstan	Agency on Regulation of Financial Markets and Organizations
Kazakhstan	Department of Internal Affairs of Almaty
Kazakhstan	Department of Internal Affairs of Astana
Kazakhstan	Financial Police of Kazakhstan
Kazakhstan	General Prosecutor's Office
Kenya	Capital Markets Authority
Kenya	Kenya Anti Corruption Commission (KACC)
Korea	Financial Supervisory Service
Korea, Republic of	Financial Services Commission of Korea
Korea, Republic of	Korean National Police Agency
Korea, Republic of	Ministry of Strategy and Finance
Kosovo	Kosovo Competition Authority
Kosovo	Kosovo Police
Kosovo	State Prosecutor of the Republic of Kosovo
Kyrgyzstan	Ministry of Internal Affairs of Kyrgyzstan
Kyrgyzstan	Prosecutor General of Kyrgyzskoy Republic
Lativa	Financial and Capital Market Commission
Latvia	Corruption Prevention and Combating Bureau
Latvia	Latvia State Police
Latvia	Security Police
Latvia	State Revenue Service
Latvia	Supreme Court
Lebanon	Special Tribunal for Lebanon
Liechtenstein	Finanzmarktaufsicht
Liechtenstein	Liechtenstein National Police
Lithuania	Central Bank of the Republic of Lithuania
Lithuania	Customs of the Republic of Lithuania
Lithuania	Financial Crime Investigation Service
Lithuania	Lithuania General Prosecutor's Office
Lithuania	Lithuanian Criminal Police Bureau
Lithuania	Lithuanian Securities Commission

Lithuania	Police department under the Interior Ministry
Lithuania	Supreme Court
Luxembourg	Commission de Surveillance du Secteur Financier Luxembourg
Luxembourg	Commission de Surveillance du Secteur Financier Luxembourg Sanctions
Macao	Commission Against Corruption
Macao	Judiciary Police
Macao	Macau Customs
Macao	Macau Security Force
Macao	Public Prosecutions Office
Macedonia	Macedonian Commission for Protection of Competition
Macedonia	Ministry of Interior
Macedonia	Ministry of Internal Affairs of the Republic of Macedonia
Macedonia	Securities and Exchange Commission of Macedonia
Malawi	Malawi Anti Corruption Bureau
Malaysia	Anti-Corruption Commission
Malaysia	Attorney General's Chambers–Enforcement
Malaysia	Bank Negara Malaysia
Malaysia	Bursa Malaysia
Malaysia	Malaysia Securities Commission
Malaysia	Ministry of International Trade and Industry
Malaysia	Royal Malaysian Police Force
Malaysia	The Companies Commission of Malaysia
Malta	Central Bank of Malta
Malta	Financial Intelligence Analysis Unit
Malta	Malta Financial Services Authority
Malta	Malta Ministry for Justice and Home Affairs
Mauritius	Mauritius Financial Services Commission
Mexico	AFI– gencia Federal de Investigacion
Mexico	CONDUSEF
Mexico	Directorio de Proveedores y Contratistas Sancionados
Mexico	Empresas y Personas Sancionadas
Mexico	Secretaria de la Defensa Nacional
Mexico	Secretaria de Marina
Mexico	Unidad de Inteligencia Financiera (UIF)
Moldova	Center for Combating Economic Crimes and Corruption
Moldova	Ministry of Internal Affairs
Moldova	Moldovan Department of Penitentiary Institutions
Moldova	Office of the Prosecutor General of the Republic of Moldova
Moldova	Supreme Court of Justic
Monaco	Service d'Information et de Contrôle sur les Circuits Financiers
Montenegro	Police Directorate of Montenegro
Montenegro	Prosecutor's Office of Montenegro
Montenegro	Securities and Exchange Commission
Morocco	CDVM
Morocco	Ethical Control of Real Estate Assets
Namibia	Namibia Supreme Court
Nepal	Nepal Credit Information Bureau
Nepal	Nepal Police Most Wanted List
Netherlands	De Nederlandsche Bank (DNB)
Netherlands	Ministry of Foreign Affairs

Netherlands	Netherlands Authority for the Financial Markets
Netherlands	Netherlands Financial Intelligence Unit
Netherlands	Politie (Netherlands Police)
Netherlands	Public Prosecution Service
Netherlands	Supreme Court of the Netherlands
Netherlands Antilles	Central Bank of the Netherlands Antilles
New Zealand	Inland Revenue of New Zealand
New Zealand	New Zealand Financial Markets Authority
New Zealand	New Zealand Police List
New Zealand	New Zealand Police Wanted
New Zealand	New Zealand Securities Commission
New Zealand	New Zealand Serious Fraud Office
New Zealand	Reserve Bank
Nicaragua	Poder Judicial República de Nicaragua
Nicaragua	Procuraduría General de la República de Nicaragua
Nigeria	Central Bank of Nigeria (CBN)
Nigeria	Economic and Financial Crimes Commission (EFCC)
Nigeria	National Insurance Commission
Nigeria	Nigeria Deposit Insurance Corporation (NDIC)
Nigeria	Nigeria National Drug Law Enforcement Agency (NDLEA)
Nigeria	Securities and Exchange Commission of Nigeria (SEC)
Norway	Authority for Investigation and Prosecution of Economic and Environmental Crime
Norway	Financial Supervisory Authority
Pakistan	Federal Investigation Agency (FIA)
Pakistan	Pakistan National Accountability Bureau
Pakistan	Punjab Police (Pakistan)
Pakistan	Securities and Exchange Commission of Pakistan
Panama	Panama Superintendency of Banks
Panama	PanamaCompra
Panama	Policia Nacional de Panamá
Panama	Superintendencia del Mercado de Valores
Paraguay	Paraguay Secretaria Nacional Antidrogas
Perú	El Peruano Official Diario
Perú	Ministerio de Justicia del Perú
Perú	Ministerio del Interior de Perú
Perú	Policía Nacional del Perú
Philippines	Department of Justice
Philippines	Philippine Department of Finance
Philippines	Philippine Deposit Insurance Corporation
Philippines	Philippine National Police
Philippines	Philippines National Bureau of Investigation
Philippines	Philippines Securities and Exchange Commission
Poland	Border Guard
Poland	Poland Police
Poland	Polish Financial Supervision Authority
Portugal	Portuguese Comissão Do Mercado De Valores Mobiliários
Puerto Rico	Departamento de Justicia
Puerto Rico	Policia de Puerto Rico
Republic of Korea	Fair Trade Commission

Republika Srpska ....Ministry of the Interior of the Republika Srpska
Republika Srpska ....Republic of Srpska Securities Commission
Romania ....Competition Council
Romania ....Directorate for Investigation of Organized Crime and Terrorism (DIICOT)
Romania ....High Court of Cassation and Justice of Romania
Romania ....Ministry of Justice of Romania
Romania ....National Anticorruption Directorate (DNA)
Romania ....National Integrity Agency
Romania ....National Securities Commission
Romania ....Police
Romania ....Public Ministry of Romania
Romania ....Supreme Council of National Defense
Russian Federation ....Chief Military Prosecutor
Russian Federation ....Courts
Russian Federation ....Federal Financial Monitoring Service
Russian Federation ....Federal Security Service of the Russian Federation (FSB)
Russian Federation ....Federal Service for Financial Markets
Russian Federation ....Investigative Committee at the Public Prosecutor's Office of the Russian Federation
Russian Federation ....Law Enforcement Portal of the Russian Federation
Russian Federation ....Ministry of Foreign Affairs
Russian Federation ....Ministry of Internal Affairs of Surgut
Russian Federation ....Ministry of Justice
Russian Federation ....Prosecutor's Office
Russian Federation ....Russia-Eurasia Terror Watch (RETWA)
Russian Federation ....The Central Bank of the Russian Federation
Rwanda ....International Criminal Tribunal for Rwanda)
Rwanda ....Office of the Prosecutor General of the Republic of Rwanda
Rwanda ....Rwanda National Police
Rwanda ....Rwanda Public Procurement Authority
Saudi Arabia......................................Saudi Arabia Royal Embassy
Serbia..Commission for Protection of Competition
Serbia..Court of Appeal in Belgrade
Serbia..Ministry of Interior of the Republic of Serbia
Serbia..Serbian Office of the War Crimes Prosecutor
Seychelles...Central Bank of Seychelles
Sierra Leone......................................Anti-Corruption Commission
Sierra Leone......................................Special Court for Sierra Leone
Singapore ....Central Narcotics Bureau, Singapore
Singapore ....Corrupt Practices Investigation Bureau
Singapore ....Customs
Singapore ....Monetary Authority of Singapore
Singapore ....Singapore, Commercial Affairs Department
Singapore ....Singapore, Ministry of Law
Singapore ....Singapore, Supreme Court
Slovakia...Ministry of Interior (Slovak Republic)
Slovakia...National Bank of Slovakia
Slovakia...The Antimonopoly Office of the Slovak Republic
Slovenia...Commission for the Prevention of Corruption
Slovenia...Republic of Slovenia, Ministry of the Interior Police

Slovenia	Slovene Securities Market Agency
Slovenia	Slovenian Competition Protection Office
South Africa	Competition Tribunal
South Africa	National Prosecution Authority
South Africa	National Treasury
South Africa	South African Financial Services Board
South Africa	South African Police Service
Spain	Dirección General de Seguros y Fondos de Pensiones
Spain	Guardia Civil Española
Spain	Interior Ministry News
Spain	La Moncloa
Spain	Ministry of Justice
Spain	National Police of Spain (Cuerpo Nacional De Policía)
Sri Lanka	Financial Intelligence Unit
Sri Lanka	Securities and Exchange Commission of Sri Lanka
St. Kitts & Nevis	Financial Services Regulatory Commission
St. Kitts & Nevis	Nevis Financial Services
St. Lucia	Royal Saint Lucia Police
St. Vincent & The Grenadines	St. Vincent & the Grenadines International Financial Services Authority
Swaziland	Financial Services Regulatory Authority
Sweden	Courts
Sweden	Swedish Financial Supervisory Authority (Finansinspektionen)
Switzerland	Office of the Attorney General of Switzerland
Switzerland	SIX Swiss Exchange
Switzerland	State Secretariat for Economic Affairs
Switzerland	Swiss Federal Police
Switzerland	Swiss Financial Market Supervisory Authority
Taiwan	Bureau of Investigation
Taiwan	Fair Trade Commission
Taiwan	Financial Supervisory Commission
Taiwan	Insurance Anti-Fraud Institute of Taiwan
Taiwan	Ministry of National Defense of Taiwan
Taiwan	Taiwan High Court Kaohsiung Branch
Taiwan	Taiwan Judicial Yuan Criminal Case Judgments
Taiwan	Taiwan Supreme Prosecutors Office
Tajikistan	Ministry of Internal Affairs
Thailand	Anti- Human Trafficking Division
Thailand	Anti-Money Laundering Office
Thailand	Narcotics Suppression Bureau
Thailand	Office of Narcotics Control Board
Thailand	Office of the Attorney General
Thailand	Royal Thai Police
Thailand	Supreme Court of Thailand
Thailand	Thai Securities and Exchange Commission
Thailand	The Department of Special Investigation
Thailand	The National Anti-Corruption Commission
Turkey	Ministry of Foreign Affairs
Turks and Caicos	Turks and Caicos Financial Services Commission
Ukraine	Department of the MIA Kherson Region
Ukraine	Ministry of Internal Affairs (MIA) of Ukraine

The Index

Notes

Meet the Author

Cynthia Hetherington, MLS, MSM, CFE has more than 20 years of experience in research, investigations, and corporate intelligence. She is the founder of Hetherington Group, a consulting, publishing, and training firm focusing on intelligence, security, and investigations. Cynthia is also the ACFE James Baker Speaker of the Year Award Recipient 2012.

Cynthia applies her expertise in library science and information systems to provide clients with strategic insight into research and complex investigations. During her career, she has assisted a vast number of clients with Internet investigations related to employee theft and intellectual property loss. Cynthia has also applied her research skills while conducting online and database research to uncover well-hidden relations between fraudulent associates, their assets, and their secrets. She has experience overseeing international investigations for Fortune 500 companies and other organizations in the Middle East, Europe, and Asia.

Cynthia is heavily involved with a number of trade associations. She is a Faculty Member of the Association of Certified Fraud Examiners (ACFE) and Chair of the Economic Crime Committee of ASIS International. She is also Past President of three organizations: Association of Independent Information Professionals, New Jersey Association of Licensed Private Investigators, and the Alpha Lambda Honor Society.

A widely published author, Cynthia authored Business Background Investigations and co-authored three editions of the Manual to Online Public Records both titles published by Facts on Demand Press, as well as co-authored Web of Deceit: Misinformation and Manipulation in the Age of Social Media published by Information Today. She is the publisher of Data2know.com: Internet & Online Intelligence Newsletter and has authored articles on steganography, computer forensics, Internet investigations, and other security-focused monographs. She is also recognized for providing corporate security officials; military intelligence units; and federal, state, and local agencies with training in online intelligence practices. Cynthia's classes are ACFE-, NASBA-, DHS-, and ASIS-approved for continuing professional education credits.

To contact Ms. Hetherington, please email her at ch@hetheringtongroup.com.